Before Forgiveness
The Origins of a Moral Idea

In this book, David Konstan argues that the modern concept of interpersonal forgiveness, in the full sense of the term, did not exist in ancient Greece and Rome. Even more startlingly, it is not fully present in the Hebrew Bible, nor in the New Testament or in the early Jewish and Christian commentaries on the Holy Scriptures. It would still be centuries – many centuries – before the idea of interpersonal forgiveness, with its accompanying ideas of apology, remorse, and a change of heart on the part of the wrongdoer, would emerge. For all its vast importance today in religion, law, politics, and psychotherapy, interpersonal forgiveness is a creation of the eighteenth and nineteenth centuries, when the Christian concept of divine forgiveness was finally secularized. Forgiveness was God's province, and it took a revolution in thought to bring it to earth and make it a human trait.

David Konstan was the John Rowe Workman Distinguished Professor of Classics and the Humanistic Tradition and Professor of Comparative Literature at Brown University. In 2010, he began teaching at New York University. Among his most recent books are *Friendship in the Classical World* (1997), *Pity Transformed* (2001), *The Emotions of the Ancient Greeks* (2006), and *"A Life Worthy of the Gods": The Materialist Psychology of Epicurus* (2008). He has also served as president of the American Philological Association and on the editorial board of journals in several countries.

Before Forgiveness

The Origins of a Moral Idea

DAVID KONSTAN

Brown University

CAMBRIDGE
UNIVERSITY PRESS

CAMBRIDGE UNIVERSITY PRESS
Cambridge, New York, Melbourne, Madrid, Cape Town, Singapore,
São Paulo, Delhi, Dubai, Tokyo, Mexico City

Cambridge University Press
32 Avenue of the Americas, New York, NY 10013-2473, USA

www.cambridge.org
Information on this title: www.cambridge.org/9780521199407

First published 2010   1006571447

Printed in the United States of America

A catalog record for this publication is available from the British Library.

Library of Congress Cataloging in Publication data
Konstan, David.
Before forgiveness : the origins of a moral idea / David Konstan.
p.   cm.
Includes bibliographical references and index.
ISBN 978-0-521-19940-7
1. Forgiveness.   2. Forgiveness–Religious aspects–
Christianity.   3. Forgiveness of sin.   I. Title.
BJ1476.K66 2011
179′.9–dc22   2010013376

ISBN 978-0-521-19940-7 Hardback

For
Larry and Marian
Michael and Carolyn
and to the Memory of
Catalina Hernández Hernández

Contents

Preface

The paucity of ethnographic references to remorse and forgiveness suggests either an appalling oversight by generations of anthropologists, or it could alert us to the modernist and western nature of the concepts under consideration.[1]

The thesis of this book is easily stated: I argue that the modern concept of forgiveness, in the full or rich sense of the term, did not exist in classical antiquity, that is, in ancient Greece and Rome, or at all events that it played no role whatever in the ethical thinking of those societies. What is more, it is not fully present in the Hebrew Bible, nor again in the New Testament or in the early Jewish and Christian commentaries on the Holy Scriptures; it would still be centuries – many centuries – before the idea of interpersonal forgiveness, and the set of values and attitudes that necessarily accompany and help to define it, would emerge. This is not to say that there were no other ways of achieving reconciliation between wrongdoers and those who are wronged, just that forgiveness in the modern sense was not among them. The absence of forgiveness in these ancient cultures is not merely a matter of terminology or theory, moreover, but involves a sharp distinction in ethical outlook, and may even be said to reflect differences in the ancient and modern conception of the self – a term that is often vague in its reference but in connection with forgiveness has a specific and clear use, and one that helps distinguish modern from

[1] Scheper-Hughes 1999: 145.

classical conceptions of ethical identity. The topic of forgiveness is thus a particularly fruitful notion on which to focus as it goes to the heart of some crucial divergences between modern moral ideas and those of classical antiquity – ideas that are often taken to be largely commensurate with each other.

Clearly, much depends on definitions, and I begin by providing a description of what I understand as forgiveness in the full modern sense of the word. In so doing, I shall also be obliged to examine a cluster of ideas that are not only closely associated with forgiveness but also essential to an understanding of it: for forgiveness is not a simple notion but is part of a constellation of ethical and emotional concepts, including remorse and personal transformation, that together constitute one aspect of modern moral consciousness. As will appear, these related ideas too are absent in classical thought or, if not wholly missing, play nothing like the role they do in relation to forgiveness today. The first chapter, then, is devoted to setting forth just how forgiveness is conceived, in the abstract and in practice, in our contemporary world.

The second and third chapters, in turn, focus on classical antiquity and seek to demonstrate that forgiveness is not among the basic ethical concepts of ancient Greece and Rome. This will involve showing that philosophical, legal, and literary texts that ostensibly give evidence of forgiveness of an offender on the part of a person who has been hurt actually manifest other kinds of reconciliation, in which anger has been appeased by other means or for different reasons from those that pertain to forgiving. In the process, I touch on the attitudes and sentiments that typically support or subtend forgiveness and show that they do not play the kind of role in the appeasement of anger in classical texts that one might expect them to play today. The second chapter, more particularly, looks at texts in which terms that are commonly translated as "forgiveness" or "forgiving" are defined or illustrated in Greek and Latin texts; here I analyze as well various passages in which these words appear, determining their meaning from the specific context. Needless to say, I cannot provide an exhaustive survey of all uses, although I have attempted to collect and consider every instance of these terms in classical literature; instead, I discuss selected examples illustrating a variety of situations and point up how and why translations employing "forgiveness" or similar expressions go astray. In the third chapter, I consider in greater detail several passages or entire works in which the fundamental elements of forgiveness in the modern sense – confession of guilt and apology, remorse, change of character, and the like – seem to be present, irrespective of whether the specific Greek and Latin terms commonly rendered as "forgive" or "forgiveness" occur. My purpose here is to show that what may appear to be forgiveness is better explained in other ways, in accord with classical ideas of anger appeasement and reconciliation of differences.

In the following chapter, I examine passages in the Hebrew Bible, alongside translations into Greek and Latin, as well as the New Testament and the writings of church fathers and other religious thinkers in the first centuries after Christ; I argue that here too, despite the powerful emphasis on a merciful God, there is not to be found a fully developed account of interpersonal forgiveness in the modern sense. God's forgiveness, it will emerge, has special characteristics, such as the ability to cancel sin entirely, even when it is inherited from the original transgression of Adam and Eve and takes the form of an innate state of sinfulness – characteristics that distinguish it from ordinary human forgiveness; correspondingly, repentance tends to take the special form of atonement. In Chapter 5 I seek to discover the origins of the modern conception of forgiveness. To my own surprise, I was unable to identify a consistently articulated conception of forgiveness in texts of late antiquity and the Middle Ages, despite an occasional intimation, or even a fairly close approximation to the modern idea. Finally, in the last chapter I consider how and when the modern idea of forgiveness arose; its relation to new conceptions, inspired largely by Kant, of moral autonomy and the consequent possibility of a radical change of character; and some of the paradoxical implications of this new image of the self. For if modern forgiveness rests on a notion of self-transformation that may be incoherent, as some have argued, then the absence of such a notion in the premodern Western tradition may point not to a deficiency in their ethical or psychological understanding but rather to a problem in the ideology of forgiveness.

The inspiration for this project derives from conversations with my friend, Charles Griswold, during the academic year 2004–5, when we were both in residence at different research centers in Stanford and Charles was writing his book, *Forgiveness: A Philosophical Exploration,* now published by Cambridge University Press (Griswold 2007b). It is thanks to these talks, and a careful perusal of his book, that I came to realize that not only had philosophers failed to examine the idea of forgiveness in ancient Greece and Rome, as Griswold had observed, but also that it was scarcely present as an idea or practice at all in classical culture – a point that seemed to have escaped the notice, or at least not attracted the attention, of other scholars. At that time, I was working on my book *The Emotions of the Ancient Greeks: Studies in Aristotle and Classical Literature* (Konstan 2006), and so I was very much engaged with ancient ideas of anger and its conciliation. Thus, I was prepared to perceive the ways in which the pacification of anger or resentment caused by an offense in classical texts differed from the account of forgiveness that Griswold had compellingly elaborated. These divergences piqued my interest, and I subsequently had the privilege of participating in a symposium organized by Griswold on the topic of "Liberty, Responsibility and Forgiveness," sponsored by the Liberty Fund in June 2007, in which the focus of discussion was precisely on ancient versus modern views of forgiveness. Griswold and I have collected the papers from this colloquium, and they will be published in 2011 by Cambridge University Press (some are cited, with the authors' permission, in this book). From that time on, I began giving talks on forgiveness in antiquity, among other venues at the XII Congreso Español de Estudios Clásicos, held in Valencia in 2007; the Johns Hopkins University; the annual meeting of the Classical Association of Canada (2008); the fourth International Conference on the Ancient Novel, held in Lisbon in 2008; the Netherlands Institute in Rome; the II Congreso Internacional de Estudios Clásicos en México (2008); and a colloquium on "Displaying Wealth and Performing Status from Antiquity to the Middle Ages," held at the University of Bristol (2009). Several of these talks appeared subsequently in the publications of the respective conferences, professional journals, and the volume edited by Charles Griswold and myself. Questions and discussions in the wake of these papers were immensely helpful to me in clarifying and testing my ideas.

I wish also to thank some (I fear I shall fail to mention all) of the friends and colleagues who lent an ear to my musings and kindly read parts or all of the present work in earlier forms. I am grateful to Alexandra Schultz, who as my UTRA (Undergraduate Teaching and Research Awards) assistant at Brown helped me collect and analyze much relevant material. Ilaria Ramelli shared with me her profound knowledge of ancient texts, including especially the church fathers, and at every stage helped me formulate my thoughts on forgiveness. I have already mentioned the encouragement I received from Charles Griswold. Nicoletta Momigliano, Vered Lev Kenaan, and Marco Fantuzzi read the entire manuscript in draft form and offered valuable suggestions and criticisms. Analise Acorn, Michael Satlow, and Laurel Fulkerson offered advice on specific passages dealing with modern law, Talmudic interpretation, and classical Greek remorse, respectively. Stavroula Kiritsi helped me find the cover image and offered various helpful comments on the text. I benefited greatly from comments by members of a seminar at New York University on "Conscience and Forgiveness," which I shared with Richard Sorabji in the autumn of 2009; enrolled in the course were Jeremy Brown, Scarlett Kingsley, Yekaterina Kosova, Kyle Johnson, Neeltje Irene (Inger) Kuin, and Calloway Scott. The two readers for the Press offered helpful comments and suggestions. My wife, Pura Nieto, bore with me as I struggled with the book. To all of these, I express my gratitude, and if I have neglected, by accident, to acknowledge a debt, I hereby beg forgiveness – or at least hope to appease any residual discontent.

1

What Is Forgiveness?

[F]orgiveness is a variable human process and a practice with culturally distinct versions.[1]

There are ideas, even relatively simply ones, that seem self-evident until one takes a closer look, and then all sorts of complications arise. Saint Augustine famously asked: "What then is time? If no one asks me, I know: if I wish to explain it to one who asks, I do not know" (*Confessions* 11.14.17: *quid est ergo tempus? si nemo ex me quaerat, scio; si quaerenti explicare velim, nescio*). I am told that Jaakko Hintikka discovered a similar puzzlement in what might seem to be a far simpler question, namely, what is the height of Mount Everest? Most people are sure they know what the question means, but when asked whether the height includes the snowcap or not, and if so at which season, and whether it is measured from sea level, and if so at what place (as this varies), or rather in respect to the center of the earth, and so forth, perplexity sets in. Forgiveness too is subject to such confusion, or perhaps it is better to call it difference of opinion. In what follows, I set forth some of the features that are essential if an act of reconciliation is to be recognized as forgiveness; to the extent that my discussion lays any claim to originality, it is only in the emphasis on those aspects that are particularly relevant to distinguishing modern forgiveness from ancient practices of conciliation.

Let me begin, therefore, with what I take to be the most elementary and fundamental condition for forgiveness, which is nevertheless open to disagreement. I take it that one only forgives

[1] Walker 2006: 152.

1

someone who has done something wrong, and that one cannot forgive an innocent person. It sounds bizarre to say, "You never did me any harm, and I forgive you."[2] Nevertheless, there are contexts in which this stipulation concerning guilt is not so clear. Take the case of executive pardon, where the governor of a state or the president of the United States exercises the right to waive a sentence: it is not necessarily presupposed that the person who is granted such clemency is guilty; it may well be that the bearer of executive authority is convinced of the individual's innocence and intervenes precisely on those grounds. Yet it is not altogether contrary to ordinary usage to say that the person has been forgiven. Still more common is the locution that speaks of forgiving a debt, which has scriptural authority in the King James translation of the Sermon on the Mount (Matthew 6:12): "Forgive us our debts, as we forgive our debtors." Here, *forgive* means *remit*, that is, foregoing the debt; it does not imply that the debtor has wronged the creditor, though this would be the case if the debtor refused to make good on the loan or otherwise sought to cheat the lender. But the creditor is free to cancel the debt, and in this case, no harm has been done or intended, and yet we use the word *forgive* naturally enough (this example will occupy our attention at some length in Chapters 4 and 5).

This is not to say that our initial intuition about forgiveness and guilt or responsibility is wrong; we can simply recognize a kind of homonymy, in which the term *forgive* has more than one use in common parlance (I return to the variety of senses of forgiveness toward the end of this chapter). The sense I wish to distinguish, and on which I shall be concentrating in this book, is the one that involves commission of a wrong and a certain kind of foregoing in respect to the wrongdoer. In singling out this meaning, I do not deny that there may well be a significant relationship among the three uses of *forgiveness* already mentioned and others not yet discussed. I do maintain that the moral, as opposed to the economic and judicial or political sense of the term, is clear and distinct enough to constitute an independent object of investigation, and what is more that this sense figures importantly in modern ethics

---

[2] Cf. Downie 1965: 128: "If A forgives B, then A must have been injured by B: this seems to be a logically necessary condition of forgiveness."

and psychology. I believe that there is sufficient agreement on this score to justify treating it as such, without mounting an elaborate defense or presuming too heavily on the goodwill of the reader. Thus, Charles Griswold writes, "To forgive someone ... assumes their responsibility for the wrongdoing," and it occurs in a context in which the wrongdoer and wronged party accept "the fact that wrong was indeed done, and done (in some sense) voluntarily."[3] Again, Alice MacLachlan, in her doctoral dissertation *The Nature and Limits of Forgiveness*, writes, "the very act of forgiving – however it is expressed – makes a number of claims: that something wrongful was done, that the wrong has caused harm, and that you (the forgiven) are responsible, even culpable, for this harm" (MacLachlan 2008: 16). Yet, just in accepting this description, and the idea that guilt of some sort is an indispensable precondition for the possibility of forgiveness, we commit ourselves to a view that, as we shall see in the following chapter, drives a deep wedge between modern and ancient strategies for overcoming the anger and urge to vengeance that arises as a consequence of wrongdoing.

Suppose that we allow that forgiveness involves a certain attitude toward a person who has wronged you – and note too that, in granting this account, we have also implicitly agreed that forgiveness is directed at people, and not inanimate entities or animals, though some may wish to extend moral responsibility, and hence forgiveness, to animals other than human beings. The nature of forgiveness is still far from settled or fully explored. For one thing, and this goes to the heart of the concept, it is necessary to determine just what is meant by *wrongdoing*. Thus, I have spoken of harm, as well as of wrongdoing: the two terms are not synonymous, and it is reasonable to ask whether one can forgive another for causing harm, even if the harm was not a matter of having done wrong. At first sight, this may seem a quibble: a person who causes you harm has wronged you. Purely accidental damage, like being struck by a bolt of lightning, does not count as an injustice, and accordingly does not elicit forgiveness; as I have said, we do not ordinarily speak of forgiving things (except incidentally, as in the usage by which we say, "I forgive you this insult," by which we mean, "I forgive you for having insulted me"; as Griswold puts it [2007b: 47–8], "we

[3] Griswold 2007a: 275; see also Griswold 2007b.

forgive the agent, not the deed"). What turns the harmful effect into a matter of wrongdoing is the deliberateness of the action on the part of the offending party. As MacLachlan states (2008: 25), "Typically, discussions of forgiveness have taken as a paradigm the straightforward case of singular interpersonal wrongdoing: an action committed by one individual against another and recognized by both as having directly and intentionally harmed the second." The requirement that the injury be intentional makes evident sense but ought not simply to be taken for granted. There are societies – and it may be the case, as some scholars have held (though not I), that archaic Greece and Rome were among them – in which the distinction between intentional and unintentional acts is said not to be drawn with the same rigor that we recognize today. If this is true, and I believe that even now we sometimes feel justified in responding angrily to, and hence at least potentially finding ourselves in a position to forgive, injuries that may not have been deliberately or voluntarily inflicted, then an important element in what we understand to be wrongdoing may vary from one culture to another. This difference could conceivably affect, in turn, the way in which forgiveness or closely related ideas are inflected, and hence go some way to explaining why a notion like forgiveness in the modern sense may not have emerged in all times and places. In the periods in the history of ancient Greece and Rome with which we are concerned here, and for which we have reliable sources, however, the difference between voluntary and involuntary actions was clearly recognized, and a strictly involuntary act, although it might do significant moral and psychological damage to an individual – think of Oedipus's unintended slaying of his father and marriage with his mother – was understood, as we shall see, to be different from the deliberate and unjust infliction of harm.

Yet, even so, the situation is not entirely uncomplicated, for it is not always easy to distinguish between intentional and unintentional acts. There are, for example, cases of diminished responsibility, as when a person is deemed not to be fully capable of moral reasoning, whether on account of immaturity, as with small children, mental incapacity, or temporary or permanent insanity. Is forgiveness relevant in cases of this kind, or shall we say that such people, or people in such states, are incapable of acting freely and independently, and because they cannot be held responsible for their behavior, they cannot be deemed guilty, and accordingly there is nothing that might count as wrongdoing for which to forgive them? Again, there are situations in which we may act under external compulsion, most obviously when we are physically constrained to perform an act but more commonly when we do so under the threat of violence or some other harm. If you assist in committing a crime because one of the people most dear to you – a child, for example – is being held hostage and menaced with death if you do not comply, to what extent are you guilty or responsible for your action? The law has developed sophisticated means of evaluating guilt and innocence in such circumstances; however forgiveness is not a matter simply of legal verdicts but has to do with personal reactions to wrongdoing: if we hold that, given the pressures brought to bear, a person cannot really be held accountable for the action in question, have we forgiven that individual? Strictly speaking, forgiveness should be irrelevant, because no wrong was done, inasmuch as wrongdoing must be deliberately and freely committed – and one can hardly speak of freedom in the kind of context just indicated. Finally, what of ignorance as an excuse or mitigating factor? There are times when we do something unintentionally, not because we are not in our right minds or because we have been forced by others, but simply because we did not know all the information relevant to the case: Oedipus's murder of his father is a classic instance of this kind of ignorance. We might sum up all these conditions as extenuating circumstances, and the question may then be phrased as follows: to what extent do such circumstances compromise the possibility of forgiveness, just to the extent that they excuse or exonerate the offender, and hence render him or her innocent? As in the case of the distinction between voluntary versus involuntary actions in respect to culpability, here again different societies may place unequal weight on these factors, and the extension of forgiveness, or the very nature of a person's responses to offenses, may vary accordingly. This last set of conditions, moreover, will prove to be highly relevant to our understanding of classical Greek and Roman practices of conciliation and the restoration of relationships.

To the premise that, for there to be forgiveness, the offense in question must be a voluntary and intentional wrong, there may be added certain further conditions, without which we do not usually suppose that foregoing a grievance constitutes an act of forgiveness. We may divide these conditions for the sake of convenience into three categories: conditions relating to the forgiver; conditions relating to the forgiven; and behavior consequent upon forgiveness, which, if not manifested, calls into question whether forgiveness has really occurred. We begin with the first of these categories, the conditions relating to the forgiver.

At the most elementary level, a person who has been wronged may never have perceived the injury, either because the effects never became palpable during her or his lifetime, or because the offense was so slight in the view of the offended party that it was truly beneath notice. A wrong has been committed, it is agreed; there is no negative reaction on the part of the victim, but no one would say that the offense has been forgiven in such a case. Somewhat more complex is the situation in which a person has perceived that harm has been done, and deliberately so, but after a period of time has forgotten all about it. Here again, we are unlikely to say that the offense has been forgiven; as Griswold puts it (2007a: 276), "Forgiving cannot be forgetting, or 'getting over' anger by any means whatever."[4] Forgiving is a far deeper and richer

---

[4] Contrast the view of Jorge Luis Borges: "I do not speak of vengeance or forgiveness; forgetting is the only vengeance and the only forgiveness" ("Yo no hablo de venganzas ni de perdones; el olvido es la única venganza y el único perdón": "Fragmentos de un evangelio apócrifo") (number 27), in *Elogio de la sombra* (included in Borges 1985: 357; first published 1969). Cf. Bioy Casares 2006, who reports that on June 30, 1966, in speaking of Job, Borges said: "With regard to offenses, the best weapon is forgetting. In forgetting vengeance and forgiveness coincide" ("Para las ofensas, la mejor arma es el olvido. En el olvido coinciden la venganza y el perdón"). The same sentiment appears in Borges's poem, "Soy," in *La rosa profunda* (included in Borges 1985: 434; first published in 1975):

Soy el que sabe que no es menos vano
que el vano observador que en el espejo
de silencio y cristal sigue el reflejo
o el cuerpo (da lo mismo) del hermano.
Soy, tácitos amigos, el que sabe
que no hay otra venganza que el olvido
ni otro perdón. Un dios ha concedido
al odio humano esta curiosa llave.
Soy el que pese a tan ilustres modos
de errar, no ha descifrado el laberinto
singular y plural, arduo y distinto,
del tiempo, que es de uno y es de todos.

phenomenon, involving, as we shall see, much more reflection and interaction between forgiver and forgiven. So too, no forgiveness exists in which the ostensibly injured party treats the offense as negligible or unworthy of attention, as though it were committed by a child. Such an attitude of aristocratic disdain may manifest itself as indifference to an insult that a lesser person would have resented more deeply; many examples come to mind, including the superior cast of mind of the ancient Stoics, who maintained, with Socrates, that "a good man cannot be wronged by a bad man" (Musonius Rufus 10). But again, this is not forgiveness but the denial that an offense was truly given, as the offender was beneath contempt. There is more to be said about the attitude of the forgiver, including the spirit in which forgiveness must be granted, but before turning to those more subjective aspects, it is convenient to consider the second set of conditions, that is, those that concern the offender.

We have said that forgiveness is granted not to those who are innocent of any wrongdoing but rather to the guilty. This is not a sufficient condition, however, at least in the most common acceptation of the idea. For it will not do if the offender fails to acknowledge the wrong but maintains that she or he is innocent. In such a situation, we are not normally disposed to grant forgiveness. Here there arises a divergence of views that has great importance for the understanding of forgiveness in the modern sense of the word and of ancient moral conceptions. For forgiveness cannot, on the terms just indicated, be construed as a mere act of dismissal of the wrong, irrespective of the attitude of the offender. We cannot simply forgive on our own, without recognition of the party to be forgiven, nor a gesture on the part of the other party. Forgiveness takes two agents, not just two persons: if I forgive you, it is because you have earned my forgiveness. How might you do that? Is it really necessary that you do?

Most recent commentators on forgiveness suppose that one must, and that the process begins with an acknowledgment of

---

Soy el que es nadie, el que no fue una espada
en la guerra. Soy eco, olvido, nada.
I am grateful to Carles Garriga for bringing these passages to my attention. So too George Herbert Mead writes (1934: 170): "A person who forgives but does not forget is an unpleasant companion; what goes with forgiving is forgetting, getting rid of the memory of it"; cited in Miller 2003: 92.

responsibility on the part of the offender, and this, not just in the
sense that one has recognized the consequences of one's action,
but also that one admits that the act was wrong. Thus, Anthony
Bash, in his recent book *Forgiveness and Christian Ethics* observes,
"Some say that there should be no forgiveness until the wrongdoer acknowledges and regrets the wrong.... Others go so far as
to say that forgiveness without repentance is morally irresponsible
because it leaves the wrongdoer free not to accept that the action
was wrong and so free to repeat the wrongdoing" (Bash 2007: 63).
So too the Jewish existentialist thinker Emanuel Levinas writes,
"There is no forgiveness that has not been requested by the guilty.
The guilty must recognize his sin."[5] Alan Thomas, in an essay on
"Remorse and Reparation: A Philosophical Analysis," remarks that
"The word 'acknowledgement' plays an important role" in the process of reparation (Cox 1999: 133), and Griswold states, "A failure
to take responsibility ... not only adds insult to injury so far as the
victim is concerned, but undermines the possibility of trusting that
the offender will not turn around and repeat the injury. To forgive
would then collapse into condonation" (2007b: 49).[6] Now, not all
agree that such acknowledgment on the part of the offender is
a prerequisite for forgiveness: there are some, for example, who
maintain that Christian forgiveness is universal, granted to all,
independent of the other's own sense of wrongdoing and any gesture, such as apology, that gives evidence of it, and they base their
argument on scripture and other ancient authorities. We shall
examine this view in relation to early Christian texts in Chapter 5,
but for the moment we may notice simply that classical Greek and
Latin had perfectly available expressions for the idea of responsibility (e.g., in Greek, *aitios*; in Latin, *in culpa esse*), and speakers of
those languages had no difficulty in assigning accountability for
actions good or bad. If they were reluctant to accept blame for
something that turned out badly, they were probably no worse in
this regard than people are today.

But to be responsible for something in the sense of having
a causal relation to the outcome is not all that is meant by the

---

[5] Levinas 1990: 19; cited in Caputo, Dooley, and Scanlon 2001: 82.
[6] On the distinction between forgiveness and condonation (and also mercy, clemency, and pardon), see Downie 1965: 130–3; Blumoff 2006.

modern writers who insist on the acknowledgment of culpability. What is demanded at the very least is regret (as in the quotation from Bash in the preceding text) – the wish that one had not performed the act and that the outcome were different. Nor does regret quite satisfy the conditions imposed on the person to be forgiven in the modern paradigm, if by regret one means nothing more than the recognition that the event has been disagreeable and that one could have wished it otherwise. The demand is for a deeper awareness, which includes the acknowledgment that what the offender did was morally wrong, complete with the rejection of such behavior in the future: not simple regret but remorse. Remorse entails sorrow for harm unfairly inflicted upon another, as opposed to postfactum misgivings concerning actions that result in one's own discomfort. It is thus a fundamentally ethical sentiment, because it involves consciousness of wrongdoing, not just of unfortunate or disagreeable consequences that might have been avoided.[7] As Michael Borgeaud and Caroline Cox put it, "*remorse* is inherently linked with an action for which the agent was responsible and for which there were no exonerating factors" (1999: 138). They quote Gabrielle Taylor (1996: 72): "The person who feels remorse sees himself as a responsible moral agent." It is this sense of culpability, not just responsibility in the causal sense, that led Adam Smith to observe, in *The Theory of Moral Sentiments*, "Such is the nature of that sentiment, which is properly called remorse: of all the sentiments which can enter the human breast the most dreadful," precisely because it entails the deepest kind of self-reproach.[8]

---

[7] Cf. the Puritan preacher William Plumer (1864: 214–15): "True repentance is sorrow for sin, ending in reformation. Mere regret is not repentance, neither is mere outward reformation. It is not an imitation of virtue, it is virtue itself.... He, who truly repents, is chiefly sorry for his *sins*. He, whose repentance is spurious, is chiefly concerned for their *consequences*. The former chiefly regrets that he has *done* evil; the latter that he has *incurred* evil." John Chryssavgis, in the introduction to his popular book *Repentance and Confession in the Orthodox Church* (2004), makes the same point in slightly different language: "Repentance is not to be confused with mere remorse, with a self-regarding feeling of being sorry for a wrong done."

[8] Smith 2002: 99. Miller (2006: 147) observes that in Clint Eastwood's *Unforgiven*, Little Bill feels no remorse: "He does, however, express a regret.... But regret is a rather different sentiment from remorse. Remorse in the Christian moral scheme of penance is *the* central self-directed moral sentiment"; as he explains (148): "Regret, though, seems to occupy a largely amoral ground, the world in which, quite simply, our luck went bad."

Concomitant upon a sense of remorse is the impulse to repentance, which involves not just grief at the action committed but also a profound moral transformation that seeks to reject the qualities of the self that were responsible for the offensive behavior. Penitence is an idea deeply rooted in the Jewish and Christian traditions and will be discussed in greater detail later in this book. Here, we may note that the modern sense of repentance, which has wide circulation as a secular notion, entails a willingness to make reparation for the injury inflicted but does so in a spirit of self-reform. The penitent not only wishes to offer compensation to the one who has been wronged but also to manifest the inner change or transformation that has occurred, and that alters the person's life hereafter to such an extent that one can almost be said to have acquired a new identity. This acquisition of a new self is not immediately visible, but it must nevertheless be revealed to the injured party, if forgiveness is to be granted; for forgiveness depends on the conviction that the offender has truly had a change of heart. It is here that the idea of confession enters in, for confession, in the religious sense, involves not simply admission of guilt but (ideally) the declaration of an inner metamorphosis, an alteration so deep as to amount to a conversion. Confession of this sort is aimed at convincing the other that the inner transformation is not a pose, or merely superficial, but that it goes to the depths of one's being and is utterly sincere. Now, sincerity by its nature invites the associated ideas of falseness and hypocrisy, and so it has always to prove itself and be convincing. The strategies for persuading others of one's own honesty in a matter such as moral conversion, which is naturally hidden within, are complex and can all be feigned in turn. Of this, the ancients were aware, when they reflected on the difficulty of distinguishing a true friend from a flatterer or false friend. Thus, Plutarch, in his essay *How to Distinguish a Flatterer from a Friend*, notes that flattery penetrates "every feeling and every gesture" and hence is "difficult to separate out" from friendship (51a). An accomplished sycophant knows that frankness is "the voice of friendship," and so he imitates that quality as well (51c). This makes it all the more challenging to discover the true friend.

But if the ancient Greeks and Romans were conscious of the difficulty in identifying the true sentiments and interests of someone who pretended to be a loyal friend or ally, they were not equally engaged, as we shall see, in seeking to discern an inward change of character as a condition for reconciliation with a wrong-doer.[9] Consequently, there is no comparable imperative to confession and repentance in classical accounts of reconciliation or the appeasement of the anger consequent upon a wrongdoing. Correspondingly, the vocabulary of regret, repentance, or a change of mind or attitude (in Greek, *metameleia* or *metanoia*; in Latin, *paenitentia*) is rarely brought into connection with the giving over of anger or with the terms typically, but misleadingly, translated into English as "forgive." As Robert Kaster remarks, after an exhaustive study of the Latin *paenitentia* and related words, the idea of "a change of heart that leads one to seek purgation and forgiveness" was unknown to pre-Christian Romans.[10] So too, David Winston observes that "Greek philosophy generally had little interest in the feelings of regret or remorse that may at times lead an individual to a fundamental reassessment of his former life path."[11] To the extent that forgiveness is part of an interpersonal exchange involving a change of heart or moral condition, the abandonment of one's former ways, and sentiments like sincere remorse and penitence, the absence of such an idea in classical antiquity is all the more visible.

The conditions that render an offender eligible for forgiveness amount to reasons why the victim should be disposed to give over anger and a desire for revenge. As Griswold puts it (2007b: 49), "The agent [of forgiveness] requires reasons in order to commit to giving up resentment, or at least, to giving up the judgment that the wrong-doer warrants continued resentment."[12] Among

---

[9] "Sincerity" as the mark of a subjective disposition, as opposed to an objective virtue manifested visibly in actions, is a modern idea dating to the late eighteenth century; see Silver 2003 and cf. Trilling 1971, who locates the origins of the modern idea rather in the Renaissance.

[10] Kaster 2005: 80–1.

[11] Winston 1990: 4.

[12] Griswold continues, "The first of these reasons consists in the wrong-doer's demonstration that she no longer wishes to stand by herself as the author of those wrongs. That is, she must acknowledge, first, that she was the responsible agent for the specific deeds in question.... Second, she must repudiate her deeds ... and thus disavow the idea that she would author those deeds again" (49). Griswold goes on to add as a third condition that "the wrong-doer must experience and express *regret* at having caused that particular injury to that particular person," and fourth, that "the

the reasons that Griswold enumerates are acknowledgment of the
wrong done, remorse, and a repudiation of one's "past self," which
taken together "constitute the *contrition* requisite to a convincing appeal for forgiveness" (50–1). So too, MacLachlan affirms,
"We forgive for reasons ...; there are better and worse reasons to
forgive," although this does not mean that "what was done is no
longer wrongful."[13] Even if these conditions are met, however, it is
not obligatory that the offended party forgive the wrongdoer: forgiveness is a voluntary act and is not constrained by the petition of
the wrongdoer, even when a sincere and credible change of heart
has occurred. As MacLachlan puts it, "The victim of a wrongdoing
has certain discretionary powers; that is, the demands of morality
leave her free to choose – within some limit – the extent to which
the generosity of her response will meet or surpass the demands
of justice" (150). For the offended party to forgive demands certain changes of character as well; to quote MacLachlan once
more: "The idea of forgiveness as a change of heart [in the for-
giver] is the image most commonly alluded to by contemporary
philosophers writing on the subject" (57).

One who forgives, in the first instance, gives over anger and the
attendant desire for revenge, or, if the resentment is not wholly
overcome (and perhaps, for there to be forgiveness, some residue
must remain, commensurate with the recognition that a wrong
has been done and not entirely avenged), then at least makes a
subjective commitment to transcend the bitterness and forego
vengeance. This transformation in the forgiver implies a willingness to restore a moral relation with the wrongdoer precisely on
the basis of the other's repentance and not on other grounds

offender must commit to becoming the sort of person who does not inflict injury,"
(50) and fifth and finally, "the offender must show that she understands, from the
injured person's perspective, the damage done by the injury" (51). For a recent
and highly publicized petition for forgiveness, one may cite the champion golf
player Tiger Woods's thirteen-and-a-half-minute apology to his fans for his extra-
marital affairs with several women, delivered on television on February 19, 2010.
The speech elicited various comments, which focused on Woods's humility, sincerity, and promise to reform (he has sought therapeutic counseling). An editorial
in *The Chicago Tribune* on the following day, "The Tiger Template," recommended
Woods's statement as a model "for the perfect apology" and explained: "Here's the
formula: Cop to your mistakes. Shun the passive voice. Ask for forgiveness, promise
to earn it, acknowledge that it might not come easily, if at all."
[13] MacLachlan 2008: 16, 18.

such as compensation, public humiliation, judicial punishment, personal retribution, or again by virtue of any of the extenuating factors indicated in the preceding text. Forgiveness is thus a dyadic relationship, involving a personal transformation on the part of the wronged and the one who has done wrong.[14] These features, as Griswold (2007b: 47) observes, "lend forgiveness highly unusual, if not unique, characteristics as a virtue," or as an emotional response or act of conscience. With such a complex set of conditions, it may be no wonder that a comparable moral scenario has not arisen, or at least become culturally salient, in all human societies, whether ancient or modern.

It may be helpful to distinguish here between forgiveness as an interpersonal process and the process of supplication, as supplication was understood in the classical world. For supplication too involves a moral exchange and reconciliation between two parties. In a recent book, F. S. Naiden identifies four steps in the supplication process.[15] First, the suppliant must approach the supplicand, that is, the person to be supplicated (or else approach an altar or other substitute, as when supplicating a god). Second, the suppliant is expected to make certain gestures or verbal appeals; clasping the knees or holding the chin of the supplicand are memorable gestures, but these are by no means obligatory or ritually prescribed, and there may be no physical contact at all between the two parties – words alone may suffice, as when the naked Odysseus supplicates the Phaeacian princess Nausicaa in the *Odyssey* (6.141–8): direct contact would be clearly inappropriate in the circumstances. In the third step, the suppliant makes his or her petition for consideration and offers arguments in support: one must make a case for deserving a positive response from the supplicand. Such reasons may include an appeal to reciprocity, kinship ties, fairness, pity (this is a recourse more common among women and children than adult males), or even threats. In the final step, the supplicand evaluates the plea and decides whether to honor it. Naiden rejects the view that the supplicand

[14] Cf. Griswold 2007b: 103: "The forgiver must not only see the injurer in a new light, but see herself in a new light. We are describing a change of heart, and in such a change not just the target of the sentiments (here, the offender) but their possessor necessarily change their aspect"; also 110.
[15] Naiden 2006: 29–169.

is required to accept a suppliant's plea if it is made in the proper
ritual fashion (the position, roughly, of John Gould);[16] on the contrary, the supplicand – like the forgiver, we may observe – is always
free to accept or reject the request. If the supplicand accepts the
suppliant's petition there arises an obligation to live up to whatever pledge has been made, for instance to spare the petitioner's
life. However, it is perfectly common for a suppliant's request to
be rejected, and no punishment, divine or otherwise, is expected
to ensue.

Naiden argues further that "The Romans differed from the
Greeks in allowing a suppliant to admit his own guilt and ask for
mercy" (240); by mercy, Naiden renders the Latin word *clementia*,
and he adds, "The difference between *clementia* and pity is ethical.
Clementia is for the pardonable suppliant, pity for the deserving
one" (243). This distinction is not quite accurate: *clementia* differs
from pity in that pity is an emotion (you feel it), whereas *clementia*
or clemency is a character trait (you possess it). Thus, clemency
came to be identified as one of the main virtues of the emperor
and was never taken as a sign of condescension, though pity might
be (in Greek, the analogous trait to *clementia* is *philanthrôpia* or
epieikeia).[17] Naiden affirms further that Greek suppliants never
admit to wrongdoing or appeal to the kindness of the person they
are supplicating, though Romans might do so, as when they throw
themselves on the mercy of a conquering general. But clemency in
these situations is not so much forgiveness as gentleness or mildness: the person in a position of power lets the offender or offenders off as a special grant of generosity, in the way that Caesar,
who was renowned for his clemency, did with a great many of his
former opponents. Caesar counted on his liberality to win these
enemies over to his side, among other reasons because loyalty to
him would now be to their advantage. They in turn might give
evidence of regret and also of submission, such as the adoption of
ragged clothing and a posture of self-abasement. But the essence
of the clemency resided in sparing the defeated, not in forgiving
in the sense indicated here.

[16] See Gould 1973: 77. Gould allows that supplication may fail, but only if the act is
somehow incomplete.
[17] For a full discussion, see Konstan 2005.

The picture of forgiveness that I have drawn is intended to represent what I have called *forgiveness* in the full modern sense of the word. As I indicated at the beginning of this chapter, we also use the term *forgiveness* in more informal ways, and at times it may signify little more than "excuse me," where there is no genuine admission of wrongdoing (though the expression may suggest an apology for a possible inconvenience caused to another) and certainly no question of a change of heart on the part of the offender or the one who forgives. We also speak of forgiving debts, as noted in earlier in this chapter, and sometimes use the word to indicate judicial or executive pardon, where there is not a necessary implication of a violation of the law. Although we draw, quite correctly, a technical distinction among *exoneration, exculpation,* and *forgiveness,* in that the last term implies a genuine offense, whereas the first two suggest that the offender may well have been innocent, in the sense that there were sufficient extenuating conditions or simply no evidence of guilt, we still sometimes apply the term *forgiveness* loosely even in these cases.[18] Then again, some people think of forgiveness as a purely individual matter in the mind of the forgiver, who may choose to forgive wrongdoing independently of an apology or request for absolution on the part of the offender: thus, for example, we may forgive the dead, or people we shall never again meet – a matter, as we sometimes say, of simply "getting over it" or "moving on." Such overcoming of resentment may be a part of forgiveness; as Bash puts it, "Interpersonal forgiveness is part of a series of experiences that have to do with moving on from the past and offering hope for the future" (2007: 168). There is also a question whether one can forgive offenses done to another, or what Griswold calls "third-party forgiveness" (2007b: 117) – do we have, as one says in legal parlance, the proper standing to forgive in such instances? A further problem concerns whether one can forgive collectively: Bash affirms flatly that "forgiveness is a person-to-person phenomenon: one does not forgive groups, and neither do groups forgive" (166). Unilateral, third-party, and collective or political forgiveness, as exemplified in the work of

---

[18] Cf. Schimmel 2002: 51: "When we *exonerate* someone we say that the harmful act that initially appears to have been performed out of malicious intent or gross negligence was not really done in that manner."

the Truth and Reconciliation Commission in South Africa, come under what Griswold labels "non-paradigmatic or imperfect forgiveness in which one or more of the logical features defining forgiveness is absent" (2007b: 113).[19]

Now, a case can be made, as Bash has done, that forgiveness is a broad idea, capacious enough to include all of the previously mentioned instances. Or, as Adam Morton (2011) puts it, forgiveness "has many varieties, all of which can come about in many ways."[20] I have no wish to legislate usage in regard to *forgiveness* or other moral terms, including *regret, remorse,* and *repentance*. I have concentrated on what Griswold calls the ideal or "paradigm" type because it represents a clearly recognizable sense of the term in modern society, even though it carries with it a considerable freight of related moral concepts, and because it is forgiveness in this sense that is, as I shall argue, missing in the classical Greek and Roman ethical repertoire. What is more, it is a hugely important conception in modern moral systems, with a long history in religious, political, and legal thought, and one that has recently acquired salience in the area of psychological therapy as well. Some of these applications of the idea of forgiveness are controversial, but it is not my purpose to enter into these disputes here: they reflect deep differences of opinion over fundamental questions of law, mental health, and attitudes toward the divine, which go beyond the scope of this book. Nevertheless, the absence of the category of forgiveness in the moral thinking of classical antiquity – if I am right to deny that it is to be found there – may shed light incidentally on some of these issues, insofar as it may direct our thinking to alternative systems for managing the consequences of injustice and resentment.[21]

[19] Cf. Davis 2007: 1: "Should Rhode Island, which sent more slave ships to Africa than any other state, apologize for its role in the slave trade?" Can a state apologize? And to whom?

[20] Cf. Bråkenhielm 1993: 15: "The term *forgiveness* is ambiguous – there is not one single concept of forgiveness by many."

[21] John Milbank writes (2001: 96), "in classical times there was mostly no real recommendation of forgiveness in a post-Christian sense. In this period, the 'overlooking' of fault referred either to a pragmatic ignoring of it for self-interested reasons, or else to the taking into account of mitigating circumstances and involuntary motions. And, in fact, acts of arbitrary 'mercy' were viewed with suspicion as exonerating malefactors and raising benefactors above the normal sway of legality." Cf. Perrin 1987, and esp. the chapters in the volume by Danièle Aubriot and Alain Michel.

We may see most of the elements pertaining to the concept of forgiveness outlined here already in play in an account that goes back to the twelfth-century AD. The Jewish philosopher and theologian Moses Maimonides asks in his treatise "On Repentance":[22] "What is repentance?" He explains, "It is that the sinner shall desert his wrong doing, remove it from his thoughts and determine in his heart not to do it again" (sec. 2.2, 111). Maimonides insists that "the penitent should cry continually before the Lord with tears and supplications ..., and isolate himself completely from the sin he has committed"; and he goes so far as to suggest that "he may change his name as if to say 'I am another person, not the man who did those things....' He may leave his home because exile atones for evil as it leads to humility and a lowly spirit" (sec. 4, 112). Here we find that emphasis on profound remorse and on a thoroughgoing transformation in the character of the wrongdoer, even to the point of a change of identity, though Maimonides is speaking of repentance before God, not one's fellow human being. Yet, according to Maimonides, there must be a corresponding change of heart on the part of the forgiver as well: "A man is forbidden to be cruel and must be conciliatory; he should be easily appeased, and hard to make angry and, when a wrongdoer begs his forgiveness, he ought to forgive with a whole heart and willing spirit" (sec. 10, 113). Here, Maimonides makes the turn to interpersonal reconciliation, and affirms that forgiving cannot be a casual dismissal of the offender, but entails – or so it seems – an alteration of moral regard, a sincere recognition of the other as a moral person despite the offense that has been committed.

To be sure, there are echoes here of the Bible, and the language is reminiscent also of Christian attitudes toward penitence and forgiveness. In Chapter 4, however, I shall offer reasons for supposing that the biblical concern with a sinful humanity and a merciful God who forgives us despite our weaknesses and errors, provided that we turn to Him – "convert" in the literal sense of the term – with our entire mind and heart, is not yet tantamount to the apparently more evolved idea of forgiveness that we find in Maimonides's account, and that the latter falls short in some respects of the fully modern concept. Setting that question aside

---

[22] Quoted from Russell and Weinberg 1983.

for now, it is worth observing that the conception of forgiveness as based on sincere repentance and moral transformation has been enshrined even in modern law, at least until quite recently. I quote from the *Código Penal* of Spain (Decreto September 14, 1973):[23] "Extenuation due to repentance, which has a religious and moral dimension, subjectively requires the manifestation of an ethical-psychological state of soul in the offender that changes his perverse criminal will for a 'sound' one, as a result of an act of inner personal contrition deriving from a felt grief and regret and from his self-condemnation."[24] The article specifies further that "repentance ... demands grief or regret of a moral nature, similar to the contrition of Christian theologians, along with self-condemnation."[25] The attenuation of guilt that such repentance enables seems to unite pardon in the judicial sense with a personal kind of forgiveness that looks to an inner change of character in the offender.

The new "Ley orgánica 10/1995, de 23 de noviembre, del código penal" represents a reaction against the religious conception of repentance, and the attendant notion of forgiveness, in the older code. Thus, we read concerning confession: "One must be truthful

---

[23] Article 9°, 9ª, "La de haber procedido el culpable antes de conocer la apertura del procedimiento judicial, y por impulsos de arrepentimiento espontáneo, a reparar o disminuir los efectos del delito, a dar satisfacción al ofendido o a confesar a las autoridades la infracción."

[24] "La atenuante de arrepentimiento, de dimensión religiosa y moral, precisa subjetivamente, de la aparición de un estado anímico ético-psicológico en el delincuente, que cambie su dolo perverso por el 'bonus,' a consecuencia de un acto de íntima contricción [*sic*] personal, derivado del dolor y pesar sentido y condena de sí mismo efectuada." The sentence continues, "que objetivamente cause una conducta material, expresada en la realización de una de las cuatro actividades exigidas en aquel tipo, y que sean externa y provechosa manifestación, de aquella virtud moral íntimamente sentida, para/ el ofendido o para la justicia" (135–6).

[25] "El arrepentimiento ... exige un dolor o pesar de condición moral, semejante a la atrición de los teólogos cristianos, con la condena de sí mismo" (136). Again, "la atenuante novena del art. 9 del C.P. consta de tres elementos o requisitos fundamentales: a) el objetivo consistente en una conducta posdelictiva reparadora ...; b) el subjetivo, psicológico o anímico conforme al cual es preciso que esa conducta objetivamente encomiable sea determinada 'por impulsos de arrepentimiento espontáneo,' es decir, por el íntimo pesar, por la contrición o aflicción del agente que, una vez perpetrado el hecho punible, apesadumbrado y dolorido, desearía borrar lo sucedido y no siendo ello posible trata de remediarlo o paliarlo en la medida de sus posibilidades; siendo también indispensable ... que actúe por determinación propia nacida en lo íntimo de su ser y no por motivaciones egoístas o interesadas ni en la búsqueda de un trato punitivo meno riguroso ...; y c) el cronológico o temporal,

in the sense that one must recount sincerely all that has happened in so far as he is aware, without concealing anything of importance and without adding false information so as to exculpate oneself or others."[26] The new code further explains, "Extenuation on the basis of spontaneous repentance has, beginning with the 1995 reform of the Penal Code, a markedly objective character, inasmuch as it attends exclusively to the fact of whether – within the conditions of the law – the relevant behavior favoring the administration of justice is realized …, thereby replacing the moral grounds represented by the demand for an urge to spontaneous repentance with a more objective criterion."[27]

el cual exige que la conducta reparadora … sea … anterior al conocimiento, por parte del culpable de la apertura del procedimiento, judicial" (137).

[26] "3.°) Ha de ser veraz en el sentido de que ha de contar con sinceridad todo lo ocurrido conforme él lo apreciara, sin ocultar nada importante y sin añadir datos falsos con los que pretendiera exculparse o exculpar a otros." The sentence is found under artículo 21, 4ª, "La de haber procedido el culpable, antes de conocer que el procedimiento judicial se dirige contra él, a confesar la infracción a las autoridades" (120).

[27] "La atenuación por arrepentimiento espontáneo tiene, a partir de la reforma del CP de 1995, un marcado carácter objetivo en cuanto se atiende exclusivamente al dato de llevar a cabo – dentro de las condiciones legalmente exigidas – comportamientos relevantes favorecedores de la administración de justicia …, como basamento para una más depurada realización de la justicia material, pilar fundamental de Estado social y democrático de Derecho …, habiéndose sustituido el fundamento moral que representaba la exigencia del impulso de arrepentimiento espontáneo por una mayor objetivación." The sentence continues, "que consolida la tendencia doctrinal de justificar la atenuación por razones de política criminal …, sustituyendo la exigencia subjetiva del arrepentimiento, por el mero acto objetivo de colaboración con la Justicia consistente en proceder el culpable a confesar la infracción a las autoridades **antes de conocer que el procedimiento judicial se dirige contra él**" (121; emphasis in original). So as to leave no room for doubt, the code goes on to specify: "El arrepentimiento como atenuante, ha seguido, pues, en la jurisprudencia una tendencia en que ha ido perdiendo importancia el factor subjetivo de pesar y constricción [*sic*], para irse valorando más el aspecto de realizar actos de colaboración a los fines de la norma jurídica, facilitando el descubrimiento de los hechos y de sus circunstancias y autores o realizando actos de disminución o reparación del daño causado" (ibid.; cf. "Tribunal Superior de Justicia de Cataluña, Sal de lo Civil y Penal, Sentencia de 17 Sep. 2001, rec. 14/2001 [3], which refers to "una **evolución jurisprudencial** que ha reducido al máximo los elementos subjetivos de pesar, dolor o contrición [*sic*] por el hecho realizado para pasar a privilegiar aspectos externos que son objetivamente facilitadores de la aplicación de la norma punitiva" [emphasis in original]; I am most grateful to Luis Francisco Nieto Guzmán de Lázaro for enlightening me concerning this aspect of Spanish law). It is worth noting that modern Canon Law has little to say about repentance and forgiveness. Thus Beal, Coriden, and Green observe (under

Outside of Spain, this anxiety over the implications of confession, which has its roots in medieval law, found expression still
earlier. Thus, the Baron de Montesquieu wrote in *The Spirit of the
Laws* (1752; trans. 1914):

> It is one abuse of this tribunal [Courts of Human Justice] that, of two
> persons accused of the same crime, he who denies is condemned to
> die; and he who confesses avoids the punishment. This has its source
> in monastic ideas, where he who denies seems in a state of impenitence
> and damnation; and he who confesses, in a state of repentance and
> salvation. But a distinction of this kind can have no relation to human
> tribunals. Human justice, which sees only the actions, has but one com-
> pact with men, namely, that of innocence; divine justice, which sees the
> thoughts, has two, that of innocence and repentance.[28]

Such a tension between a judgment that takes into account confession, repentance, and forgiveness on the one hand, and one based
simply on evidence of guilt or innocence on the other, is absent in

"Preceptive Penalties") that a judge can abstain from imposing a penalty or impose
a lighter one "if the offender has reformed and repaired the scandal" (2000: 1560 =
Canon 1344); this comes closest to pardon on the basis of reform of character.
Canon 1535 (1672) defines "Judicial Confession" as "the written or oral assertion of
some fact against oneself before a competent judge"; there is no mention of repentance here, only the "probative force" of confession (Canon 1536, p. 1673), and the
conditions for its validity (e.g., it must not be extorted, Canon 1538, p. 1673). Cf.
also Chapter 2, n. 21.

[28] Book 26, "Of Laws in Relation to the Order of Things Which They Determine,"
Chapter 12, "That Human Courts of Justice Should Not Be Regulated by the
Maxims of Those Tribunals Which Relate to the Other Life, Continued"; quoted in
Acorn 2007. Acorn comments, "Thus as early as the 18th Century we see a strong
aversion to a focus on confession in the criminal justice system. There is also in
Montesquieu's words the suggestion of an aversion to the law inquiring at all into
the emotional state of the wrongdoer. This sensibility – the one that believes that
the criminal law should be focused on the question of whether the state has proof
of the offence – is exemplified by the Western right against self-incrimination. This
right – which protects an accused person from ever being required to give evidence
of his own guilt – is fundamental to Western ideas about criminal justice." Even
today, nevertheless, advocates of the so-called restorative justice method, in which
conflict resolution is achieved by way of apology and forgiveness, continue to insist
on the authenticity of confession. Thus, Carl Schneider (2000: 266–7) lists among
the conditions for a sufficient apology (1) that the apology must acknowledge that
a wrong has been done and harm has been suffered; (2) that the apologizer must
accept personal responsibility for the wrong; and (3) the apologizer must feel sincerely sorry: an apology that is not accompanied by an internal feeling of remorse is
no apology at all (Schneider adds that the apologizer must also be vulnerable). For
a balanced critique of this approach, see Acorn 2007, and in greater detail Acorn
2004.

ancient legal discourse and forensic speeches.[29] Defendants in a court of law may appeal to the pity of the judges, but such an appeal never involves an admission of guilt, and so there is no place for remorse or forgiveness (see Konstan 2001a: 34–43). Forgiveness in the principal modern acceptation, let it be recalled, is not reducible to the appeasement of anger, which may be achieved by compensation, acts of self-abasement, the offer of plausible excuses for one's conduct, and other means; rather, it is a bilateral process involving a confession of wrongdoing, evidence of sincere repentance, and a change of heart or moral perspective – one might almost say moral identity – on the part of the offender, together with a comparable alteration in the forgiver, by which she or he consents to forego vengeance on the basis precisely of the change in the offender. To demonstrate the absence of forgiveness in this ample sense in classical antiquity, whether in law or in other forms of discourse including narrative literature, is the object of the following two chapters.

[29] Langbein 2005: 6, in explaining why judicial torture was common in Europe from the thirteenth to the eighteenth centuries, observes that when trial by ordeal was abolished by the Fourth Lateran Council of 1215, there resulted "a profound change in thinking about the nature of government and law.... Henceforth, humans were going to replace God in deciding guilt or innocence, humans called judges." The new system demanded proof; however, the standards were too high, because proof required confession and two witnesses. Judicial torture helped solve this problem. But the conception of proof changed in turn: "Torture could be abolished in the eighteenth century because the law of proof no longer required it" (12).

Before Forgiveness

Greeks and Romans on Guilt and Innocence

"I'd like to say to the court and my family and friends, my former colleagues and all the citizens of Rhode Island how sorry I am. I was raised to accept responsibility," he continued, quavering, as one of his brothers patted him in support. "For me, this is the first step in the process of forgiveness and healing."[1]

In the article "Forgiveness," Berel Lang writes, "It is possible, of course, to imagine a world without forgiveness or any of its allied concepts. But that world would, it seems to me, either be more than human (that is, one in which no wrongs are committed or suffered) or less than human – one where resentment and vengeance would not only have their day, but would also continue to have it, day after day after day" (Lang 1994: 115; quoted in MacLachlan 2008: 2). This seems an extreme pair of alternatives: either godlike perfection or the perpetual cycle of the feud. The classical societies of Greece and Rome represent neither of these extremes, and yet, as I am about to argue, forgiveness in the modern sense was not a feature of their moral life – and it is the modern sense of the word that Lang intends in his article, when he affirms that, in forgiveness, "two agents are involved, both of whom recognize a failure by one of them in fulfilling an obligation to the other.... The person responsible for the injury acknowledges his responsibility, expressing regret, with this implying an attempt to avoid the act's recurrence; the person injured responds to this overture ... by 'forgiving' the

---

[1] Stanton 2007: 1; Gerard Martineau, who had formerly been leader of the House majority in Rhode Island, is quoted.

failure" (105).[2] How did the ancient Greeks and Romans manage anger and vengeance, then, and how were their strategies different from the modern conception of forgiveness?[3]

In the second book of Aristotle's *Rhetoric*, which provides the most extensive analysis of the emotions that has survived from ancient Greece, the first emotion to be examined in detail is anger (*orgê*); following this, Aristotle devotes a section to *praotês* or *praünsis*, "calmness" or "calming down," which he treats as the emotion opposite to anger. As many critics have observed, calmness does not sound much like an emotion; however, if we think of the *pathê* as responses to the behavior of others that have the effect of altering our judgments, which is the way Aristotle defines them (adding that they must be accompanied by pleasure and pain: cf. *Rhetoric* 2.1, 1378a20–3), then we can more easily see why the elimination of anger might also figure in Aristotle's inventory of the passions.

In this section, Aristotle discusses various ways of appeasing another person's anger. First of all, given that anger (or *orgê*), as Aristotle defines it, is a response to a slight or belittlement, and because, as he points out, "a slight is a voluntary thing," it follows that people are peaceably disposed "toward those who do not belittle them, or who do so involuntarily, or who at least seem like that" (2.3, 1380a10–12). Thus, you should try to show that you meant just the opposite, or that however you behaved toward the other person you also behave toward yourself, because, as Aristotle says, people do not normally belittle themselves. He then adds that our anger is lessened toward those who admit that they were wrong and show that they regret it (1380a14: *kai tois homologousi kai metamelomenois*). For, Aristotle explains, it is as though they have paid the penalty for the pain that they caused you.

---

[2] Lang continues (105–6), "Three conditions thus appear in the process: 1) Wrongful (and so avoidable) harm is caused by one person to another, with that act recognized as harmful and wrong by each; 2) the person who caused the harm (a) acknowledges responsibility for it, (b) expresses regret and (tacitly or explicitly) offers assurance about future conduct, and (c) either through the combination of (a) and (b) or in addition to them, asks the person harmed to forgive him; and (3) the person harmed assents to the request – that is forgives – implying with this that the original act has in some sense been nullified or repaired."

[3] I use *anger* rather than *resentment* to render the classical Greek and Roman terms, because *resentment* today carries a special freight of meaning, due in part to Nietzche's analysis of "ressentiment"; for discussion, see Konstan 2001b and Konstan 2002.

Now, Aristotle would seem to be recommending that, in order to assuage anger, one should apologize and express remorse and by implication ask forgiveness of the person who has been offended. But the situation is not so clear. For he goes on to offer as evidence of the effectiveness of such an approach the treatment of slaves who have aroused the ire of their masters: "we rather punish those who talk back and deny what they have done, but we leave off being angry at those who confess that they are being justly punished" (1380a17–19).[4] Aristotle explains that, by denying what is obvious, the slave seems to be acting shamelessly, and shamelessness in turn resembles contempt – which Aristotle identifies as one of the major stimuli to anger, because contempt is nothing other than a kind of belittlement. So too, Aristotle says, we give over anger toward those who adopt a humble attitude (*tapeinoumenoi*), because this is a sign that they are beneath us and so fear us, and "no one belittles a person he fears" (1380a24). In the same way, we tend to relax our anger against those who beg and plead, because in doing so they humble themselves. Clearly, Aristotle is not so much interested in the sincere expression of regret or remorse, which might elicit forgiveness, as he is in the demonstration that any hint of insult was unintentional, because, by abasing yourself, you openly exhibit your recognition of the other person's superiority – and this is just the opposite of a slight.[5] Furthermore,

---

[4] Cf. "The Second Plague Prayer by Mursili II," dating to the second millennium BC: "Storm-god of Hatti, my lord, Gods, my lords, as it happens, people sin. My father too sinned. He broke (his) word to the storm-god of Hatti. I, on the other hand, did not sin at all ...; if some servant has sinned, but confesses his sin to his lord, his lord will have his way with him as he wishes, but since he confesses to his lord, the lord's mind will be satisfie[d and] his [lord] will not punish that servant"; trans. Theo van den Hout in Chavalas 2006: 265. For other translations, cf. Gary Beckman in Hallo and Younger 1997: 158–9; Itamar Singer in Hoffner 2002: 60. I am grateful to Theo van den Hout for these references.

[5] Acorn 2007 cites Wagatsuma and Rosett 1986 for an extraordinary case study of the different meanings of apology in Japan and the United States. Acorn observes that the article indicates "that the failure of cultural understanding between Japanese and North Americans may lie in the fact that apologies have different meanings in the two cultures. In North America a 'good' apology is usually understood to mean something like this: 'I have done something wrong. That wrong has caused you harm. I am responsible for the wrong and I caused the harm you have suffered. I accept that responsibility and I feel remorse.' In Japan, however, Wagatsuma and Rosett's analysis suggests that an apology may mean something quite different. It may mean something more like this: 'I willingly submit to your authority. I humble myself to you and ask submissively that you not to use your authority to harm me.

Aristotle notes that it is not just humility that allays anger: a show of strength can do so as well. As Aristotle puts it, "it is impossible to be afraid and be angry at the same time" (1380a33–4), the point being that if you are afraid, you have already acknowledged your inferior status, and so have no grounds on which to resent the insult. A manifestation of one's superior power is the way to treat anger on the part of a slave, for example, should a slave ever presume to feel or show such a proud sentiment.[6]

Aristotle's analysis of the appeasement of anger is, as we see, focused entirely on relations of status and power, which is in

I value our relationship and recognize your superiority.' Wagatsuma and Rosett note that this second sort of apology does not necessarily acknowledge that a wrong was done at all; nor does it acknowledge that the person apologizing is responsible for a wrong; nor even that any harm was done. It is more like a symbolic self-lowering that appeases the aggrieved party or authority figure without addressing precise issues of personal responsibility." Acorn notes that, according to Wagatsuma and Rosett, "the Japanese idea of apology combines the concepts of remorse and gratitude.... Usually in Japanese the same word can be used to say: 'thank you' and to say: 'I am sorry.'" She notes further that "North Americans purport to be committed to the idea of an egalitarian society and they purport strongly to reject notions of social hierarchy. These commitments make it impermissible for North Americans openly to admit to want an apology from another person in order to see them adopt a stance of submission and inferiority." It is worth emphasizing that despite the radical democracy of classical Athens, self-abasement was openly acknowledged as a strategy for appeasing the anger of another.

6 In Herodas's fifth *Mimiamb*, the slave Gastron denies that he has committed a wrong (namely, sleeping with a woman other than his mistress), but Bitinna is set on having him whipped anyway; Gastron then changes tack and confesses, pleading for mercy on the grounds that he has done it just once, to err is human, and he will never repeat the offense. Although this may seem like an appeal for forgiveness, it resembles Aristotle's advice that a slave will do best to humble himself by admitting his error, in order not to offend the master. Bitinna, however, concludes that because Gastron has confessed to wrongdoing, he deserves to be punished – a perfectly reasonable position, though it shows undue harshness not to be mollified by Gastron's manifest show of subservience. Gastron's claim that his error is merely human is a standard ploy for evading responsibility, as Aristotle and others make clear. Nor does Gastron suggest that he has undergone a change of character: he will simply be on guard against committing another such offense, given the magnitude of the punishment that is threatened. Later, another slave will intercede for Gastron, on the grounds that a festival is coming on which punishments should be remitted; any question of Gastron's inner transformation or restored moral relationship with his mistress is moot.

  Acorn 2007 cites Walker 2000, who argues that battered wives tend to apologize to their husbands in order to avoid being beaten; they appease the husband's anger by demonstrating that they are not seeking undue power in the relationship. If the husband beats the wife, he is likely to apologize in turn, which, Acorn argues, elicits the forgiveness of the wife and the perpetuation of the battering syndrome.

accord with his conception of anger as a consequence exclusively of a slight or diminishment.[7] His definition of *orgê*, we recall, is "a desire, accompanied by pain, for a perceived revenge, on account of a perceived slight on the part of people who are not fit to slight one or one's own" (*Rhetoric* 2.2, 1378a31–3).[8] Thus, his discussion of the ways to assuage the anger of another has little to do with begging forgiveness for an admitted wrong, and Aristotle makes no mention in this context of pardon or *sungnômê*. This is not surprising, given that, in the *Rhetoric* (1.6, 1358b32–3), Aristotle asserts a litigant in court "would never concede that he has done wrong, for if he did there would be no need for a trial" – nor for forgiveness.

In the *Nicomachean Ethics*, Aristotle briefly mentions that *sungnômê* – the Greek term most commonly rendered as "forgiveness" – is appropriate when people act either under external compulsion or in excusable ignorance of the facts or circumstances (1109b18–1111a2). Aristotle begins by observing that, "since virtue concerns emotions and actions, and praise and blame are due in the case of voluntary acts, whereas *sungnômê*, and sometimes pity [*eleos*], are due in the case of involuntary acts, it is obligatory for those investigating virtue to define what is voluntary and what is involuntary" (1109b30–4), and he adds at once that "it is believed that involuntary acts are those that occur either by force or through ignorance." Both actions performed under compulsion and those done in ignorance admit of various descriptions and evaluations, and Aristotle does not shy away from these complexities. Thus, if one's ship is driven astray in a storm or pirates take over the vessel, no one would accuse a passenger of voluntarily changing course, for she or he has not contributed anything at all to the result, neither actively nor passively. But in the kind of case I mentioned in the previous chapter, in which one acts out of fear, as when a tyrant who has power over one's parents and children orders one to commit a shameful deed, then there is some ambiguity as to whether

---

[7] Evelyne Scheid-Tissinier (2007: 181), notes that "Dans le monde inégalitaire que met en scène l'épopée, la colère reste ... liée au statut"; and despite the democratic reforms going back to Solon, in Aristotle anger and revenge continue to be "des attributs que caractérisent la condition de l'homme libre" (182). In response to an insult, it is incumbent upon a citizen to restore his honor; anger is "pour l'homme libre non seulement un droit, mais plus encore une obligation, et elle constitue de ce fait l'un des fondements de la morale aristotélicienne" (183).

[8] For discussion of Aristotle's view of anger, see Konstan 2006: 41–76.

the act is voluntary. Aristotle says that "such actions are mixed, but they rather resemble voluntary ones" (1110a11–12). Even so, an act may be worthy of praise if one has submitted to something disagreeable for the sake of what is great and noble, though, as Aristotle concedes, it is not always easy to judge precisely what should be chosen in such situations (1110b7). Aristotle then notes that "in some cases, praise is not given, but *sungnômê* may be, when someone does things one ought not to do on account of circumstances that are beyond human nature and which no one could endure" (3.1, 1110a23–6). So too, Aristotle later observes that we are more inclined to grant *sungnômê* to people who surrender to the kinds of desires that are natural and common to all human beings (7.6, 1149b4–6), because they are presumably irresistible.[9]

Aristotle's discussion of involuntary action in the case of ignorance is equally nuanced. For example, if one commits a wrong in ignorance but later feels no regret (*en metameleiâi*), then the act hardly counts as unwilling, because one would have done it even had one been fully aware; Aristotle labels such an act, accordingly, "not voluntary," as opposed to "involuntary" (1110b18–23). So too, wrongs done when one is drunk or in a rage are in some sense done unawares but are not genuinely involuntary.[10] Aristotle, thinking no doubt of the Socratic postulate, says that in a certain sense anyone who does something evil is ignorant of what ought to be

---

[9] Metzler 1991: 44–5 cites various passages in which *sungnômê* is granted for an action that is all too human, or common to all people ("Allgemeinmenschliches," 44), e.g., Euripides *Andromache* 955, *Bacchae* 1039, *Heracles* 981, *Hecuba* 1107, ps.-Xenophon *Constitution of the Athenians* 2.20: δημοκρατίαν δ' ἐγὼ μὲν αὐτῷ τῷ δήμῳ συγγιγνώσκω· αὐτὸν μὲν γὰρ εὖ ποιεῖν παντὶ συγγνώμη ἐστίν ("I grant the common people [*dêmos*] *sungnômê* for their democracy; for *sungnômê* is due to anyone for favoring himself"); there is no implication here of pardoning a wrong action.

[10] Cf. Philippides fragment 27 Kassel-Austin: "One cannot obtain *sungnômê* by saying, 'I was drunk, father, I erred'; for someone who acts violently against a weak person, Pamphilus, is thought to mistreat [*hubrizein*], not merely to err [*hamartanein*]." Drunkenness is dismissed as an excuse, but the larger point is that only an error is deserving of *sungnômê*, not deliberate wrongdoing. We may compare Fingarette and Hasse 1979: 77: "In a purely formal sense, it can be maintained that in the common law there is no such thing as an 'intoxication' defense – indeed the fact that a defendant was intoxicated at the time he commmitted a crime has classically been rejected as a defense to the commission of that crime.... In the nineteenth century, however, English and American judges attempted to introduce an element of flexibility into the law to allow partial – but not complete – exculpation of the inebriated offender." So too, "English law ... reasoned that if intoxication resulted in the

done but does not on that account act unwillingly. As opposed to such character-based or generalized ignorance, Aristotle specifies that what renders an act involuntary is a lack of knowledge of particulars, and this is the kind of situation in which there arise pity and *sungnômê* (1110b33–1111a2). One might, for example, mistake one's son for an enemy or mistakenly strike someone with a deadly weapon when one had reason to suppose that it was harmless, and such cases will naturally result in regret.

This is about all that Aristotle has to say about *sungnômê* in the *Nicomachean Ethics*, which is significant. But far more to the point is that Aristotle's conception of *sungnômê* fails to meet the minimal condition for forgiveness, as set out in the previous chapter. For leaving aside any question of confession, remorse, repentance, or change of heart, of which Aristotle takes no account here (*metameleia* clearly signifies in this context simply regret over what one has done unwittingly and not guilty compunction), the kind of action that induces *sungnômê* is specified as involuntary in the most strict and narrow sense of the term. Truly involuntary acts do not count as instances of wrongdoing but rather are innocent. Oedipus makes the point in Sophocles's tragedy, *Oedipus at Colonus*, in his reply to the reproaches of Creon, insisting that he murdered his father and married his mother unwillingly (*akôn*, 964). Because he did not know what he had done or to whom, one cannot rightly blame an action that was on these grounds involuntary (976–7; cf. 983, 986–7). There is no reason to suppose that Oedipus's speech here represents some new stage in Athenian legal theory, as though the difference between voluntary and involuntary acts in regard to guilt or innocence had been unknown in Greece prior to this moment (we shall see later that the distinction was clear to Homer).[11] Oedipus is replying to a manifestly unjust and self-interested accusation on the part of Creon and expects

absence of a required state of mind (*mens rea*) for the alleged crime, the defendant logically cannot be found guilty of that crime" (79). The story is ongoing: "For well over a decade, courts have debated the scope of the criminal responsibility of those addicted to alcohol, narcotics, and other mind-altering drugs. Today the issue remains unsettled" (137).

[11] Cf. the Sophocles Fragment 665, from the lost tragedy Tyro: "No person is evil for having erred involuntarily." Sissa 2006: 57–75, suggests that Sophocles's *Oedipus the King* and *Oedipus at Colonus* exerted a strong influence on later discussions of guilt and responsibility, and in particular Aristotle's.

bystanders to approve his argument, as the chorus of Athenian elders does. If it is true that we do not forgive people who are innocent, because there is nothing to forgive, then the term *sungnômê* in the preceding passage of the *Nicomachean Ethics* cannot signify "forgiveness."

What then does *sungnômê* mean here? The sense must be that a harmful or inappropriate act that was performed involuntarily is excusable or understandable and does not count as a case of wrongdoing for which the agent is responsible. The pairing of *sungnômê* with pity suggests as much as well. For Aristotle, pity is defined as "a kind of pain in the case of an apparent destructive or painful harm in one not deserving to encounter it" (*Rhetoric* 2.8, 1385b13–16); so too, the *Rhetoric to Alexander*, nowadays ascribed to the rhetorician Anaximenes and believed to have been composed somewhat earlier than Aristotle's *Rhetoric*, stipulates that "all people pity those whom they suppose to be well-disposed toward themselves and whom they believe to be undeserving [*anaxioi*] of misfortune. One must show that those whom one wishes to render pitiable have these qualities, and demonstrate that they have suffered or are suffering or will suffer wrongly [*kakôs*], unless the hearers help them" (34.4–5). Were the agent to be held responsible for the unjust act, there would be no occasion for pity.

The noun *sungnômê* and the related verb *sungignôskô* are compounds based on the root for the word meaning "to know" (*gignôskô*), with the addition of the prefix *sun-*, which broadly speaking signifies "with" or "together with." The compound thus naturally bears the sense of "know with another," that is, to think alike or comprehend, or, to use a Latin word that is composed of the same elements etymologically, to be cognizant (from *cognoscere*). The Latin *ignoscere*, also commonly (but erroneously) rendered as "forgive," has a similar formation, composed of the prefix *in-* and the root *(g)nosco*, and here too, the root sense is sometimes evident.[12] Etymology is not a reliable guide to current meanings of a word, but in this case, as can be shown by a host of examples, it provides a useful insight into the sense of *sungnômê*.[13]

---

[12] See Cicero's letters *To His Friends* 1.6.2 and 13.2.3, cited later in this chapter.

[13] Metzler 1991 puts considerable stress on the origin of the term *sungnômê*, as well as of *ignoscere*, as compounds signifying "recognize" or "realize," with the additional connotation of "think the same as" or "be in accord with" ("erkennen" in the sense

Aristotle's point is that with truly involuntary acts, one can see the agent's point of view and not deem him or her culpable; that is why, in such cases, one does not assign blame, as one ordinarily would for a deliberate injustice. It is not the victim of the offense who is the subject of the verbal expression *sungnômê* here, but any observer, again as in the case of pity; once more, the relevant response in the context is comprehension or understanding on the part of a presumably, or at least potentially, disinterested party, who judges the deed undeserving of blame. Forgiveness is not in question here.

The extended discussion of Aristotle's mention, almost *en passant*, of *sungnômê* is intended to illustrate why the notion of "forgiveness," in the full sense of the modern word, is not the right rendering of the Greek term here. To have shown this is, to be sure, a far cry from demonstrating that the word in question never

of "übereinstimmen, zugestehen," 29), and she argues that from the very beginning (e.g., in Indo-European), the terms carried a cognitive and a moral meaning: "In der frühen griechischen Belegen gibt es nämlich eine doppelte Brücke zwischen den Bedeutungen 'erkennen' und 'verzeihen'" (31). The Greek noun and especially the associated verb *sungignôskô* undoubtedly do carry this significance in many passages, duly collected by Metzler, e.g., Thucydides 8.24.5 (*meta pollôn ... tên hamartian xunegnôsan*); Herodotus 7.13, in which *sungnous* means to share an opinion or sentiment (so too Herodotus 4.3, of entire peoples); cf. Thucydides 2.60.4, 2.74.2, in which the sense is that "man sich die Meinung des anderen zueigen machen kann" (36). Nevertheless, Metzler notes (37) that Herodotus's usage is often ambiguous between "agree" and "forgive," e.g., at 2.110 (these senses are noted in Liddell and Scott, the authoritative Greek-English dictionary), and Metzler affirms that the noun, at least, normally carries a connotation of Verzeihen (38). For *sungnômê* as "Einsicht in die Rolle des anderen," Metzler cites (41–6), *inter alia*, Herodotus 1.39, in which Croesus's son professes to understand his father's concern for his welfare, Aristophanes *Acharnians* 578, *Wasps* 959, Thucydides 4.61.5, Euripides *Medea* 814. Metzler's analysis, although very useful, suffers from adopting too wide a definition of forgiveness: "Fragt man nach dem Begriff des Verzeihens in einer fremden Sprache und Kultur, so erwartet man, dass er auf Situationen angewendet wird, die durch (mindestens) dreierlei ausgezeichnet sind: eine Tat, einen Täter und einen Betroffenen; genauer gesagt: eine Tat, die eine Schädigung darstellte, als sie begangen wurde, deren Urheber und denjenigen, den die Schädigung betroffen hat (oder dessen Vertreter) und der jetzt die Möglichkeit einer Vergeltung hätte, auf diese aber – darin besteht im Kern das Verzeihen – verzichtet" (47). But one can forego retaliation for various reasons, and not all cases amount to forgiveness. Thus, at Xenophon *Hellenica* 5.4.30 (discussed on pp. 48–54), there is no evidence of an apology or repentance; Sphodrias simply asks his son to intervene with the son of the Spartan king Agesilaus in order to gain him acquittal despite his misconduct; and this Agesilaus agrees to do, to the extent that it is possible without loss of honor. One can speak of pardon here, but not of forgiveness proper.

means forgiveness, or, much more radically, that the very idea of forgiveness, irrespective of the meaning of the Greek *sungignôskô* (or the Latin *ignoscere*), was not a salient moral concept in the classical world. But before proceeding to the larger question, we may indicate the specific significance of the ancient terms with reference to a few more passages.

Let us take a Stoic passage. John Stobaeus, in his collection of excerpts from the classical works *Eclogae* (2.7, 95.24 W. = *SVF* [the standard edition of Stoic fragments] 3.640), reports in connection with the attitude of the Stoics:

Φασὶ "μηδὲ συγγνώμην ἔχειν <μηδενὶ τὸν νοῦν ἔχοντα"· τοῦ γὰρ αὐτοῦ συγγνώμην τε ἔχειν> καὶ νομίζειν τὸν ἡμαρτηκότα μὴ παρ' αὐτὸν ἡμαρτηκέναι, πάντων ἁμαρτανόντων παρὰ τὴν ἰδίαν κακίαν· διὸ καὶ δεόντως λέγεσθαι τὸ μηδὲ συγγνώμην ἔχειν τοῖς ἁμαρτάνουσιν.

Roberto Radice, in his translation of the complete fragments of the Stoics (Radice 1998), renders the passage as follows (I have turned Radice's Italian into English): "For them (scil. for the Stoics) a person with sense ought not to experience compassion [*sungnômê*] for anyone. For to experience pity [*sungnômê*] is the attitude of one who believes that no sinner sins voluntarily, whereas <the truth is> that all sins depend on the wickedness of the individual: this is why it is right to assert that one must not have pity [*sungnômê*] for one who sins."[14] Now, the first thing to note is that Radice translates the noun *sungnômê* once as "compassion," and twice as "pity" – but never as "forgiveness" or "pardon." It is easy to see why, for if we substitute *forgiveness* for those words, the argument will turn out to be confused (here I present my own, slightly more literal version of the Greek): "a man of reason ought not to entertain forgiveness for anyone. For forgiveness is the attitude of a person who believes the one who has committed a wrong has not done so on his own account, and yet all who do wrong do so because of their own vice; this is why it is right to say that one does not forgive those who do wrong." Let us leave aside the question of free will in general in

---

[14] "Per loro (scil. per gli Stoici) l'uomo di senno non debe provare compassione per nessuno. Provare misericordia, infatti, è l'atteggiamento di chi crede che nessun peccatore pecca volontariamente, mentre <la verità è> che tutti i peccati dipendono dalla malvagità dell'individuo: ecco perché è corretto affermare che non si deve avere misericordia di chi è nel peccato."

Stoic thought and the fact that they maintained that only the sage really acts deliberately whereas the foolish, as the Stoics labeled all the rest, are wholly ignorant and therefore do not have free will in the strict sense of the term (cf., e.g., Stobaeus *Eclogae* 2.111.18 W. = *SVF* 2.548; 2.68.8 W. = *SVF* 3.663). The point on which Stobaeus is insisting here is that *sungnômê* is due solely to those who have not deliberately or freely done wrong: and in this respect, the passage agrees perfectly with the preceding discussion of Aristotle. But it is precisely in cases of this kind that we do not apply the term *forgive*, but rather *exculpate* or *absolve*. It is thus clear why Radice chose to translate *sungnômê* here by using *compassion* and *pity*, although Greek has other, perfectly good words for these latter concepts, as we have seen.[15]

The Stoics regarded anger, like other passions, as unbecoming to a sage (Chrysippus defined *orgê* as "the desire to take vengeance against one who is believed to have committed a wrong contrary to one's deserts," *SVF* 3.395 = Stobaeus 2.91.10). A wise man will disdain a slight on the part of a fool, as the Stoics called those who fell short of virtue. But this does not mean that he will be inclined to accept excuses, for that would be to ignore the claims of justice: in effect, to condone the crime. Seneca, in his treatise on clemency, asks, "Why will a wise person not excuse [*ignoscet*]?" He explains, "Pardon [*venia*] is the remission of a deserved penalty." However, the wise man acts according to what is due, and so he will not remit the penalty for an intentional wrong (*De clementia* 2.7.1). Seneca does allow that a sage will spare (*parcet*) an offender, and try to improve him (*corriget*); and thus "he will act as though he excused, but he will not excuse, since he who excuses confesses that he has failed to do something that should be done" (2.7.2).[16] Cicero, in his speech *In Defense of Murena* (61–66), ascribes to Zeno the idea that a sage is never moved by generosity or favor (*gratia*) nor will he ever pardon another person's error (*numquam cuiusquam delicto*

---

[15] Compare Philo of Alexandria *QGen* 1.68: "He who has done something involuntarily confesses and asks for *sungnômê*; he who has done it voluntarily denies the deed"; *Quod Deus sit immutabilis* 134: "*sungnômê* is for those who have erred on account of ignorance or lack of experience of what one should do."

[16] In this passage, the term *ignoscere* might seem to approach that of *forgive* because Seneca means that the sage will not excuse a deliberate act of wrongdoing, but Seneca does not allow for the possibility that confession or remorse might sway the sage's judgment.

ignoscere); so too, only a fool will feel pity. What is more, all faults are equal (*omnia peccata esse paria*), but the wise man never repents of anything nor ever changes his mind (*nullius rei paenitere ..., sententiam mutare numquam*). Cato, he avers, not only thinks but also lives by these principles. If someone admits having done wrong and asks his pardon (*venia*), Cato says, "it is wicked to excuse a crime [*nefarium est facinus ignoscere*]." Nor will a sage ever get angry – and so this cannot be an excuse for error. Those who adhere to Plato's and Aristotle's teachings are of the view that a good man can feel pity, and that there is a place for pardon (*esse apud hominem constantem ignoscendi locum*). Cato maintains, "excuse nothing [*nihil ignoveris*]," to which Cicero replies, "some things – but not everything [*immo aliquid, non omnia*]." Yet the great men of old, schooled in Stoicism, were milder, given to humaneness (*humanitas*).

Musonius Rufus, a Stoicizing philosopher who was a contemporary of Seneca, sees a mild and humane temper and a disposition to pardon any offenses against himself (*hôste sungnômês axious ei tis plêmmelêseien eis auton*, 10), rather than go to trial, as proper to a philosopher. Although by bringing the case to court he may seem to be defending himself, in truth he betrays his own inconsistency, because the philosopher claims that "a good man cannot be wronged by a bad man, and yet he brings charges as if he believed that he, though a good man, were being wronged by people who are wicked." The Socratic premise of the argument obviates the need for forgiveness.[17]

Plato took no more interest in forgiveness (in the modern sense) than the other thinkers we have mentioned. Griswold remarks that "Plato never sees it as a virtue or commendable quality – certainly not one of any significance" (2007a: 279). The reason for Plato's neglect, according to Griswold, is that a good person is invulnerable to harm and so has nothing to forgive; and because he will not hurt others voluntarily neither will he be in need of forgiveness.

So much for the philosophers – and again, what stands out is their near total neglect of forgiveness, or even of *sungnômê* in its more limited sense, as a means of achieving reconciliation

---

[17] See Ramelli 1998, and cf. Graver 2007: 6, who notes that, for the Stoics, "there is no recourse to emotion as a means of discounting or lessening responsibility for actions taken by reasoning adults."

between offender and victim. Let us now turn to some examples
of pardon, or rather of *sungnômê* and its cognates as well as the
Latin *ignoscere*, drawn from legal discussions in rhetorical treatises
of a period rather later than Aristotle. These theorists, beginning
at least with Hermagoras (second century BC), sought to classify
and systematize the various kinds of judicial cases they found in
the Greek orators of the classical period and later, including the
school exercises, which were the stuff of rhetorical education in
Greece and Rome. There are subtle and not always clear differences in the arrangements they preferred, most of which we need
not explore in detail in this context. All tended to divide the fundamental strategies of argumentation (or "issues," in Malcolm
Heath's rendition of the Greek *stasis* and the Latin *status*) into
three broad categories: questions of fact, definition or terminology, and counterargument. Most simply, in the first of these –
questions of fact – the issue is: did the defendant do it or not? In
the second, one acknowledges the deed but argues that it does not
constitute an offense or crime. In the third, labeled "qualities" or
perhaps "qualifications" (*poiotês, qualitas*), one acknowledges the
deed and the legal description of it but denies responsibility.[18] It
is the third class of issues – the one that concerns us in the present context – that is most complex, both for the large and various numbers of subcategories, ranging from five or seven up to
thirteen subdivisions with later writers, and for the different clas-
sifications adopted by successive authorities. The specific defense
that is relevant here is that of *sungnômê* or, in the Latin versions,
the *status venialis*, the issue involving *venia*, from which derives the
English word *venial*.

   The only Greek treatise on *staseis* or issues that survive complete
is by Hermogenes, who lived from ca. AD 160 to 225, but there are
numerous references to the theory in commentaries and scholia
to ancient texts, above all in the scholia to Demosthenes,[19] and

---

[18] For a lucid account of these categories, see Heath 1995; also Heath 2004: 4–10.
   Metzler 1991 discusses *sungnômê* in various rhetorical tracts, citing (*inter alia*) Hyper-
   ides 5.26, PFlor 61.15, Anaximines 4.7–9, 36.35–6, and 4.5–6, Aristotle *Rhetoric*
   1373a28 and 1384b3, Hermagoras 31.2, and Iulius Victor; see Metzler 1991: 91–103
   for these and other references.
[19] On the scholia to Demosthenes, see especially Heath 2004: 109–12. E.g., ad 1.21,
   1.37, 2.46, 4.12: εἰκότως ἂν συγγνώμης] καίτοι ἀποδείξας ὡς οὐχ ἁμαρτάνει
   διὰ τὸ ταπεινοφρονεῖν, "συγγνώμην" τὸ τοιοῦτον καλει; 15.8–10, where

in Latin in commentaries on Terence and Virgil, among other
sources; in Latin too, Cicero (and the more or less contemporary
rhetorical treatise called *Ad Herennium* or "To Herennius") and
Quintilian (especially *Institutio Oratoria* 3.6) provide us with systematic accounts, much indebted to earlier Greek analyses but also
in part reflecting, as seems likely, customary Roman legal practice.
Hermogenes, in his essay, gives one of the standard examples of
a defense based on *sungnômê*, alluding to a famous real-life case
in which the Athenians collectively condemned ten commanders
for having abandoned the corpses of marines and sailors at sea
after the sea battle at Arginusae (406 BC) rather than gather them
up for proper burial (for the episode, see Xenophon *Hellenica*
1.6.1–36): "A paradigmatic instance of [the appeal to] *sungnômê* is
the ten generals who were unable to retrieve the bodies on account
of a storm, and were convicted" (*Peritôn staseôn* 2.67–9: συγγνώμης
δὲ παράδειγμα οἱ δέκα στρατηγοὶ οἱ διὰ τὸν χειμῶνα μὴ ἀνελό-
μενοι τὰ σώματα καὶ κρινόμενοι). Hermogenes's point is that
the storm was an external circumstance that absolutely prevented
the recovery of the bodies, and hence the generals were not guilty
of dereliction of duty. The argument is very like that of Aristotle,
although one might allege in reply that the storm did not prevent
at least an attempt at rescue, and that it was not so much the storm
per se in this case as the fear induced by the storm that led the
generals to abandon the corpses (Hermogenes does not make this
point here but other rhetoricians do: cf. Heath 2004: 109–12).[20]
The distinction is subtle, and goes back to Aristotle, who notes
in the passage of the *Nicomachean Ethics* discussed earlier that a
storm might cause passengers to cast their luggage overboard in
order to lighten the ship, a thing they would not ordinarily do,

Demostheses is said to justify forgiveness on the grounds that the Rhodians were
deceived (the same excuse as in the Olynthian orations); 18.14, where Demosthenes
appeals to a passion that is common to all human beings as justfication for *sungnômê*; 18.221, where the justification is said to be by necessity, and by the absence
of pleasure associated with the action (so too in Aristotle); 19.228 for a citation
of Hermogenes on the connection of *sungnômê* with passions, and an extended
discussion of various bases for *sungnômê*, including deception (εἰ δὲ <συγγνώμης
τυχεῖν> ἀξιοῖ ὡς ἐξηπατημένος, συγγνωμονικὸν γίνεται), drunkenness, erotic
passion, ignorance, and foolishness. Many additional passages in the scholia might
be cited.

[20] The other problem with the trial of generals at Arginusae was that they should not
have been tried collectively (Aristotle, *Constitution of Athens* 34.1).

needless to say, and yet they did decide on this course of action (1110a8–12) – it is one of those "mixed actions" that nevertheless "rather resemble voluntary ones." This distinction was not lost on later rhetoricians.

In addition to such external examples of overwhelming force or necessity, as the rhetoricians often labeled it, ignorance too – again as in Aristotle – could serve as a reason for *sungnômê*. One such defense reported by Hermogenes is based on the inability to know the future, and hence the outcome of certain actions (5.81–97): "no one knows what will happen, and so I am not guilty if I was ignorant of it" (οὐδεὶς οἶδε τὸ μέλλον· οὐκοῦν οὐδὲ ἐγὼ ἀγνοήσας ὑπεύθυνός εἰμι). However, there was one important development in the defense on the basis of ignorance that departs from Aristotle's discussion, for although he considered the argument, he viewed it as invalid: this is ignorance based on inner state or *pathos*, a term that in this context includes not just emotions such as anger or erotic passion but also madness, drunkenness, sleepiness, and similar psychological states of diminished responsibility. We can see most clearly the effect of this new conception on the Latin writers, beginning with Cicero. Thus, in his treatise *On Invention* (1.41) Cicero notes that, in reference to the state of mind in which an action is done (*quo animo factum sit*), the relevant division is between knowledge and ignorance (*prudentia et imprudentia*). Ignorance is relevant to a plea involving *purgatio*, which is to say, the case in which the deed is acknowledged, but responsibility or guilt is denied (*purgatio est, cum factum conceditur, culpa removetur*, 1.15), more or less what *sungnômê* signifies in the Greek tradition, though as we shall see, there are certain differences. *Purgatio*, in turn, is subdivided by Cicero into ignorance, chance, necessity, and state of mind or emotion, including irritation, anger, passionate love, and other perturbations of the sort (*inscientia, casus, necessitas, et in affectionem animi, hoc est molestiam, iracundiam, amorem et cetera, quae in simili genere versantur*, 1.41).[21] The treatise *To Herennius* (formerly ascribed to Cicero but composed by an unknown author more or less a contemporary of his) again refers to passions as an excuse, but this time only to

---

[21] At 1.15, however, Cicero divides *purgatio* simply into ignorance, chance, and necessity (*imprudentiam, casum, necessitatem*).

dismiss them, much in the manner of Aristotle: thus, in a plea of ignorance (*imprudentia*), one will want to know whether the defendant was unaware accidentally or culpably: "For a person who will claim to have acted irrationally on account of wine, love, or anger will appear to have been unaware [*nescisse*] as a consequence of vice, not of ignorance [*imprudentia*]." One has the strong impression that the author of this treatise had found in his sources a justification of the defense based on passion and is here rejecting it.[22] In the *Topics*, written toward the end of his life, Cicero notes that "passions of the mind fall under unawareness and ignorance [*cadunt enim in ignorantiam atque imprudentiam pertubationes animi*]" (64); Cicero adds that, "although these emotions are voluntary – for they are subject to reproach and admonition – they nevertheless possess such energy [*motus*] that even voluntary acts [committed under such impulses] sometimes appear compulsory or done in ignorance [*ut ea quae voluntaria sunt aut necessaria interdum aut certe ignorata videantur*; cf. *De partibus* 1.43]."[23] It may be, as Luigi Pirovano suggests (108), that excuses based on passion came into conflict with Roman legal and moral traditions and were rejected by Roman authorities on this account. Later writers, including the previously mentioned Latin commentators from the fourth century onward, do allow for *venia* on the basis of inebriation, passionate love (cf. Quintilian *Declamation* 291.3), and youth (cf. Quintilian *Declamation* 260.8, 286.8), all under the heading of ignorance, and to these they add, very plausibly, out and out insanity or *furor* (cf. Quintilian *Institutio oratoria* 7.4.9–10).[24]

---

[22] See Pirovano 2006: 105; I am much indebted to this fine study.

[23] See ibid., 106–7.

[24] Details in ibid., 96–104, 108–10. Pirovano notes (128–9), "Stupisce invece constatare che in nessun manuale retorico tardoantico sia dato rilevare la presenza del *furor* nell'ambito della *venia per imprudentiam*, che dunque – allo stato attuale delle nostre conoscenze – sembrerebbe rappresentare un peculiarità delle *Interpretationes Vergilianae* [sc. of Tiberius Claudius Donatus]." On the excuse of youth, see Antilochus's apology to Menelaus for his unsporting behavior in the chariot race in which he cut off Menelaus's team (*Iliad* 23.587–8). Antilochus further humbles himself by offering his prize to Menelaus by way of compensation. Menelaus observes that Antilochus is not normally this way, and adds that he is the more ready to be reconciled because Antilochus, along with his father and brother, have suffered so much on his behalf (607–8) – another standard ploy among the rhetoricians.

Roman writers made one distinction in regard to issues or types of argument that is not found in surviving Greek sources, namely that between *purgatio* proper, in which guilt is not acknowledged, and what they call *deprecatio* or "appeal," in which it is. As Cicero defines it, "*deprecatio* is when the defendant admits that he has committed a wrong and done so deliberately [*consulto*], and yet nevertheless asks that he be granted pardon [*ut ignoscatur*]"; but Cicero adds at once that "this type occurs very rarely" (*On Invention* 1.15; cf. 1.46, 2.94). In a later passage, Cicero affirms (2.104) that the use of *deprecatio* "can scarcely be approved in trials, since if the crime is conceded it is hard to ask the person who is supposed to be the punisher of crimes to grant pardon [*ut ignoscat*]" (cf. Quintilian 7.4.17: "The last recourse is *deprecatio*, a type of argument that most deny should ever be employed in a trial" [*ultima est deprecatio, quod genus causae plerique negarunt in iudicium umquam uenire*]).[25] Cicero recommends that in such cases one mention one's services to the republic and the like so as to seem not to be resorting to *deprecatio*, even if one is;[26] one can even allege the benefits bestowed by one's ancestors, and in any case will insist that the deed was not done out of hatred or cruelty but foolishly or on impulse, or for some other decent and commendable reason (2.106: *non odio neque crudelitate fecisse, quod fecerit, sed aut stultitia aut inpulsu alicuius aut aliqua honesta aut probabili causa*). One should also show that one has learned from one's error – a move that might suggest a change of heart on the part of the offender. But the argument

[25] Shortly before this, Quintilian remarks that, when all other means of defense have been exhausted, there remains what he calls *excusatio* (7.4.14): "This may be either ignorance (as when a man brands as a slave a runaway who is afterwards adjudged to be a free man, and then denies that he knew he was free); or necessity (as when a soldier overstays his leave and says he was delayed by floods or by illness)" (trans. Russell, Loeb vol. 3 [2001], 245). It is only if this strategy too should fail that Quintilian recommends the desperate measure of *deprecatio*, or a plea for mercy, which as he says is very rarely resorted to. Quintilian quotes Cicero's *Pro Ligario* (30) as an instance: "I have pleaded many Causes, Caesar, and indeed with you, while your political career kept you active in the courts, but never have I said, 'Members of the jury, pardon [*ignoscite*] this man, he erred, he lapsed, he did not think [*non putavit*].'"

[26] Cicero, in a letter addressed to Q. Metellus Celer (*Letters to His Friends* 5.2.6), writes, "if I have opposed your brother in any matter for the good of the Republic, *ut mihi ignoscas!*" Clearly, Cicero is not asking for forgiveness but excusing his conduct on the basis of a wholly honorable and adequate motive.

would seem to look to a different effect, for Cicero continues (the translation is by Yonge 1888):

> [The defendant is advised] to promise and undertake that he has been taught by this error of his, and confirmed in his resolution also by the kindness of those who pardon him, to avoid all such conduct in future. And besides this, he may hold out a hope that he will hereafter be able, in some respect or other, to be of great use to those who pardon him now; he will find it serviceable to point out that he is either related to the judges, or that he has been as far back as possible an hereditary friend of theirs; and to express to them the earnestness of his good-will towards them, and the nobility of the blood and dignity of those men who are anxious for his safety.

The claim is not so much to have reformed morally as to have given over treating the offended party in a hostile way, putting oneself rather at the other's service: it is a kind of argument that Cicero evidently sees as being similar to other pragmatic advantages that the defendant has available.

The distinction that the Romans draw between *purgatio* and *deprecatio* is absent in the Greek sources; as Pirovano states, "Tale suddivisione non trova però alcun riscontro in ambito greco, dove compare solo il termine συγγνώμη" (93–4). The Greek writers, in turn, give evidence of a type of classification that is missing in the Latin authorities. Among the types of argument that the accused might employ there is not only that based on *sungnômê* but also one involving a transference (or in Greek *metastasis*) of responsibility, as when one alleges that the accuser bears the blame or else some third party. Hermogenes (6.69–81) reports that "Some have divided off *sungnômê* from *metastasis* not on the basis of responsibility and non-responsibility (*tôi aneuthunôi kai hupeuthonôi*), but have simply called all those things that transfer the crime to something coming from without 'transferences' [*metastatika*], whether it is a storm and torture and any other such thing, and define only those things that transfer to some private passion of the soul [*idion ti pathos psukhês*] as pertaining to *sungnômê*, for instance pity or sleep or anything of this sort." Hermogenes comments that this may not be wrong (*kakôs*), for "they differ in nothing but name from *sungnômê*." It is highly likely, on the basis of independent sources (cf. Anonymous in *Rhetores graeci* 7.583.4–14), that the authority to whom Hermogenes is alluding is Minucianus, a second-century

AD rhetorician (see Pirovano 111–16; Heath 2004: 109). A little later, Apsines (276.3–7) records a similar distinction, including among the reasons for *sungnômê* drunkenness and madness. Finally, Porphyry (third century AD), who wrote a commentary on Minucianus, proposed to distinguish simply between crimes that are avoidable, which he listed under *metastasis*, and those that are not, and that fall under *sungnômê*, for example the case of the ten generals at Arginusae who were absolutely prevented by the storm from retrieving the bodies (Anonymous in *Rhetores graeci* 7.203.22–204.4; cf. Heath 2004: 110; Pirovano 116–19).[27]

One can go into much greater detail in tracing the genealogy of the various distinctions, but for present purposes the point is sufficiently made that *sungnômê*, whether it includes such external pressures as storms and tortures or is restricted to internal factors such as drunkenness, passion, or insanity, has nothing to do with asking forgiveness for a confessed wrong, but rather looks to denying or evading responsibility for the action, ascribing the cause to circumstances beyond the agent's control. One can see why Malcolm Heath, in his translation with commentary of Hermogenes's treatise on issues, renders *sungnômê* as "mitigation" (1995: 256, in the glossary) and explains that it comes under the category in which "an acknowledged *prima facie* wrong is excused as due to factors outside the defendant's control, and not capable of being brought to account (or, according to some, due to internal factors outside the defendant's control, such as emotion)." Michel Patillon, in turn, in his French translation of all the works that have come down under the name of Hermogenes, renders *sungnômê* as "excuse."[28] The latter comes closer, in my view, to capturing the sense of *sungnômê* in these texts, for the object in this kind of argument is not to diminish or extenuate responsibility for the crime but to seek complete exoneration by virtue of something equivalent to what

[27] It is interesting to compare modern Canon Law in this connection. Thus, Beal, Coriden, and Green (2000: 1542) list under "Factors Exempting from a Penalty" (Canon 1323) conditions such as being under age, nonnegligent ignorance, acting under physical force, being coerced by grave fear, self-defense, and lack of the use of reason; on 1543, under "Factors Diminishing Imputability" (Canon 1324), are listed people who "had only the imperfect use of reason," thanks to drunkenness or the like, or who acted under the "grave heat of passion," intense fear, etc.

[28] Patillon 1997: 617, in the "Index de noms grecs."

jurists call *force majeure* or, in Latin, *vis maior.*[29] It is true that the deed is conceded, and that the act is defined legally as wrongdoing, but responsibility is wholly denied, except in the special case of Latin *deprecatio*, and even here, one does everything possible to avoid accepting responsibility for the action. Whatever *sungnômê* or Latin equivalents may signify in these documents, it has nothing to do with the rich sense of forgiveness set forth in the previous chapter.

Manuals dedicated to forensic rhetoric are perhaps not the place where one might most expect to find references to forgiveness, as opposed to judicial pardon (and even that only very rarely), and thus the fact that *sungnômê* or *ignoscere* in these contexts means something less than *forgiveness* in the full modern sense of the term does not in itself show that the words cannot bear this significance in connection with more informal or personal relations. I therefore proceed now to consider some additional occurrences of the relevant terms in nontechnical literature, selecting cases in which *forgiveness* might seem a plausible rendering. Here, it is not a matter of explicit definitions or descriptions such as we have encountered in the philosophical and technical treatises but rather of inferring the meaning of the terms under discussion from the wider context. Such a philological or lexical analysis, which explores the denotations and connotations of particular words, constitutes a necessary preliminary to the investigation, in the following chapter, of more general situations in which forgiveness might seem to be at work, irrespective of the occurrence of the terms under consideration here. For so long as it is assumed that the terms in question do refer to forgiveness, it makes little sense to undertake the broader study.

The basic Greek-English dictionary that scholars employ today is by Henry George Liddell and Robert Scott (1940). This is the best modern dictionary of classical Greek in any language and will remain so until the completion of the Greek-Spanish dictionary being published in Madrid.[30] Under the lemma *sungnômê*, Liddell and Scott give as the first set of definitions "fellow-feeling, forbearance, lenient judgement, allowance," followed by a variety

---

[29] On this concept in Roman law, see Molnár 1981 and Pirovano 2006: 129–41.
[30] Adrados and Rodríguez Somolinos 1989–.

of phrasal combinations that they render as "judge kindly, excuse, pardon" (*sungnômên ekhein*) or "be excusable." For the adjective *sungnômôn*, in turn, the lexicon gives not only "agreeing with" but also "disposed to pardon *or* forgive, indulgent." Finally, Liddell and Scott define the verb *sungignôskô* as "think with, agree with," and the like, reflecting the etymology of the term as a compound based on *gignôskô*, "to know or think," and also as "confess," "have fellow feeling" with someone, "excuse," and "pardon."[31] The reticence to use the word *forgive* in the definitions of these Greek terms is noticeable and commendable and stands in contrast to the more recent and prestigious Latin-English dictionary, also published by the Oxford University Press (1968) and edited by P. G. W. Glare. Although Glare normally offers highly nuanced definitions of the lemmas, broken down into multiple submeanings, in the case of *ignosco* he gives only two: first, "To forgive," with more than fifty citations; and second, at the end of the entry, "(in a weakened sense) To make allowances, grant indulgence," with eight examples. *Excuse* can mean to exonerate and carries no necessary implication of a fault in the other, whereas *forgive*, in the stricter sense under consideration here, does imply guilt. Let us then examine some uses in context and see whether they bear out the claim that I am making.

To limit the data, I shall consider first some passages from tragedy and from the historian Herodotus and the orator Lysias.[32] In Sophocles's *Women of Trachis*, there is a touching scene in which Iole, whom Hercules has brought home as his slave and concubine after destroying her city, stands mutely in the presence of Hercules's wife Dejanira; the messenger who has accompanied her explains (327–8): "She has suffered a cruel misfortune, but it invites *sung-nômê*." Her silence may be indulged because it is not a sign of arrogance (as Clytemnestra, in Aeschylus's *Agamemnon*, interpreted Cassandra's silence) but of shock. In the *Ajax*, Agamemnon

---

[31] Cf. Dover (1994: 195): "a misdeed could be thought to deserve forgiveness if it was committed without malicious intent.... A further motive for forgiveness, however, was compassion, the sensitivity which makes us identify ourselves with a sufferer and advance his interests even to the detriment of our own." The latter element is less in evidence in the texts I have examined, though it may play a role in comedy (see the discussion of Menander in the next chapter).

[32] On tragedy, besides the discussion in Metzler 1991, see Gutzwiller (2011).

asks Odysseus whether he is justified in responding angrily to Teucer's reproaches, to which Odysseus replies (1322–3): "I rather have *sungnômê* for someone who answers insults in kind," the point being that Teucer's words are justified because he has been provoked. Needless to say, nothing like forgiveness is involved here. In Sophocles's *Electra*, the heroine tells the chorus of women that she is ashamed at her outbursts of grief but asks their indulgence (*sungnômê*) because "compulsion obliges me to behave this way [*hê bia gar taut' anankazei me dran*]" (256); the appeal is to necessity, which renders an action involuntary, according to Aristotle, and hence innocent. In the *Philoctetes*, Neoptolemus tells the ailing hero that one must bear what the gods send us, but those who bring on deliberate suffering deserve neither *sungnômê* nor pity (1316–20): the pairing with pity is, as we shall see, common among the orators. Here again, *sungnômê* is due when there is no recourse. However, it was a different matter when Philoctetes screamed out in the throes of his disease. Aspasius, the second-century AD commentator on Aristotle's *Nicomachean Ethics* (133 Heylbut, on *Nicomachean Ethics* 7.8), remarks in connection with softness of character that "it is not remarkable 'if a person is overcome by excessive pain or grief' [*Nicomachean Ethics* 7.8, 1150b6–7]; rather, this deserves *sungnômê*, for example when someone, like Philoctetes in Theodectes' tragedy [fr. 5b Snell], having been bitten by a serpent, endures it up to a certain point, since he wishes to conceal it from Neoptolemus and his men, but afterwards, when he cannot tolerate such intense pain, gives himself away. Sophocles and Aeschylus represented him in the same way. Carcinus too seems to have represented Cercyon [fr. 1b Snell] as overcome by severe pain. These men are not soft; one is soft rather if one cannot bear up under pains that the majority can endure, but is overcome by those." In a fragment (fr. 352 Radt) from Sophocles's *Creusa*, a character declares that it is not right to lie, but when telling the truth entails one's ruin then it is pardonable (*sungnôston*). In all these instances, what might seem like inappropriate behavior is held to be excusable because it is humanly impossible, or at least contrary to human nature, to react otherwise (for grief as an excuse, cf. Livy 3.48.4).

A similar range of excusable actions is manifested in Euripides' employment of the terms under consideration. In a fragment of his *Polyidos* (fr. 645), a character affirms, "The gods are believed to be *sungnômones* [adjective] when someone seeks by swearing an oath to escape death or chains or the violent harm of enemies" (for the idea that the gods, being wiser, should grant *sungnômê* to a young man's thoughtless boast, see Euripides *Hippolytus* 117–20). In the *Alcestis*, it is said to be understandable that slaves should weep at the misfortunes of their masters (136–9). Medea, in the tragedy named for her, allows that Jason might reasonably have sought the bed of another woman if she had been childless (490–1); again, she can see why the chorus would seek to discourage her from killing her children, because they have not suffered what she has (814–15; cf. also 703, 869–71). In the *Children of Heracles*, Iolaus acknowledges that it is pardonable or understandable if the king does not wish to offer up in sacrifice a member of his own city on behalf of the exiles he is harboring (435–6), and the chorus affirms that Alcmene, Hercules's mother, harbors an understandable hostility to Eurystheus, who was responsible for his labors and had just now sought to put his surviving family to death (981–2). In these cases, we see that the idea associated with *sungnômê* and more particularly with the adjective *sungnôston*, that is, deserving of *sungnômê*, is that of an action that is comprehensible in the circumstances (cf. also *Andromache* 840, 954–6). In the *Hecuba*, the chorus declares that it is understandable (*sungnôst'*) that one should wish to die when one suffers misfortunes that are too great to be borne (1107–8), the emphasis once again falling on the limits of human endurance. In the *Suppliant Women*, the chorus introduce an excuse that turns up again in the writers of rhetorical manuals: "he did wrong; but this is characteristic of young people, and one should have *sungnômê*" (250–1; on youth as an excuse, cf. Lysias 24.17). In the *Heracles*, Hercules's wife, Megara, begs her father-in-law's pardon (*sungnôthi*) for speaking before he does on the grounds that "women are more pitiful [*oiktron*] than men" (534–7). In the *Phoenician Women*, on the contrary, young Menoeceus excuses his father's unwillingness to give his life for his country on the grounds of his advanced age (994–6). In the *Trojan Women*, Helen argues rather cynically that her passion for Paris is pardonable, because Zeus is slave to Aphrodite (948–50) – this is the argument from *pathos* or strong emotion that, as we have seen, some later rhetoricians considered to be the specific domain of *sungnômê*.[33] In *Helen*, Teucer, who has just landed on the shore of Egypt, concedes his error in cursing the woman he takes to be Helen (she is Helen, who was wafted away to Egypt while a phantom of her was carried off to Troy, but Teucer does not know this) and begs her pardon on the grounds that he was carried away by anger (135–7) – another of the passions that might overpower a person and hence render his or her actions involuntary.[34]

In Herodotus (1.39), Croesus's son, whom Croesus had forbidden to engage in hunting or warfare because of a prophetic dream that the youth was to die by an iron spear point (1.34), declares that his father's reaction is deserving of *sungnômê*, because he failed to take into account the detail that his death would come from iron – but boars' tusks are not iron-tipped, and so the restriction on hunting, as opposed to warfare, is needless; Croesus's mistake was a natural one, in that it is easy for an anxious father to overlook such particulars, and so his error is deemed to be understandable (the boy will die when struck by the javelin of another of the huntsmen, and so the prophecy is fulfilled). In giving advice to Cyrus on how to tame the Lydians, Croesus first shifts the blame for their rebellion from them onto the satrap Pactyes (1.155), thereby making partial use of the strategy called *metastasis* or transference, which, as Hermogenes notes, is very close to *sungnômê*, because it effectively indicates the innocence of the supposed offender. At another point (7.13), Xerxes asks the Persians' *sungnômê* for his quick change of plan; he explains that he was under pressure from many advisers to the contrary, and that he resisted the wise counsel of Artabanus with a young man's overheated irritation;

---

[33] Cf. Plato *Republic* 3.391E, quoting a fragment of Aeschylus; Propertius 2.2.1–4; Tibullus 1.6.29–30: *non ego te laesi prudens: ignosce fatenti,/ iussit Amor: contra quis ferat arma deos?* ("I did not deliberately harm you; excuse me even as I confess – it was Love that bade me, and who can bear arms against the gods?").

[34] In Simonides's poem on Danae, which contains perhaps the earliest example of the term under consideration (here in verbal form), Danae, who has been cast into the sea in a small boat along with her infant son Perseus, prays that her child and the sea remain calm, and that there be a change of plan (*metaboulia*) on Zeus's part; she then adds, "if I am uttering, in my prayer, a word too bold or without justice, *sungnôthi* (imperative) me!" Danae is not exactly apologizing but rather expressing the hope that she has hit upon the right tone or formula in petitioning Zeus's favor. For further discussion and earlier interpretations, see Metzler 1991: 68–70.

but now he will accept it, having come to agree with him (*sung-nous*): the participial form of *sungignôskô* carries something of the root meaning of the verb.

I now take a sample of uses from the speeches of Lysias, a younger contemporary of Herodotus, Sophocles, and Euripides. In the first speech (1.3), in which a man of relatively humble station defends himself on the charge of having killed his wife's lover when he was caught in the act, he says that everyone agrees that a person responsible for such deeds (i.e., adultery) does not deserve *sungnômê* or a mild penalty: presumably *sungnômê* here means something like being "let off the hook." Later (1.18), he recounts how he told his slave that she must either tell him the whole truth about the affair, and so receive *sungnômê* for her misdeeds, or else be beaten and sent to hard labor in the mill. This looks like a demand for confession, but clearly that is not what is at stake: the speaker simply wishes to get her to reveal what she knows so that he can take proper action; in this, it resembles the spirit of the new "Ley orgánica 10/1995," cited in Chapter 1, which rejects confession as an extenuating factor and insists instead that "One must be truthful in the sense that one must recount sincerely all that has happened in so far as he is aware." In the third oration (3.12–13), the speaker addresses the council and declares, "In my view, if I have done wrong, I deserve no *sungnômê*." A little later (3.19), he seems to take the opposite view, asserting that a group of people, who together with his opponent had gotten quite drunk and beaten him, asked *sungnômê* of him, not because they had been in the wrong but because what they had done was terrible. Were they confessing their guilt? I suspect rather they were relying on the excuse of *methê*, drunkenness, to affirm their innocence, a standard strategy for appealing for *sungnômê*, as we have seen. In any case, the speaker immediately thereafter declares that his antagonist, Simon, is to blame for the whole problem. In the peroration to the ninth speech (9.22), the speaker urges the jury to put justice above all else, and, bearing in mind that they often grant *sungnômê* even for manifest wrongs, not to ignore those who have done no wrong but have unjustly suffered at the hands of their enemies. If I understand the passage rightly, the speaker means to say that, given that the jury tends to be understanding even in the case of admitted offenses, they ought to be especially considerate of his

situation, because he has wronged no one. At the beginning of
the tenth oration (10.1–2), the speaker says he would have granted
sungnômê to his antagonist if he had accused him of killing his
(the antagonist's) father, because he was a worthless fellow, but he
could not do so when charged with the murder of his own father,
who had done such great services for the city (on benefactions to
the community, cf. 19.56, 30.1, 30.7; in the Roman tradition, Livy
28.41.1). The idea behind this witty barb is something like "making allowance" for the low status of his opponent. At 10.26, *sungnômê* is paired with pity, as in Aristotle (1110b33–1111a2; cf. 11.9,
12.79, 14.40 [the latter two in the peroration]); like pity, *sungnômê*
may be contrasted with anger toward the wrongdoer (14.13; cf.
25.1, 29.5; for Latin examples, cf. Livy 2.3.3, 3.40.1).[35] At 10.30, the
speaker claims that the lawgiver explicitly excluded the granting
of *sungnômê* in the case of things said in anger – but this claim is
made precisely because, as the speaker affirms, his opponent had
resorted to just this argument (cf. the same formulation at 11.11;
on anger as justifying inappropriate speech, 18.19).[36]

In Lysias's indictment of Eratosthenes (12.29), he allows that had
a higher authority than the city ordered it, one might be granted
sungnômê for having committed a murder. Again, at 12.30 he says
that one may have *sungnômê* for someone who has destroyed others for the sake of the safety of his own family – just the kind
of case that Aristotle thought of as "mixed," in which the act is
primarily to be construed as voluntary, though there is clearly an

---

[35] Metzler 1991 suggests that the pairing of *sungnômê* with pity might at first seem
odd ("Die Zusammenstellung von συγγνώμη und ἔλεος dürfte zunächts wun-
dern," 106) because, of the two, pity need not have a rational basis, but she then
observes that the same is true for forgiveness (107); the difference between the
two is a matter of degree: "Der Grad der Freiwilligkeit der Handlung und damit
der Verantwortlichkeit des Täters unterscheidet sich bei Mitleid und Verzeihen"
(108). But this is not entirely so: pity too is due to those who suffer undeservedly,
as Aristotle and many other classical writers affirm (see Konstan 2001a: 34–44),
and is not rendered indiscriminately. What pity and *sungnômê* have in common
is that both are granted to people who are not responsible, or fully responsible,
for the situation in which they find themselves, and so are in principle innocent.
Demosthenes 21.100 argues that only one who pities deserves pity, and likewise
for *sungnômê*. See Demosthenes 25.81 for the combination of pity, *sungnômê*, and
philanthrôpia.

[36] For additional examples of motives for and against *sungnômê*, including anger
(Demosthenes 21.38), love (Lysias 3.4), and lack of information (Demosthenes 45.7
and 59.83), see Metzler 1991: 83–7.

element of compulsion. Where the action is no more than a minor infraction (which is not the case here), and the harm threatened is vastly greater, such a deed, according to Aristotle, though wrong in itself, can even be viewed as praiseworthy (cf. 18.20). At 13.53, it is suggested that *sungnômê* may be reciprocal: one is more disposed to grant it to those who have been indulgent toward oneself (cf. Cicero *Against Verres* 2.3.2; Horace *Satires* 1.3.73–5; Seneca *On Anger* 2.34.4; *On Benefactions* 7.28.3).

We may conclude this selected survey of the uses of *sungnômê* with a passage in the thirty-first discourse, which is Lysias's most detailed and explicit treatment of the subject (31.10–12). The case involves the prescribed scrutiny of public officials upon taking office. Lysias writes (modern commentators generally agree that the speech is authentically his), "All those who, on account of their own misfortunes, had no part in the dangers within the city at that time [the oligarchy of 404 BC], are worthy of receiving *sungnômê*. For no one suffers a voluntary misfortune. But those who acted intentionally deserve no *sungnômê* at all, since they did so not out of hardship but in conspiracy. For it is a just custom among all human beings to be especially angry, with respect to the same crimes, at those who are in a position not to do wrong, but to show *sungnômê* toward the poor or the physically incapacitated, in the belief that they err involuntarily. Thus, this man here deserves no *sungnômê*, since he is neither physically disabled nor struggling to survive, as you yourselves see...." The powerful emphasis here on voluntary action versus acts committed under constraint or coercion is consistent with all other testimony concerning *sungnômê*, whether analytical, as in the case of Aristotle and the rhetoricians, or literary and descriptive, as in the tragedians and historical writers.[37] This is as one might have expected in a society in which

---

[37] Compare Antiphon *On the Murder of Herodes* 92.1–2: Ἔπειτα δὲ τὰ μὲν ἀκούσια τῶν ἁμαρτημάτων ἔχει συγγνώμην, τὰ δὲ ἑκούσια οὐκ ἔχει ("Unwilling offenses, then, gain *sungnômê*, but willing ones do not"); cf. *Tetralogy* 3.1.6.1–2: Εἰ μὲν γὰρ ἄκων ἀπέκτεινε τὸν ἄνδρα, ἄξιος ἂν ἦν συγγνώμης τυχεῖν τινός ("For if he killed the man unwillingly, he is worthy to receive *sungnômê*"); also Isocrates *Plataicus* 14.20, Demosthenes 24.49, 24.67, and 58.24. In Thucydides's account of the debate over the fate of Mytilene, which had revolted from Athens during the Peloponnesian war, Cleon affirms that only an involuntary action is forgivable (*xungnômon d'esti to akousion*, 3.40.2); cf. 1.32.5: "*xungnômê* if not accompanied by vice"; 3.39.2, where *xungnômê* (an alternative spelling of *sungnômê*) is associated

judicial procedures had taken the place of blood price and other forms of private compensation for harm. For gaining the goodwill of a jury, or of one's adversary, by confessing to guilt without the least justification of one's actions, on the sole basis of a declared change of heart and promise of reform for the future, is not a self-evidently winning maneuver.[38] At the conclusion to this chapter we shall see that even where it might have been applicable, such a strategy did not commend itself to an experienced pleader. The modern idea of forgiveness has it roots in a religious conception of sin and conversion that was foreign to classical ways of thinking – but this is the subject of Chapters 4 and 5 of this book.

For now, let us examine evidence for the use of the Latin verb *ignoscere* (the corresponding noun, *ignoscentia*, is found for the first time in the second-century AD writer Aulus Gellius and is very rare before the Christian writers, e.g. Tertullian *De paenitentia* 7.10), which, in contrast to *sungnômê* and its congeners, is defined by the most authoritative Latin-English dictionary as principally bearing the meaning of "forgive." Rather than leap into forensic or rhetorical texts, which, important though they are to the argument of this book, reflect a juridical context in which, as we have seen, those accused of wrongdoing feel obliged to defend their innocence and hence are unlikely to confess to a crime or offer an apology, let us begin with a genre that, although highly artful and sophisticated and that is based on adaptations of Greek models (as far as surviving examples go, at any rate), nevertheless offers

with actions performed under compulsion; also 4.98.6, 4.114.5, 5.88.1, 7.15.2. In Xenophon's *Cyropaedia* (The Education of Cyrus) 3.1.38, Cyrus affirms, "all those wrongs that human beings commit out of ignorance, I deem to be involuntary"; a further excuse is that the actions in question were *anthrôpina*, that is, all too human, and hence beyond a person's ability to avoid, as Aristotle points out. Gaiser 1977 compares Jesus's words, "They know not what they do ..."; we shall discuss this passage from the Gospel in more detail in Chapter 4.

[38] Fulkerson 2004 argues that remorse, and not just regret, is essential to the idea of *metameleia*: "*metagignosko* simply involves a change of mind, *metanoeo* is a more serious reconsideration (especially where there is some harm done), and *metamelei* is a result of *metanoeo*, specifically the realization, upon reconsideration, that one has made a serious mistake and that it cannot be fixed" (256). Fulkerson defines *remorse* as "the emotion one has after having done something felt to be bad (or, sometimes, not having done something good) that one now wishes not to have done (or to have done).... [T]rue remorse looks beyond the self to the larger world, while regret simply wishes things were different" (244); a moral sense is thus built into the concept.

what is perhaps the closest reflection in ancient literature of every-day interactions among ordinary Romans. I mean the comedies of Plautus and Terence, which are reworkings of Greek comedies by Menander and his contemporaries but employ colloquial or conversational Latin (subject to the significant constraint of poetic meter, to be sure) and stage situations that at least resemble the misunderstandings and reconciliations or arbitrations that occur in ordinary life, short of going to court. For in these texts characters often do seek to excuse themselves for offensive words or actions, and do so face to face with the injured party, as opposed to speaking before a judge or jury or in the context of a rhetorical exercise.

I begin with an example from Plautus's *Aulularia* (Pot of Gold) and a famous scene that was later adapted by Molière in his play *L'Avare* (The Miser). A young man, Lyconides, has raped the daughter of a stingy old miser named Euclio, who has been hoarding a pot of gold he discovered in his fireplace. In the meantime, his treasure has been stolen. Having discovered that the girl has given birth, Lyconides decides to approach Euclio and confess his crime, at the same time asking for the girl's hand in marriage, thereby rectifying the situation, in accord with the conventions of New Comedy (as the genre is called). Euclio, however, mistakenly understands him to be confessing to the theft of his gold, and the resulting confusion makes for a hilarious exchange. For our purposes, the interest lies in Lyconides's attempt at an apology. He begins, "I confess that I have done wrong [*fateor peccavisse*] and I know that I deserve blame [*me culpam commeritum*]; I have come here to tell it to you, in hopes that you may kindly pardon me [*ut animo aequo ignoscas mihi*]" (738–9). The miser asks how he could have dared touch what did not belong to him – he means his gold – to which Lyconides replies that done is done, and adds that the gods must have wished it, for otherwise it would not have happened (741–2). This is excuse number one; Lyconides's second recourse is to affirm: "I did it under the influence of wine and love [*vini vitio atque amoris feci*]" (745), an argument that will scarcely seem plausible to Euclio, because he is thinking of his gold, but that, as we have seen, is one of the standard arguments in support of a request for *sungnômê*. Euclio will have none of it: "if this is fair and you can use this as an excuse [*si istuc ius est ut tu istuc excusare possies*]" (747), he says, then anyone can commit a robbery in broad daylight and get off scot-free on the grounds of drink and passion. Once the confusion over what Lyconides is confessing to is resolved, the young man states, "no one who has committed a crime [*culpam admisit in se*] and is ashamed of it [*pudeat*] is so worthless as not to justify himself [*purget sese*].... If I have unwittingly wronged [*imprudens peccavi*] you or your daughter, pardon me [*ut mi ignoscas*] and give her to me as my wife, as the laws require. I confess that I abused [*iniuriam fecisse*] your daughter at an all-night festival of Ceres, thanks to wine and the ardor of youth [*per vinum atque impulsu adulescentiae*]" (790–5).[39]

Lyconides comes as close as any character on the ancient stage to making a frank avowal of culpability and to seeking something like forgiveness. But it is clear that he does not base his appeal to consideration on repentance and a change of heart per se but rather offers a series of what are by now familiar excuses to acquit himself of responsibility: inebriation, passion, and youth, all contributing to unwitting or involuntary (*imprudens*) behavior – the language could have been taken straight from the rhetorical manuals; and because he now proposes to make good on the harm he has done by marrying the girl, Lyconides feels wholly exonerated. So too, in Plautus's *Mercator* (The Merchant), Demipho, an old man in love, says to his neighbor Lysimachus: "There is no reason why you should be angry at me: eminent men have done the like before. It is human to love – human also to pardon [*humanum amarest, humanum autem ignoscerest*]. Please stop reproaching me, it was not my own free will [*voluntas*] that drove me to it" (317–20).[40] Once again, love exempts a man from responsibility and admits

---

[39] On wine as an excuse, cf. Terence *Phormio* 1014–20; on youth, cf. Plautus *Mercator* 997; *Mostellaria* 1255–7; Terence *Hecyra* 736–8; Livy 2.18.10; Seneca *On Anger* 2.10.1–2; Cicero *In Defense of Sextus Roscius Amerinus* 3, and cf. 51 on rusticity as a defense: Cicero argues that, "given that, among our ancestors, the most eminent and famous, who ought to have been continually at the helm of the Republic, nevertheless dedicated a part of their labors and their time to caring for their own land, one should pardon a man who confesses that he is a farmer [*rusticus*]." Clearly, *ignoscere* here means something like "make allowance," not "forgive."

[40] For the argument from precedents, cf. Terence *Eunuch* 42–3 (from the prologue); that one should grant *sungnômê* because it is natural for human beings to err [*hamartein eikos anthrôpous*], see Euripides *Hippolytus* 615, along with the passages from Aristotle, Xenophon, etc., cited in the text.

of exculpation (cf. *Miles Gloriosus* 1252; *Poenulus* 140–1; Terence
Eunuch 878–81). So too, anger (*Poenulus* 1410–13) – once more in
line with the strategies recommended in the rhetorical treatises –
and fear (*Rudens* 702–3) may be invoked as grounds for acquitting
a person of blame (on fear, cf. Propertius 2.6.13; Ovid *Letters from
Pontus* 2.7.7).

Simply by way of contrast, I cite an article in a local Spanish
newspaper (*La Gaceta* of Salamanca, 88, no. 28,289 [July 5, 2008],
56), concerning a case in which a prison chaplain smuggled hash-
ish into the jail; the priest's lawyer is quoted as declaring that
his client "recognizes that he has done something wrong and is
deeply sorry for what has happened.... He begs the pardon of all
those whom he may have disappointed, for he accepts that he has
done something he ought not have done."[41] Granted, the chaplain
was caught in the act and is throwing himself on the mercy of the
court, but he and his lawyer assume that the mere affirmation of
contrition has some value in gaining forgiveness for his action.[42]

In the final scene of Plautus's *Epidicus*, the title character, the
clever slave who has manipulated the action to a successful conclusion, demands, rather absurdly, that his master Periphanes beg
permission to free him. Periphanes obliges, "I beg you, Epidicus,
to pardon me if I have unwittingly been responsible for having
done wrong [*oro te, Epidice, mihi ut ignoscas, siquid imprudens culpa
peccavi mea*]" (728–9). Once again, the emphasis is on *imprudentia*
or nonculpable ignorance, and Epidicus yields, as he says, under
compulsion of necessity (cf. *Menaechmi* 1073). In the *Miles Gloriosus*
(Braggart Soldier), the slave Sceldrus has been duped into believ-
ing that his master's courtesan, whom he saw in the arms of another
man, is really her twin sister, and he begs: "pardon my ignorance
and foolishness [*inscitiae meae et stultitiae ignoscas*]" (542–3). When

---

41 "[E]l capellán de la cárcel salmantina 'reconoce que ha hecho una cosa mal y está
profundamente arrepentido por lo occurido.... [P]ide perdón a todas las personas
a las que puede haber defraudado porque asume que ha hecho una cosa que no
debe."
42 In Aristophanes's *Wasps*, the protagonist, Trygaeus, confesses that he and his fellow
Athenians erred in rejecting peace earlier and asks for *sungnômê*, offering as an
excuse the fact that, at that time, their minds were all on leather, that is, the counsels of Cleon, who was mocked as a tanner; the move is a good example of *metastasis*,
or shifting the blame. So too at *Clouds* 1479, Strepsiades asks for *sungnômê*, explaining that he was mad and under the influence of Socrates' nonsense.

he promises never again to utter a word, even if he is certain of what he has seen, his fellow slave Palaestrio accepts that he did not act out of malice (*malitiose*, 569) and grants him pardon. The issue does not turn on a change of heart in Sceledrus, who has not deliberately done wrong, but on his complete submission to Palaestrio, who is the artificer of the action in this play.[43]

An extended discussion toward the end of the *Truculentus* (Irritable Man) sums up neatly the sense of *ignoscere* in Plautine comedy. Diniarchus, a young man who has raped the daughter of an Athenian citizen, begs her father to "put up sensibly what was done senselessly [*ut istuc insipienter factum sapienter feras*]" and pardon him for what he did when he was out of control and under the influence of wine (*mihique ignoscas quod animi impos vini vitio fecerim*, 827–8). Callicles, like Euclio in the *Aulularia*, is loath to accept the excuse, arguing that this is to transfer the blame to a mute party that cannot defend itself, and adding, in accord with Aristotle, that decent men control their drinking, and the fault for inebriation lies with the person, not the wine (829–33). Diniarchus concedes that he is responsible for the deed (*fateor culpae compotem*, 835), and Callicles decides to bring the matter to trial. Diniarchus replies, "Why would you take me to trial? You are my judge! But I beg you, give me your daughter as wife" (840–1). Callicles agrees, on condition that he reduce the dowry by six talents on account of Diniarchus's stupidity (*inscitia*, 845). Once Diniarchus admits his guilt, he no longer seeks pardon but proposes the only remedy still available, short of conviction in court: that he marry the girl, again as in the *Aulularia*. Because he has previously broken an engagement to her, Callicles is understandably suspicious, but makes the best of a bad deal. Forgiveness seems beside the point.

Turning now to Terence, in the *Andria* a slave explains that his duty is to run risks in the service of his master, while the master ought to pardon him if things go contrary to his plans (675–8). Terence's *Heautontimorumenos* (Self-Tormentor) is about a father who repents of having been too strict with his son, thereby inducing him to enroll as a mercenary in a foreign campaign. The neighbor's son, Clitopho, complains meanwhile of his own father's

---

43 Quintilian, in one of his declamations (307.11), affirms, "Earlier you could have been exonerated [*ignosci*], when you were still unaware [*cum ignorabas*]."

overly strict discipline and insists that when he is an old man, he will remember what it is like to be young and will make allowance for mistakes (*ignoscendi dabitur peccati locus*, 218; for a daughter justifying her passion by reference to her father's, cf. Ovid *Heroides* 8.37–8). In the same play, we see a wife arguing that her husband's sense of justice should offer some protection for a mistake done out of foolishness (644–8) – the error in question is that she did not leave her infant daughter to die, as her husband had ordered, though in the way of comedy it turns out for the best. In the end, the tough neighbor agrees not to disinherit his son for consorting with a courtesan but only on the condition that he take a wife and do all his father demands of him (1049–59): this does represent a change of attitude in the son, but it is achieved solely under constraint, and so hardly represents a clear case of repentance as the condition for forgiveness. Terence's *Phormio* involves a man who seeks to conceal from his wife the fact that he raped a young woman while drunk fifteen years in the past and has since been supporting her and the child she bore (cf. 1014–20 for the excuse of drink). When the secret is out, his brother pleads with the wife for indulgence: "Since the deed cannot be undone by leveling charges, pardon him. He's begging, confessing, clearing himself [*orat confitetur purgat*]; what more do you want?" (1034–5). The sense of *purgat* here is clear from Cicero's definition in *On Invention*, discussed earlier, as well as from many other passages: it is a matter of *purgatio* (as opposed to *deprecatio*) when the deed is conceded but guilt is denied (*purgatio est, cum factum conceditur, culpa removetur, De inventione* 1.15; cf. 1.46, *Rhetoric to Herennius* 1.24, 2.23). So too, Cicero, in writing to Atticus, explains that his brother Quintus has justified his conduct in a letter to him in which he insists that he never said anything inappropriate about Atticus to anyone (*Letters to Atticus* 1.19.11: *Quintus frater purgat se mihi per litteras et adfirmat nihil a se cuiquam de te secus esse dictum*; cf. 1.17.7).[44]

One of the contexts in which pardon may be implored is in war, typically on the part of those who have been defeated. For example, in the *Bellum Alexandrinum*, probably composed by Julius

---

[44] In Seneca's tragedy, *Oedipus on Mount Oeta*, Hyllus tells his mother: "pardon [*ignosce*] the fates – the mistake is free of blame" (*error a culpa uacat*, 983), and Cicero, in his speech *Against Verres* (2.4.126) equates *ignoscere* with legitimate justification (*iusta excusatio*).

Caesar's officer, Aulus Hirtius, the author recounts how the king of Lesser Armenia, when summoned to appear before the Senate, turned to Caesar and, having adopted the dress and posture of a suppliant, begged *ut sibi ignosceret* (67.1), explaining that he had been forced (*coactus*) to join Pompey's camp and that, besides, he was not in a position to act as judge in a civil war among Romans but had to obey the local authority. The argument is thus based on coercion (something like the excuse that Roman law identified as *vis maior*, and that Aristotle and the Greek rhetorical writers called *bia*, or force), and simultaneously on the fact that, under the circumstances, the king was under no obligation to take Caesar's part; thus he was innocent and not deserving of punishment. Although the term *pardon* might be employed in such a context, the Armenian monarch is exonerating himself rather than confessing to having done wrong (cf. Plautus *Amphitryo* 253–9). In war, *ignoscere* is sometimes more or less equivalent to showing "clemency" (*clementia*), humaneness (*humanitas*), or pity (*misericordia*); for example, in the *Bellum Africum* (92), possibly also composed by Hirtius, various leaders come to beg Caesar to spare them (*orantque ut sibi ignoscat*); he grants them pardon (*venia*), and as a result word of his mildness (*lenitas*) and clemency spreads round. Something like this idea is present in Anchises's famous instruction to his son Aeneas in their underworld conversation in Virgil's *Aeneid* (6.853): "spare the defeated and overwhelm the proud" (*parcere subiectis et debellare superbos*).

Like *sungnômê, ignoscere* is composed, as we have noted, of the prefix *in-* (probably intensive) and the root *(g)nosco*, the latter meaning "to know." As with *sungnômê*, the root sense of the Latin term is sometimes evident, as in the following letter from Cicero to Lentulus (*To His Friends* 1.6.2): "I am consoled by the memory of my times, which I see reflected in your affairs; for although your dignity is being sullied in a matter of less importance than the situation in which mine was infringed, there is such a great similarity between the two that I may hope that you will pardon [*ignoscere*] me for not fearing things that you never regarded as frightening." Cicero is not asking for forgiveness but rather indicating that he expects Lentulus to understand his attitude because he has had much the same kind of experience. In another letter (*To His Friends* 13.2.3), Cicero writes, "you will understand [*ignosces*] my anger, which is just when directed against men and citizens of that stripe." Cicero does not believe that his anger is excessive; on the contrary, he says explicitly that it is perfectly justified.

The Latin *ignoscere* has various nuances, like the Greek *sung-nômê* or the English *pardon* or *forgive*, which is often equivalent to a casual "excuse me!" So too, *ignoscere* may signify little more than "allow" or "accept." For example, Quintilian (*Institutio oratoria* 1.8.14) affirms that even though certain words are barbarisms and should be avoided in speeches, they are permissible (*ignoscitur*) in poetry, where they may be used for the sake of the meter. Again, Quintilian says (5.13.10) that he approves (*ignoscam*) of "a pretense of having forgotten" something in the course of a speech on the part of a good orator, if he feigns the lapse of memory for the purpose of saving his client.[45]

I conclude this chapter with a passage in which the word *ignoscere* does not occur explicitly, but which sheds light on the question of forgiveness precisely by virtue of its absence. In the last book of the *Institutio oratoria*, Quintilian states that there are times when even the best orator – who, according to Quintilian, must also be a morally perfect man (*vir bonus*) – will lie, if it is necessary in order to save or protect an innocent client. In the words of Quintilian, "a *vir bonus*, in his defense speech, will seek to withhold the truth from the judge" (12.1.36). Quintilian insists that even the sternest (*gravissimos*) philosophers – clearly a reference to the Stoics – held this view (ibid.; cf. 12.1.38). Quintilian was right about this: though it may seem paradoxical, the Stoics held up as a model of the ideal sage the figure of Odysseus, who was notorious for his propensity to fabricate fictions, and they specified various contexts in which a philosopher was actually obliged to deceive others, for example in conditions of war, when it is perfectly permissible to mislead the enemy.[46] One may also lie to prevent a murderer from killing someone (Quintilian 12.1.39). In respect to judicial cases, Quintilian adduces the instance – virtually a commonplace – of a plot against a tyrant, in which the orator has to defend one of the conspirators (12.1.40); another situation is when what the defendant did was

---

[45] I wish to thank Javier Gómez Gil for having shared with me his thoughts on the role of *excusatio* in Quintilian.

[46] Cf. Cicero *De officiis* 2.51; *SVF* 3 148; further references in Aubert (2011).

just, but the only way to achieve his acquittal is to deny that he did it at all (12.1.41). However, the most interesting case in the present connection is the following (12.1.42): Quintilian argues that if a guilty individual can change for the better – and he takes this to be possible – then it will be in the interest of the republic that he be absolved rather than punished. Consequently, if the orator is certain that the defendant will be a decent and law-abiding citizen in the future, then, even if the accusations against his client are true, he must do all he can to save him, up to the point of falsely affirming his innocence (*si liqueat igitur oratori futurum bonum virum cui vera obicientur, non id aget ut salvus sit?*). It never occurs to Quintilian to try convincing the judge to acquit the defendant precisely on the basis of the transformation in his character, that is, of his remorse for what he did and sincere rejection of his former behavior and his former self. It would appear that a demonstration of heartfelt contrition has no role to play in court trials, even if the orator is wholly convinced that his client has genuinely reformed and will behave honorably henceforward. There is no place, at all events in a judicial context, for what we call "forgiveness" in the full sense of the word.[47]

I hope to have shown that the Greek and Latin terms most frequently rendered as *forgive* do not bear that meaning in the strict or ample sense of the English word, which for us implies a confession of guilt on the part of the offender, along with clear signs of sincere remorse and repentance. This complex of sentiments is so deeply ingrained in us, thanks in large part to the Judeo-Christian tradition (as we shall see), that we are inclined to interpret the ancient Greek and Latin vocabulary as though the same set of

---

[47] Cf. 11.1.81–3: "If there is no excuse available, only repentance has any plausibility [*quod si nulla contigit excusatio, sola colorem habet paenitentia*], since a man who has come to be disgusted with his own previous errors may be regarded as sufficiently reformed. There are in fact circumstances which, in the nature of the case, make this not unbecoming: for example, when a father disowns a son <whom he had by a prostitute, because the son has now married> a prostitute; this is a theme from the schools, but it is not <one that might not occur in court>. There are many things the father can say here with perfect decency: that it is the prayer of all parents to have children better than themselves ...; that he himself was of humble status (it was allowable in him to marry a prostitute); that he had no father to advise him ...," etc. (trans. Russell 2001: 51–3). Quintilian is interested here not so much in repentance as in regret, perhaps, and above all in showing that the action of the father was excusable whereas that of the son was not.

concepts already existed in the pagan world. In my view, this is a mistake, and we run the risk of misrepresenting not only the sense of the words *ignoscere* and *sungnômê* but also of misunderstanding the prevailing ethical system in the classical world, which had its own moral categories and criteria – criteria that did not include a fully developed conception of forgiveness, properly speaking. But to show this, it is, as I have said, not enough to examine a select set of words or expressions; we must also examine situations in which forgiveness in the modern sense might appear to be in play and determine whether it is so or whether some other form of reconciling offender and victim is operative. This is the burden of the next chapter.

3

Did They Forgive?

Greek and Roman Narratives of Reconciliation

Surely confession and penitence must precede reconciliation? Amnesty yes, reconciliation maybe, but forgiveness no.[1]

I have argued in the previous chapter that the ancient Greek and Latin terms *sungignôskô* and *ignosco*, usually rendered as *forgive* in English, do not properly bear that meaning, as forgiveness is commonly understood today – that is, a response to an offense that involves a moral transformation on the part of the forgiver and forgiven and a complex of sentiments and behaviors that include sincere confession, remorse, and repentance. I suggested that, on the contrary, the appeasement of anger and the relinquishing of revenge were rather perceived as resting on the restoration of the dignity of the injured party, whether through compensation or gestures of deference, or else by way of discounting the offense on the grounds that it was in some sense involuntary or unintentional. Is it true, then, that remorse and repentance played little or no role in the process of reconciliation between wrongdoer and victim? If not, did the Greeks and Romans have some moral equivalent to our modern forgiveness in their vocabulary and ethical system?

In this chapter, I approach an answer to these questions through an examination of scenes of reconciliation and the assuaging of

[1] *The New York Review of Books*, February 14, 2008, 55, from a letter to the editor by Bernard Lytton, Professor Emeritus of Surgery and Urology at the Yale University School of Medicine, responding to a review by Freeman Dyson entitled "Rocket Man" that appeared in the issue of January 17, 2008; Dyson, reviewing a book by Michael Neufeld on the German rocket scientist Werner von Braun, indicated a certain sympathy for von Braun. Lytton replied: "Von Braun never publicly renounced

anger, where we can perhaps catch a glimpse of how these processes worked in practice. I begin with Homer's *Iliad*, the earliest surviving work (along with the *Odyssey*) of classical literature – and a text that offers a classic case of the renunciation of anger, when Achilles gives over his wrath against Agamemnon for having arbitrarily deprived him of his war prize and rejoins the battle against the Trojans to avenge the death of his friend Patroclus. Does Achilles forgive Agamemnon? Many modern critics have thought that he does not. The time for forgiveness, had Achilles been so disposed, was when Agamemnon offered him countless gifts, and the hand of one of his daughters in marriage, using the trio of messengers or ambassadors Odysseus, Ajax, and Phoenix. But at that time Achilles rejected the offer of reconciliation, still angry at the way Agamemnon had insulted him before the rest of the Achaeans. Some scholars have supposed that the reason why Achilles was unappeased is that Agamemnon's offer seemed like a buyout, an effort to purchase Achilles's favor without a proper apology or recognition of his own guilt, accompanied by appropriate gestures of remorse and repentance. They find support for this interpretation in Agamemnon's insistence, as he dispatches the three envoys to Achilles's tent, that Achilles defer to his superior status (9.160–1): "Let him yield to me to the degree that I am more kingly (*basileuteros*) and claim to be greater in lineage," words that Odysseus discreetly suppresses when he repeats Agamemnon's message. True, Achilles has not heard this comment directly, but he seems to intuit Agamemnon's attitude when he sarcastically suggests that some other Achaean wed Agamemnon's daughter – one who is "more kingly" than he (9.391–2; the comparative adjective *basileuteros* occurs only in these two passages in the *Iliad*, reinforcing the sense that Achilles's comment contains an echo of Agamemnon's). So too, Achilles's curt remark, as he begins his reply to Odysseus, that "he is as hateful to me as the gates of Hades who hides one thing in his mind but says another" (9.312–13) has suggested to commentators that he senses that Odysseus is concealing Agamemnon's real feelings in the matter, although these

his role in the Nazi regime, of whose sadism and brutality he seems to have been fully aware. Surely confession and penitence must precede reconciliation? Amnesty yes, reconciliation maybe, but forgiveness no. Neither did we need to reward such a man with a presidential medal for his acts of redemption for unforgivable sins."

words are perhaps better interpreted as Achilles's way of preparing his friends for his own forthright rejection of their plea. On the preceding reading, in any case, Achilles refuses to forgive the wrong done to him because the proper conditions for granting forgiveness have not been met – that is, a personal and sufficient acknowledgment of Agamemnon's own responsibility for having deliberately and arbitrarily offended his finest warrior. When Achilles finally does become reconciled with Agamemnon, it will be because a more powerful emotion – his grief at the loss of Patroclus – has driven out his resentment at the insult he suffered, and by that point in the poem the question of forgiveness has become moot.[2]

But is it true that Achilles expects such a confession from Agamemnon as the basis for forgiveness? Might we not be projecting values onto the poem that, however self-evident they may seem to us, are not relevant to Homer's world? After all, we may also interpret Achilles's response as simply revealing the depth of his mortification for the way he was humiliated by Agamemnon, which will take him more time to overcome; this is precisely what he says when he finally dismisses his comrades and their appeal: "my heart swells with anger when I recall those things, how the son of Atreus treated me as a fool in front of the Achaeans, as if I were a vagabond without honor" (9.646–8).

There is perhaps another reason to think that an apology in the modern sense is not what Achilles or anyone else expects of Agamemnon in these circumstances. For Odysseus suppresses not only the final words of Agamemnon's charge to the ambassadors but also his opening remarks in which he replies to Nestor.[3] It was Nestor who recommended the attempt to assuage Achilles's wrath and reproached Agamemnon: "You yielded to your arrogant spirit and dishonored the noblest of men, whom the gods themselves had honored" (9.109–11). To this Agamemnon responds: "Old man, you have accused my madness [*emas atas*], and not mistakenly: for

---

[2] Compare the interpretation of the scholiast (preserved in the manuscript tradition bT) *ad Il.* 18.112–13: "of the two emotions besetting Achilles' soul, anger [*orgê*] and grief [*lupê*], one wins out.... For the emotion involving Patroclus is strongest of all, and so it is necessary to abandon his wrath [*mênis*] and avenge himself on his enemies." For further discussion of anger in the *Iliad*, see my *The Emotions of the Ancient Greeks*, 48–56.

[3] I am grateful to Steven Scully for bringing this passage to my attention.

I was mad [*aasamên*], I myself do not deny it…. But since I was mad when I was swayed by my grim mind, I wish now to please him [*aresai*] once more and give him numberless gifts" (9.115–20). If it was Odysseus's wish to represent to Achilles Agamemnon's genuine and deeply felt regret, why did he not communicate to him this confession of responsibility on Agamemnon's part? For those who would see implicit in the scene a modern ethic of forgiveness (and its failure), the answer is that Agamemnon has not admitted his fault but has exculpated himself by ascribing the cause of his behavior to a spell of folly. Later, when Poseidon seeks to encourage the Achaeans to fight more resolutely, reminding them of the shame of defeat as they are beginning to lose confidence, he adds, "But if the heroic son of Atreus, wide-ruling Agamemnon, was in truth wholly responsible [*aitios*], in that he dishonored the swift-footed son of Peleus, there is nevertheless no way that we can relax from battle" (13.111–14). Here then is a clear statement of Agamemnon's responsibility for the offense to Achilles and the reversals suffered by the Achaeans. Yet it would seem that Agamemnon is not entirely prepared to accept it; for when Achilles has already decided, after the death of Patroclus, to lay aside his anger (19.67) and rejoin the battle, Agamemnon declares, "I am not responsible [*aitios*], but rather Zeus and Fate and the Fury that strolls through the air, who cast this violent madness upon my wits in the assembly, on that day when I myself took away Achilles's prize" (19.86–90). Agamemnon launches on a lengthy narrative about Ate and concludes, "Since I was mad and Zeus stole my wits away, I wish to please [Achilles] once more and give him numberless gifts" (137–8), thereby reaffirming the offer he had made when he sent forth the ambassadors to Achilles's tent.

If we consider this episode from the perspective of the ancient philosophers and rhetoricians, however, Agamemnon's words take on a different significance. In attributing his error to a god-sent fit of fury, he is insisting that his offense against Achilles was involuntary – precisely the strategy for appeasing anger that Aristotle and others consistently recommend. If no one can resist the will of Zeus, then what Agamemnon did was understandable and to this extent excusable – a fault common to all, as Aristotle puts it (*Nicomachean Ethics* 7.6, 1149b4–6). This does not absolve him, in his own mind, of the obligation to make compensation to Achilles: in this respect, he recognizes his role in causing the conflict. Though the term does not appear here, what Agamemnon is seeking is *sungnômê*, not forgiveness in the modern sense; and for this, one wants precisely to disclaim full liability. The advantage of this interpretation of Agamemnon's self-justification is that it is consistent with ancient Greek conceptions of the appeasement of anger and does not introduce ideas of remorse and repentance that are extraneous to the epic – and to Greek moral thought generally.[4]

The *Odyssey* is hardly the place to look for the forswearing of revenge. In return for the abuse of his home, Odysseus slaughters every last one of the 108 suitors for his wife's hand. After he has slain Antinous, the nastiest and most aggressive of the lot, the second-most prominent among them, Eurymachus, tries to appease Odysseus's wrath by displacing the blame onto Antinous: "he lies dead now, the one who was responsible [*aitios*] for all of it, Antinous" (22.48–9), and he alleges that Antinous's real motive was to rule over Ithaca. Eurymachus also offers, on behalf of all the suitors, to compensate Odysseus many times over for what they ate and drank in his house. But Odysseus is implacable and prepares to kill them. Clearly this is not a scene of forgiveness or of reconciliation; I wish only to point out that Eurymachus's argument in his defense resembles that of Agamemnon in the *Iliad*: displace the blame onto another and offer remuneration for the damage done. This is not to say that Eurymachus should have tried a different ploy, pressing the earnestness of his remorse upon Odysseus: it is not that Eurymachus would not have meant it – he recognizes that what he and the others did was wrong (cf. *polla atasthala*: 22.46–7) – but rather that remorse and a change of heart do not enter into the strategies for anger appeasement in classical literature. Eurymachus does what every pleader after him

---

[4] There is an analogous difficulty in interpreting the exchange between Achilles and Priam in *Iliad* 24 as a function of remorse and forgiveness. For an analysis in terms of restorative justice, see Van Ness and Strong 2006: 55–69; see also the cogent refutation of this interpretation in Acorn 2004: 91–8. To put the case most simply: Priam does not come asking to be forgiven and does not even seek to disown responsibility for his prior conduct – nor is it clear what it is he might apologize for. One must not look for the pattern of forgiveness behind every scene of reconciliation and least of all in classical Greek and Roman literature.

will do: he seeks to exonerate himself, not to prove that he is now a different person.

Before leaving the *Odyssey*, we may consider one further example of reconciliation, namely that between Menelaus and Helen, who preside over their household in Sparta in an atmosphere of domestic tranquillity; Menelaus appears to have given up whatever rancor he may have entertained over Helen's elopement with Paris. Helen here, as in the *Iliad*, blames herself for the troubles she has caused the Greeks and the Trojans (4.145–6), and she makes no excuses; but neither does she offer what might amount to an apology.[5] She joins Menelaus and Telemachus in weeping over the memory of Odysseus (4.183–5), which suggests a harmony of sentiment. Yet her decision to doctor the wine that her husband and his guests will drink with a drug that dulls sorrow and anger and induces oblivion of all problems, even the death of one's parents or children (4.220–32), perhaps implies that Menelaus requires some such sedative to get over his resentment. If so, then we may repeat the words of Charles Griswold that "forgiving cannot be forgetting."

Tragedy is not the place in which one necessarily expects to find reconciliations, and so forgiveness is likely to be marginal to the genre.[6] Still, there are some situations in which characters who are at odds abandon the desire for revenge. In Aeschylus's *Eumenides*, the final play of the *Oresteia* trilogy, Orestes defends himself on the charge of having murdered his mother. The chorus maintain that he is wholly responsible for the deed (*panaitios*, 200), and that Apollo had no share in it (he was not *metaitios*, 199); in court, however – the trial is to be the model for future tribunals in Athens – Orestes admits the deed (463) but insists on the fact that Apollo was coresponsible (*metaitios*, 465). This is precisely the strategy of transference or *metastasis* that the rhetoricians endorse and that Orestes employs alongside the argument from definition, in which one avows the act but claims that it does not constitute

---

5 Much time has passed since the fall of Troy, and perhaps an apology at this late date is no longer appropriate; perhaps too the audience recalls that she acted in some sense under divine compulsion (cf. *Iliad* 3.383–420, where Aphrodite, in what can be read as a reprise of the original elopement, compels Helen to go to bed with Paris).

6 See further Metzler 1991; de Romilly 1995: 62–77.

a crime according to the law. In Sophocles's *Ajax*, Odysseus is moved by pity for his former antagonist (121–2) when he sees him reduced to madness, despite Ajax's attempt to murder him and the other Achaean commanders, and he goes so far as to defend his right to a proper burial, against the wishes of Agamemnon and Menelaus. Because Ajax is dead, there is no question of an apology for what he intended; more important, there is no indication that he felt remorse for it while he was still alive: he killed himself not because he repented or was ashamed of the attempt but because he was humiliated by his failure to carry it out (see Konstan 2006: 105–6). Odysseus bases his case on the laws of the gods and the duty to respect a noble warrior in death (1343–5), irrespective of the question of Ajax's guilt.

In a brief but characteristically thoughtful paper on remorse in classical Greece, Douglas Cairns observes that the plot of Sophocles's *Philoctetes* "turns to a large extent on the dilemma of Neoptolemus, who is forced, as a deep affinity develops between him and his victim, painfully to confront the recognition that his deception of the noble Philoctetes is incompatible with his own nature, and who eventually ... seeks to make good his offence by sacrificing his own interests in support of the man he has wronged."[7] Having tricked Philoctetes into surrendering the bow on which his life depends, Neoptolemus turns around and gives it back, moved by pity and shame (929, 965–8, 1228, 1248–9, 1282, 1288) at having betrayed his true character or *phusis* (902–3). In this recognition of a moral lapse, Neoptolemus may well acquire a deeper understanding of human decency; in any case, Philoctetes will be reconciled with him, despite his initial shock at his treacherous behavior (1280–3). Does he forgive him? His reaction depends in the first instance on the return of his bow. As Neoptolemus says, "Look, you have the bow: you have no reason to feel anger or blame toward me" (1308–9). Philoctetes agrees and praises his noble nature as a true son of Achilles (1310–12): there is no indication of lingering resentment or an effort to overcome it. Neoptolemus at once undertakes to persuade Philoctetes to give over his anger at the Greek commanders who abandoned him en route to Troy, arguing that the cause really lay with divine fate

---

[7] Cairns 1999: 173–4; cf. Konstan 1998a.

(1326) – the standard ploy of deflecting blame. But Philoctetes
will have none of it and insists on going home – Greek victory at
Troy be damned. Toward those who really harmed him he remains
adamantly hostile. Forgiveness hardly seems to be the message of
this play.[8]

In the previous chapter, I referred to the episode in Herodotus
in which the son of Croesus, whom his father had sequestered
from all warlike activities on account of a dream, is accidentally
slain by the javelin of another man while on a hunting expedition.
The killer turns out to be Adrastus, a man whom Croesus had
received hospitably, ritually purifying him of prior blood guilt,
and to whom he had entrusted his son's safety. Overcome with
sorrow, Adrastus hands himself over to Croesus and begs him to
butcher him on the very corpse of the boy. But Croesus rather
takes pity on him, declaring that he is not responsible (*aitios*, 1.45)
for the misfortune, but rather some god, who had earlier warned
him of the event through the dream (again, the argument from
metastasis). Nevertheless Adrastus, recognizing (*sungignôskomenos*)
that he is the most unfortunate of human beings, kills himself
shortly afterward at the boy's tomb. There is no change of heart
on Adrastus's part – his innocence is acknowledged, and there is
nothing to forgive. His suicide is rather like the self-blinding of
Oedipus in Sophocles's tragedy; it reflects incapacity to live with so
wretched a fate even if the action that brought it about was unwitting and predestined. Regret he certainly felt but not remorse, if
by remorse we understand a sentiment "inherently linked with an
action for which the agent was responsible and for which there
were no exonerating factors."[9]

It was noted in the previous chapter that the genre of New
Comedy, represented in Latin by the plays of Plautus and Terence,
is particularly rich in scenes of day-to-day conflict and reconciliation. This is equally true of the comedies by Menander, the greatest

---

[8] See Fulkerson 2006a.

[9] Borgeaud and Cox 1999: 138 (cited also in Chapter 1). Contrast Cairns 1999: 171–2,
who defines remorse as "a species of regret over actions for which one considers
oneself responsible, which one wishes one had not performed, and whose damage
one would undo if one could"; Cairns's account does not sufficiently distinguish
remorse from simple regret for something one has done, irrespective of will or
intentionality.

of the Greek New Comedy playwrights, whose works can now be read with some appreciation since the discovery, for the first time, of a papyrus containing a complete play of his in 1959 and, subsequently, of major fragments of several other comedies that had been partially known since the late nineteenth century.[10] I begin with the *Samia* (Samian Woman), which comes nearest to exhibiting a genuine apology and what looks like a sincere appeal for forgiveness. To summarize the plot: two Athenian men, Demeas and Niceratus, have been traveling abroad for several months. In their absence, Demeas's adopted son, Moschio, has raped the daughter of Niceratus, as a result of which she became pregnant and gave birth to a child. In fear of their parents' reaction, they conspire with Chrysis, Demeas's concubine, to pretend that the baby is hers and that Demeas is its father. This too poses a problem: Chrysis is a courtesan and a foreigner – she is from Samos, as the title indicates – and Demeas has no reason to wish to raise a child of hers, because by Athenian law only the offspring of two citizen parents was eligible to inherit property, and besides, Demeas already has a legitimate heir in Moschio, acquired by adoption. Nevertheless, Chrysis rightly predicts that he will get over it, because he is in love with her, and "this quickly leads even the most anger-prone person to reconciliation" (82–3: *touto d'eis diallagas agei takhista kai ton orgilôtaton*). When Demeas finds out about it, he is furious: "It seems that, unbeknownst to me, I have a lawfully wedded courtesan [*gametên hetairan*]" (130–1). He declares that he is not one to raise a bastard son [*nothos*, 136] for someone else (the Greek word *nothos* designates the issue of just such mixed parentage, irrespective of the formality of marriage), and that he is prepared to cast Chrysis out of the house. Moschio, however, objects, "which of us is a bastard, by the gods, and which legitimate, given that we are born human?" (137–8). The following bit is mutilated, and so we cannot tell what further arguments the boy may have offered, but Demeas is ultimately persuaded to relent. What explains his calming down?

Chrysis's offense, in Demeas's view, consists in having nursed the infant rather than expose it. In so doing, she behaved as if she and Demeas were social equals – husband and wife instead of

[10] For a somewhat different approach to forgiveness in Menander, see Gutzwiller (2011).

Athenian citizen and foreign concubine – and as if she had the right to decide the baby's fate. This is in effect to demean Demeas; hence, his rage. Two factors, in turn, work to mollify him. First, there is his love for Chrysis, which, as Chrysis predicts, softens him. As Aristotle remarks in the *Rhetoric*, "we do not render judgments in the same way when we are in pain or rejoicing, or when we love or hate" (1356a15–16). Second, there is Moschio's argument that the child is as good as legitimate: hence, Chrysis's behavior – and by implication her own status – are less inappropriate than they seemed. This is a radical claim, because it undermines one of the fundamental social distinctions in classical Athens: that between citizen and noncitizen, and Demeas is understandably amazed at it.[11] Still, he gives in. Has he forgiven Chrysis? It is hard to say. There is no sign that she is apologetic (she does not appear to be on stage during this exchange). If he accepts Moschio's argument, then Demeas has changed his mind about the nature of the offense, and no wrong was done (the argument from definition, according to the rhetoricians). More likely, he is bowing to the preference of his beloved stepson and avoiding a rupture with his devoted mistress, and so simply swallows his irritation.

However, a greater shock is in store for Demeas. For when he accidentally overhears his old nurse say that the real father of the child is Moschio, he concludes that Moschio had an affair with Chrysis during his absence. At first, he explores the possibility that he may be leaping to a mistaken conclusion – a good Aristotelian strategy for allaying anger. Addressing himself to the audience as if they were judges he declares, "I am not yet upset. For I know the boy, by the gods, and he has always been well behaved until now and as respectful as possible toward me." Yet the evidence of what he has heard seems indisputable, and he ends up beside himself with rage (*exestêkh' holôs*, 279). Nevertheless, he still seeks ways of exonerating his son: "Why are you shouting, you fool? Control yourself, bear up. Moschio has not wronged you" (327–8). He reasons

---

[11] Although the evidence is indirect, it may be that the law going back to Pericles (in 451) restricting the rights of progeny not born of two citizen parents was effectively in abeyance by the time in which Menander was composing his dramas. Nevertheless, New Comedy seems to have maintained the convention, perhaps because it suited the plots concerning marriage and status that were a staple of the genre; cf. Traill 2008: 246–8.

that Moschio did not act deliberately, because in that case he would have opposed the idea of marrying Niceratus's daughter, but he consented at once, when Demeas proposed the idea to him (146–9). Moschio, he adds, was doubtless drunk and not in control of himself (340: *ouk ont' en heautou*) when Chrysis seduced him; besides, he is still young – another mitigating factor in regard to anger and, again, a well-documented strategy of exculpation in the handbooks on legal argument. Demeas repeats that it is not at all plausible (*pithanon*, 343) that a youth who was always well-behaved and modest should treat his own father badly, "even if he was ten-times over adopted, and not my own son by birth: for I look not to this, but to his character [*tropos*]" (346–7). Demeas is applying something like the logic that Moschio employed to persuade him to condone Chrysis's decision to keep the child, though adoption was a common practice and carried no stigma.[12] Unfortunately, this time it works to opposite effect. Having convinced himself of Moschio's innocence, Demeas turns violently against Chrysis: it is she who is "responsible for what happened" (338) – we recognize the procedure of *metastasis* or transferring responsibility to another. "You must be a man," he admonishes himself: "forget your desire [*pothos*], stop being in love" (349–50). He resolves to expel Chrysis from his house, while keeping the real cause concealed for his son's sake, pretending that the reason is her presumptuousness in raising the child (374–5).

In pacifying his anger toward his son, Demeas convinces himself of the boy's innocence: a young man is easy prey for an experienced courtesan, and to resist her charms would be, as Aristotle puts it, beyond the powers of a human being. Demeas, then, does not so much forgive as exonerate Moschio in this episode.

But Demeas's problems are not over. When Moschio, unaware of Demeas's suspicions, pleads vigorously on behalf of Chrysis, Demeas concludes that he is joining Chrysis in wronging him (*sunadikei*, 456). Hence, he must have been a willing partner in the affair, after all. Moschio, aware of Demeas's growing agitation, declares, "it is not right to give everything over to anger" (to which Niceratus adds, "he's right," 462–3). Bursting with rage (475), Demeas finally blurts out that he knows the child is Moschio's.

---

[12] See Rubinstein 1993.

But, Moschio, supposing that Demeas knows the whole truth,
declares that what he did is nothing terrible – tens of thousands
have done likewise (485–7). The argument from precedent is a
standard one, especially given the implied motive of erotic passion, which is one of the admissible pretexts for *sungnômê*, though it
backfires here because Demeas thinks he means to justify sleeping
with Chrysis, and this he deems to be off limits. Finally, Moschio
catches on to his father's error (522) and reveals that the mother
is Niceratus's daughter. With this, Demeas's anger against his son
and Chrysis evanesces, because he realizes that both are innocent
of any offense against him.

Now it is Niceratus's turn to be furious. When Demeas tries
to protect the infant, the two old men almost come to blows, as
Niceratus concludes that Demeas has wronged him and was in
on the scheme from the beginning (582–4). This is untrue, but
there is no way of denying that Moschio was at fault. The only
way to appease Niceratus's rage is for Moschio to marry the girl
(586, 599), and this sets matters right.[13] Once more, forgiveness is
beside the point.

We come now to the final act – and a further surprise. Moschio is
furious, now that he has reflected on the matter (cf. *logismos*, 620),
that his father suspected him of sleeping with Chrysis (620–1).
Only his passion (*erôs*) for Niceratus's daughter, he says, prevents
him from leaving Athens for good and entering military service in
remotest Bactria (modern Afghanistan): once again, love serves
to inhibit anger and revenge. Nevertheless, he desires some vengeance, if only in words, and so he pretends that he is off to the
wars: this way he can give his father a fright (*phobêsai*, 635), so
that he will hesitate to treat him unfairly (*agnômonein*, 637) in the
future. When Demeas emerges from the house, he neither begs
Moschio to stay nor dismisses him angrily (as Moschio had feared,
682–4). Rather, he acknowledges that Moschio has reason to be
angry and hurt at having been wrongly accused (694–6), though
he goes on to call Moschio's attention to the circumstances of
the case (*all' ekein' homôs theôrei*, 697). Here, then, is something

---

[13] Cf. the approving comment of Diogenianus in Plutarch's *Quaestiones convivales*
712C: "In all his [i.e., Menander's] plays there is no passionate love for a male
youth, and the violation of virgins ends up decently in marriage."

new: Demeas frankly admits that he was in the wrong. Is he appealing for forgiveness? Let us take a closer look at his arguments.

Demeas first reminds Moschio that he is his father, and that he reared him from childhood: because Demeas gave him all that was pleasant in his life, Moschio should also put up with something painful. This is a plea for fairness, not a denial of guilt, and Demeas again flatly confesses: "I accused you unjustly: I was deluded, wrong, out of my mind" (702–3). Demeas next points out that even when he believed the worst of Moschio he kept it to himself, whereas Moschio is making his father's mistake public; thus Moschio's response is immoderate. Demeas does not challenge his reason for being angry, only his readiness to advertise a family quarrel to their enemies. Finally, Demeas urges Moschio not to dwell on the memory of a single day and forget all the rest. With this, he ends his apology, concluding that a son should obey his father willingly, not reluctantly.

Demeas clearly confesses his error. It is true that he alleges extenuating factors, pointing out that his reaction was moderate – unlike Moschio's now – and that he is owed filial respect, all the more so in that he had always treated his adopted son generously. But if these arguments serve to mitigate Demeas's guilt, they do not entirely exonerate him – these are not the strategies commonly recommended for soliciting *sungnômê*. Is he asking rather for forgiveness? If so, does Moschio in turn relent and accept his father's plea, generously dismissing the wrong he feels was done to him? It is impossible to evaluate the effect of Demeas's arguments on Moschio, because at this point Niceratus appears, furious that Moschio is about to make off for foreign parts and abandon the girl he got with child. Harry Sandbach, in his great commentary on Menander, explains the action as follows:

> Demeas' speech puts Moschion in a difficult position. There is no answer to the accusations that he has allowed one incident to outweigh many years' good treatment, and that he has been ready to injure his father's reputation, while his father had done all he could to preserve that of his son. Reason requires that he should abandon his dramatic pose and apologize. But this is a thing that Moschion, like many young men, would find very hard. He is saved by the sudden appearance of Nikeratos, which relieves him from the necessity of an immediate reply.[14]

[14] Gomme and Sandbach 1973: 628 ad 713ff.

As Sandbach reads the scene, Demeas has in effect turned the tables on Moschio, and put him in the position of the wrong-doer; thus, it is Moschio, rather than Demeas, who should be apologizing and asking his father to forgive him. If this is right, then Demeas has pulled a neat trick, defending himself by exposing a greater fault on the part of his son (what the rhetoricians call the argument from comparison). In any case, Demeas finally convinces Niceratus that Moschio is prepared to marry his daughter and asks him to bring out the bride. With this, Moschio says, rather impertinently: "If you'd done this right away, you wouldn't have had the bother of playing the philosopher just now" (724–5). We are reminded of his earlier claim that his real motive for not leaving home is his passion for Niceratus's daughter, not consideration for his own father.

Does Moschio realize that he was wrong to be so angry with his father? Sandbach's view that it is he who ought to apologize is not entirely satisfactory, because Demeas has admitted that he was at fault: his earlier accusation can be seen as a slight against Moschio's character, which Moschio had reason to resent; this surely is what Demeas's confession invites the audience to suppose. But if Moschio does give up his anger at this point, it is not because he has perceived a change of heart in his father or responded to his expression of regret – he remains too smug and pert for that. Rather, he would seem to relent because Demeas, in conceding that he was at fault, has humbled himself, and this, as Aristotle makes clear, is an effective means of reducing ire (see Chapter 2). In New Comedy, older men – of the age of Demeas and Niceratus – were imagined as especially irascible. Quintilian informs us that "in comedies … the father who has the principal role has one eyebrow raised and the other flat because he is sometimes wrought up and sometimes calm, and it is the actors' custom to expose mainly that side of the mask which suits the part they are playing" (11.3.74). This stereotype has its basis in the social fact that free adult males had a recognized status and authority in Athenian society: they were *kurioi* or heads of household, with positions to defend and the right to respond with indignation to what they regard as a diminishment of their reputation or prestige. As Danielle Allen observes, "the individual citizen who was sensitive to his honor and guarded it with anger was also guarding his personal independence, greatness, and equality" (Allen 2000: 129). Though Demeas appeals to the obligation of filial piety, he is treating his son as an equal, precisely by recognizing that he has as much right to be angry when insulted as he does. Correspondingly, by demanding this show of respect Moschio demonstrates that he is now a man, ready to assume the responsibilities of a married head of household – and a father in his own right. Throughout the previous acts, Moschio had been ducking the wrath of his elders, hiding, prevaricating, pleading, sometimes arguing, as he did when he denied the distinction between legitimate and illegitimate children, but he was always on the defensive. In expressing anger, he is laying claim to the dignity of a mature member of the civic polity. The finale, then, dramatizes Moschio's change of status from boy to man. If he seems oversensitive to insult, this may be chalked up to a young man's excess – he is still trying on the role of irate senior (it was a commonplace that boys are easily moved to anger and as quickly set it aside: cf. Horace *Art of Poetry* 159–60).

This interpretation, moreover, makes sense of the final act, which otherwise has the appearance of an arbitrary coda to the principal action of the play. After all, the basic entanglement of the plot had been resolved by the end of the fourth or penultimate act: the secret of the rape was out, the marriage was on, and all parties were in agreement. The *Samia* concludes with a satisfying reconciliation between father and son, but the appeasement of anger rests not on the remorse of the offender and the forgiveness that it invites but on a display of humility that shows a proper regard for the affronted party's status and authority. As a moral basis for the giving over of anger, it works. But it is not the modern paradigm of remorse, repentance, and forgiveness.

There is an analogous moment in the final act of the Menander's *Dyscolus* (The Grouch), the only complete example of Greek New Comedy. The young hero, Sostratus, has fallen in love with the daughter of the title character, a cantankerous misanthrope named Cnemo who thinks that no man is good enough for his daughter – or any good at all. By the end of the fourth act, however, Sostratus has won her hand, because after Cnemo falls down a well and is rescued by his stepson Gorgias, he hands over to the latter responsibility for his estate (in Greek terms, he makes him *kurios* or head of his household). Gorgias, for his part, is happy to see the girl wed to a decent and wealthy, if rather naïve, young man. As the fifth act begins, Sostratus and his father, Callipides, are engaged in an argument as they emerge from a shrine dedicated to Pan, with Sostratus declaring: "Things have not all turned out as I had wished or expected of you, father" (784–5). Because Sostratus had entered the shrine in order to break the news of his intended marriage to his father, the audience will inevitably suppose that Callipides has objected to the idea, as Gorgias had feared, though the cocksure Sostratus was certain that his father would go along with it (760–1). But it turns out that Sostratus has also demanded that his sister be given in marriage to Gorgias, and it is this that Callipides opposes; as he puts it, "I don't want to accept both a bride and a groom who are paupers: one is enough for me" (795–6). Sostratus responds with an earnest lecture on the proper use of wealth, which is to help others prosper. Callipides listens to his son with a kind of amused respect and yields at once with a gentle: "You know me, Sostratus" (813).

This unexpected twist in the plot has various functions, no doubt, including that of endorsing marriage across class lines and so promoting the unity of the citizen body (see Konstan 1994: 93–106). But it also lets Sostratus take on the role of counseling his father, in the sententious manner of young people, and allows Callipides to make the gesture of yielding to his son and to affirm that all his possessions really belong to Sostratus (813–15), and he may do what he pleases with them (818–19). He is effectively rendering Sostratus *kurios* of his property, just as Cnemon had done with Gorgias, thereby signaling Sostratus's transformation from child to responsible adult. This altercation between father and son, truncated though it is, thus serves the same function as the quarrel between Moschio and Demeas in the final act of the *Samia*: in both cases, a father pacifies his son's indignation by acknowledging his new status as an adult.

Anger could be excessive, however, and at the end of Menander's *Perikeiromene* (Shorn Girl), there is a scene that comes, I think, as close to a genuine apology and appeal for forgiveness as any in classical literature. The plot is as follows: Glycera, the "shorn girl" of the title, has been living as a concubine with a mercenary soldier named Polemo. Her brother Moschio lives in the house next door. He has been raised as the son of a prosperous citizen couple and does not know that he is actually Glycera's brother. Both children had been left to die as infants; however, the old woman who rescued them gave the boy over for adoption but passed Glycera off as her own daughter (130–1) and later handed her over to the soldier as his mistress. Before she died, she informed Glycera, but not Moschio, of the truth. The action proper begins when Moschio tries to embrace Glycera, and she – knowing he is her brother – does not prevent him. When Polemo learns of this, he cuts off her hair in a jealous rage. Glycera takes refuge with Moschio's mother, whereas Polemo abandons his house for the company of friends, including a certain Pataecus. After various events, it is revealed, thanks to some keep-sakes that were left with Glycera when she was exposed, that she is Pataecus's daughter. Two consequences follow on this discovery and bring about the denouement: first, Pataecus persuades Glycera to give over her anger at Polemo, and second, as her legitimate father he betroths her formally to a deeply contrite Polemo.

Does Glycera forgive Polemo? It is a complicated question. It is worth remarking that, according to the conventions of the genre, she has little choice but to accept him, because she would other-wise find herself in the awkward position of being a citizen woman with a history as a concubine. In New Comedy, a woman (apart from widows) can only be given in wedlock if she is a virgin or else, if she has had a prior sexual experience, then to the one man whom she has known carnally. This is why young women who have been raped invariably end up married to the men who vio-lated them, and courtesans, if, like Glycera, they turn out to be citizens after all, are always novices and marry their first lover. Glycera only consents to be reconciled with Polemo (the word is *diallakhthêsomai*, 1006) after her citizen status is known, at which point her father declares that to accept a settlement (*dekhesthai tên dikên*) when one is well off is the mark of a Greek character (1008). Immediately after this, he betroths Glycera to Polemo and throws in a generous dowry.

But the story does not end here. Pataecus at once warns Polemo: "From now on, forget that you are a soldier, so that you don't do any-thing rash," to which Polemo replies, "By Apollo, would I do anything rash again, given that I practically died just now? Nor will I blame Glycera. Just be reconciled, my darling" (1016–20). At this point someone – either Pataecus, as I think likely, or Glycera – declares,

"Yes, since now your mad brutality (*paroinon*) has turned out to be a source of good for us." Polemo replies, "Right you are!" and either Pataecus or Glycera fires back: "This is why you have earned *sungnômê*" (1021–3). There follows a brief mention of a marriage for Pataecus's son Moschio, and here the papyrus breaks off.

In a subtle Aristotelian analysis of this scene, William Fortenbaugh observes, "forgiveness is justified solely on the grounds that Polemon's act has been a source of blessings. This justification is to be taken at face value. The blessings resulting from Polemon's act simply nullify any possible moral indignation Glykera may have felt" (Fortenbaugh 1974: 441). Noting that Aristotle does not recognize sudden changes of character, Fortenbaugh adds (443), "We are not meant to scrutinize Pataikos' injunction in terms of a consistent theory of human personality." That things have turned out well in the end can contribute to excusing an ill-considered action, or at least mollifying the offended party (cf. Terence "Self-Tormenter" 666–7). In addition, the hint that Polemo behaved madly or like a drunkard (the word *paroinon*, from *oinos* = wine, suggests inebriation) offers a possible justification of his action on the basis of emotion or *pathos*, which the rhetoricians recognized as a basis for granting *sungnômê*. Still, it is noteworthy that there is no mention of Polemo's best defense in the situation, namely his ignorance that Moschio was Glycera's brother. Instead, Menander shifts the emphasis to Polemo's promise not to repeat his offensive conduct. This too was standard procedure for requesting pardon; Cicero, as we saw in the previous chapter, counsels a defendant "to promise and undertake that he has been taught by this error of his, and confirmed in his resolution also by the kindness of those who pardon him, to avoid all such conduct in future" (*On Invention* 2.106; trans. Yonge). Are we to understand, then, that Polemo has really changed, and that this is a consequence of his remorse for an acknowledged transgression? Is Glycera's newfound generosity – that sign of "Greek character" that Pataecus praised in her – an indication that she too has had a change of heart? It is probably wiser to take the characters at their word and see at work here conventional moves for appeasing anger, without resorting to modern notions of repentance of forgiveness.[15]

---

[15] We may note that the prologue, delivered by Agnoia or "Ignorance," states that Polemo is not given to anger by nature, but that she induced it in him so that

There is a tragic instance of reconciliation between parent and child in Euripides' *Hippolytus*, which bears a structural resemblance to the situation in Menander's *Samia*. Theseus, under the impression that Hippolytus has attempted to rape Phaedra, his wife and Hippolytus's stepmother, calls down a fatal curse upon the boy. In the end, Artemis, the goddess dearest to Hippolytus, reveals the truth – that Phaedra's deathbed accusation of Hippolytus was a lie – and she blames Theseus for having rushed to judgment rather than investigate the slander more closely. Theseus exclaims, "O Mistress, I am destroyed," to which the goddess replies, "You have done a terrible thing, but nevertheless you can obtain *sungnômê* for it. For Aphrodite wished it to turn out this way, being filled with rage [*thumon*]" (1325–8; cf. 1406: "he was deceived by the schemes of a goddess"; also 1414). Pardon is once again predicated on a transfer of blame, in this case onto a goddess, who has acted under the impetus of anger, so that even her action may be at some level excusable. In a deeply touching finale, Hippolytus exclaims that he suffers more for his father than for himself, and Theseus wishes that he could die in place of his son (1409–10). Artemis promises to slay one of Aphrodite's favorites in return (1420–2) and bids Theseus take his dying son in his arms: "you slew him involuntarily [*akôn*]: it is understandable [*eikos*] for human beings to err when the gods allot it" (1433–4). She tells Hippolytus in turn to cease hating his father, for his death was fated. Hippolytus replies, "I revoke the strife with my father, since you ask it of me" (1442). Once more, the basis of reconciliation is the negation of guilt, not forgiveness of blameworthy misconduct.

There are examples in classical literature of genuine remorse, in the sense of regret for the harm one has done to another as opposed to a self-interested displeasure at the result of one's actions. In the anonymous *Life of Aesop* (version G), dating to the late Hellenistic or early Roman period, Aesop's son Linus falsely denounces his father for conspiring against king Nectanabon of

Glycera and her brother might discover their identities (164–7). This suggests that Polemo has not changed character at the end of the comedy but recovered his normal self. In this, he is like Agamemnon, who claims to have been motivated by *atê*, or delusion. In the classical pattern, offenders typically explain their misbehavior as a lapse due to external factors – a kind of blip in the linear continuity of character; the modern paradigm of forgiveness, on the contrary, tends to presuppose a radical change of direction or conversion of the self.

Egypt; the king condemns Aesop to death, but he is put in prison
instead. Later the king, in need of Aesop's advice, regrets his decision, and Aesop is saved. Aesop then delivers a sententious lecture to his son on how to behave (109–10), concluding with the
advice that one not bear a grudge against one's enemies when
one is prospering but rather do them a good turn, so that they
may feel regret (*metamelôntai*) when they realize the kind of man
they have wronged; in addition, one should not hesitate to show
pity (because fortune is unstable), trust slanderers, rejoice over
great possessions, or be upset with small. Linus, grieving (*lupoume-
nos*) over the wrong he has done and the scolding he has received,
starves himself to death. It is reasonable to suppose that Linus felt
the kind of remorse that Aesop described at mistreating a good
man, but instead of seeking forgiveness (Aesop has already pardoned him for his offense) he condemns himself. Acknowledged
guilt brings punishment, not reprieve.

The Epicurean philosopher Philodemus, in his treatise *On Death*
(preserved on a papyrus roll that was scorched during the erup-
tion of Mount Vesuvius in AD 79), explains that a wise man knows
very well that many good people have suffered at the hands of
tyrannical rulers, but he trusts that "those who condemned (him)
have been punished throughout life by the vice in them [*pros tês
en autois kakias*], and that they will be pained by many regrets
on his account [*kai di'auton metameleiais pollais odunêsesthai*], and
perhaps even be punished more unpleasantly by others."[16] Here
again we see regret for having harmed another, although the reference to potential punishment at the hands of others suggests
that the pangs of conscience may be due to fear of future repri-
sal, a notion with good Epicurean credentials (*Vatican Saying* 7;
Principal Doctrines 34–5; Lucretius 3.825–7, 3.1014–15, 5.1154–7;
Seneca *Letters to Lucilius* 97.13–15). In any case, remorse does not
lead here to a request for forgiveness. Doubtless there are many
other examples of what we would recognize as genuine remorse
in the rich ethical sense of the term, though they do not always
come equipped with the kind of internal commentary found in
the two passages just examined (the cases adduced by Douglas
Cairns, which include "Achilles' pain at having failed Patroclus"

---

[16] Text and translation in Henry 2009: col. 35.6–11.

[1999: 173] at *Iliad* 18.98–126, are subject to alternative inter-pretations). An other-regarding sensibility of guilt was surely a concept available to ancient Greeks and Romans (even if Robert Kaster is right that the Latin *paenitentia* never securely bears this sense). But it does not seem to have been configured as "a change of heart that leads one to seek purgation and forgiveness" (Kaster 2005: 81).[17]

Before turning to some Latin cases of the conciliation of anger, let me cite a couple of purple passages in Greek sources that illus-trate the rhetoric of appeasement. Dionysius of Halicarnassus, in his *Roman Antiquities* (first century BC), puts in the mouth of the mother of Marcius Coriolanus a long speech designed to persuade him to give over his wrath against Rome, after he was driven into exile on trumped-up charges. I take the liberty of quoting from it *in extenso*, to give something of the flavor of such appeals:

> (8.50.1) Let us concede to those who have suffered something terrible the right not to distinguish whether the harm was done by friends or by strangers, but that they may bear an equal anger toward all. Have you not exacted a sufficient penalty from those who abused you by having turned their best land into sheep fodder, destroyed their allied cities which they acquired and retained with enormous effort, and for three years now kept them penned up in an extreme lack of basic necessities? But you drive your wild and insane anger beyond the enslavement and destruction of their city. (8.50.2) You did not even respect the old men who were sent by the Senate bearing you

---

[17] Remorse or regret is understood in some sources to be a route to moral reform, independently of forgiveness; a fragment (43 Diels-Kranz) attributed to Democritus reads: "remorse [*metameleia*] for shameful deeds is the salvation of life." Lactantius (*Divine Institutes* 6.24.2–3) cites Cicero as holding that repentance or regret (*paenitere*) does not lead to the correction of error, though Lactantius maintains that it does; God, in turn, will "remit, wipe away, and pardon [*remittere, obliterare, condonare*]" sins that have been repented of. I am most grateful to Richard Sorabji for these references. Sorabji is in the process of writing a history of the idea of con-science and has assembled a wide array of passages to demonstrate that the ancient Greeks and Romans were clearly aware of its pangs and torments, and not only for fear of exposure and punishment; from his wealth of examples, I cite only Plutarch *On Divine Vengeance* 556A–B, in which he describes the soul of the wicked person as obsessed with "how it may escape from the memory of its injustices, expel from itself the consciousness [*to suneidos*] of them, become pure and live another life all over again"; and Cicero *Pro Roscio Amerino* 24.67, in which he explains the Furies who populate tragedy as "the anguish of conscience [*conscientia*] and the torture deriving from guilt [*fraus*]" and insists that this inner torment derives not from the threat of penalty but from human nature.

absolution from the charges and a return to your own property, though they came as friends and good men, nor again the priests whom the city finally sent, bearing and extending before them the holy garlands of the gods, but you drove them away as well, having delivered to them an inflexible and despotic reply as though to vanquished subjects. (8.50.3) I cannot praise these harsh and arrogant justifications [*dikaiômata*], which have gone beyond the nature of mere mortals, when I see that excuses [*kataphugas*] and apologies [*paraitêseis*] have been found for all human beings, whatever wrongs they may have done to one another, and also supplication and entreaties [*litas*], by which all anger is quenched and instead of hating one's enemy one pities him. But all those who are obstinate and trample down the entreaties of suppliants are visited with retribution by the gods and reduced to miserable circumstances. (8.50.4) For the gods themselves, who first established and handed down to us these rules, are *sungnômones* toward human faults, and are easily reconciled, and many who have sinned greatly against them have propitiated their anger by prayers and sacrifices. Or is it that you, Marcius, believe that the anger of the gods is mortal, while that of human beings is immortal? You will do what is just, and fitting both for yourself and your country, if you excuse [*apheis*] the charges that she laid against you, now that she has repented [*metanoousêi*] and been reconciled and is restoring to you all that she took away before. (8.51.1) But if you are irreconcilable toward her, then grant this honor and favor, my son, to me, from whom you have received no small benefits nor those which another man might claim, but rather the greatest and most valuable, and by virtue of which you have acquired everything else: that is, your body and soul. For you have these as loans from me, and no man nor place nor time will deprive me of them. For neither the good services and favors of the Voluscians or of all other human beings combined, not even if they are sky high, are so powerful as to wipe away and surpass nature's justice. But you will be mine for all time and you will owe me first of all gratitude for your life, and whatever services I may ask of you, without excuse [*prophaseôs*]. (8.51.2) For the law of nature has defined this as just for all those who possess perception and reason, and it is trusting in this, Marcius my son, that I beg you not to make war upon your country, and I plant myself in your way if you use force. So either sacrifice me first, your mother who opposes you, to the furies by your own hand, and then wage war against your country, or if you fear the stigma of matricide, yield to your own mother and grant me this favor willingly, my son.

This passage may suggest the Christian idea of divine forgiveness as a model for human clemency, but a closer look reveals that it is grounded rather in the most archaic (but not for that reason more primitive) Greek conceptions of assuaging anger.[18] To begin with, Coriolanus's mother argues that he has already avenged himself sufficiently on his country, and that its losses should be compensation enough; if it is now beseeching him not to wage war against it, it is because it has been driven to desperation. In addition, the most august representatives of Rome, and men who are friends of Coriolanus, have made a personal appeal to him and promised the restoration of all that he lost. It is not hard to see in the background of this speech the pattern of Achilles's rejection of the embassy sent by Agamemnon in Book 9 of the *Iliad*, and, in case the reader missed it, Dionysius's use of the poetic word *litai* or "entreaties" gives it away, with its clear reference to their personification in the parable that Phoenix relates to Achilles (9.502–12). Coriolanus is being asked to forego his anger and vengeance, not because his countrymen have admitted their mistake, but because they have come to him in all humility; Coriolanus's fault lies in treating them like slaves rather than equals who have abased themselves before him. The gods operate in the same way: they look not to moral reform in those who have offended them, but to outward signs of deference, in prayers and sacrifices, just as Aristotle had recommended as the way to render angry people mild. Coriolanus's mother's final argument returns to the idea of reciprocity and compensation: because she gave him life, he owes her limitless gratitude and should yield to her petition. Forgiveness in the modern sense is scarcely on the horizon.

Inventing speeches for historical characters was part of the ancient chronicler's stock in trade, and although they do not necessarily reflect what the purported speaker said or thought, they do indicate what the writer believed to constitute a plausible argument, and in that respect they are highly useful to the cultural historian today. Dio Cassius, a Roman senator who lived in the late second and early third centuries AD and wrote, in Greek, a massive history of Rome (of which only a portion survives), staged a conversation between the first Roman emperor, Augustus, and his wife Livia, in which they debate whether clemency or severity is the best policy to follow in respect to Augustus's enemies

---

[18] For a detailed discussion of this passage in relation to divine forgiveness, see Várhelyi (2011).

(55.14–21; cf. the similar conversation reported by Seneca in *On Clemency* 1.9.6–12). As Dio would have it, Augustus had been suffering sleepless nights, worrying at the number of people who were opposed to him; Livia, in turn, explains that it is natural for someone in power to have enemies, because he must inevitably have harmed many, not to mention the consequences of envy and other base passions. She maintains that his opponents are hostile to his rule, rather than to him personally: were he a private citizen, no one would attack him unprovoked. Such jealousy is a bad thing, but it is also unavoidable, and neither law nor fear can remove it. Livia concludes her first speech (55.14.8): "take this into account and do not get upset about the errors [*hamartias*] of others, but rather establish a careful watch for yourself and your monarchy, so that we may keep it safe not by punishing people energetically but by watching over it energetically." To this Augustus replies (55.15.1): "I myself know, my wife, that nothing great is established without envy and plots, and least of all autarchy. (55.15.2) For in fact we would be equal to the gods, were it not that we have troubles, worries, and fears beyond all private citizens. And it is this very thing that pains me, that it is necessary that this be so, and impossible to find any remedy for it." Livia points out they have armies for external defense and self-protection, but Augustus counters that they live in fear not just of enemies but even more so of those who are friendly (*philious*, 55.15.4). Livia, who alone has the courage to speak frankly to Augustus (if he will accept advice coming from a woman), argues that because it is human nature to err (55.16.3), the best strategy is humanity (*philanthrôpia*) rather than cruelty, and she adds (55.16.5–6), "people love those who are *sungnômones* – not just those who have received their pity and are eager to recompense them, but everyone else as well, who both respect and revere them [i.e., those who are *sungnômones*], and thus do not dare to wrong them. (55.16.6) But those who entertain implacable anger are hated not only by those who have something to fear, but everyone else is disgruntled with them too, and as a result they plot against them so that they may not be killed first." The term *sungnômôn* here means something like "mild" or "clement": a kindly disposition rather than a response to wrongdoing and apology. Livia offers the analogy of doctors and insists that gentle treatment is effective for the *pathêmata* or afflictions of the soul (55.17.3): "when *sungnômê* is granted it relaxes even the very impetuous, just as punishment vexes even the very mild; for violent treatment invariably provokes everyone, even if they are utterly just, but decent treatment makes them docile." Once again, *sungnômê* here is simply gentleness – Livia notes that animals too are domesticated in this way.

Livia continues (55.18.1–2): "I do not say that one must simply spare all who do wrong: rather, one must cut out root and branch anyone who is reckless, meddlesome, malevolent, misguided, or who is immersed in incorrigible and lasting mischief, just as we do with wholly incurable parts of the body. But those others, who err because of youth, stupidity, ignorance, or some other circumstance, whether voluntarily or involuntarily, one must counsel with arguments or chasten with threats or manage in some other judicious way." This argument goes back to Plato, who also saw death as the answer to intractably corrupt individuals.[19] We recognize the exculpatory factors of youth, ignorance, and the like from the rhetorical handbooks on "issues" as well as from popular literature such as comedy, though the inclusion of voluntary offenses, to be controlled by intimidation, goes beyond the scope of *sungnômê* proper. Livia notes that those who have been cheated or their hopes and plans often become sensible afterward, and concludes that Augustus (like Caesar's wife) must not only do no wrong but also not even seem to (55.19.3). In the end, Augustus is persuaded (55.22.1). The discussion revolves entirely around the advantages of strategic clemency in a ruler; the idea of forgiveness as a response to sincere repentance is moot.[20]

Finally, before proceeding to Latin literature, we may take a glance at a particularly challenging passage in Plutarch's essay *On*

[19] Cf. Cairns 1999: 175–6; in greater detail, Saunders 1991: 139–95.
[20] It is worth noting that here and in the preceding passage concerning Coriolanus it is a woman who preaches the need for clemency and the foregoing of anger. An analysis of gender roles in relation to ancient anger is a desideratum, but lies outside the scope of this book; see Milnor (2011), who discusses this passage, and its pair in Seneca, and observes that "by speaking for public forgiveness from her place within the domestic sphere, Livia is able to frame the emperor's *clementia* as that shown by a father to his family rather than that displayed by a triumphant general to a foreign enemy. Not only does this assist the ideological redescription of the Roman state under Augustus as an enormous household with the *princeps* at its head, it also allows forgiveness to become less a display of power and more a gesture of healing and mutual respect." Instead of "forgiveness," I am more inclined to speak here of "mildness" or "leniency."

Brotherly Love (489B4–D2). Plutarch is arguing that where differ-ences have arisen among kin they should relegate the day it happened to oblivion (*amnêstia*) and recall the many good days passed in common rather than a single ill one; this is the reason that nature has endowed us with gentleness (*praotês*), which is above all to be displayed toward relatives. He continues,

> When those who have done wrong request and accept *sungnômê* it reflects goodwill and affection no less than when one grants *sungnômê* to those who have done the wrong. Thus, we must neither be unconcerned about those who are angry with us, nor hold out against those who beg us, but often those who have done wrong must anticipate the other's anger by entreaty, and those who have been wronged, in turn, must anticipate the entreaty by *sungnômê*.

Plutarch recommends that members of the same family hasten to appease the anger of those they have offended, by pleading for their pardon: this is a sign of their affection and will work to effect reconciliation. Similarly, even before such a petition or supplication is offered, the offended party should give over his or her antagonism: this is the sense of *sungnômê* here, because there is no question in this latter case of apologies or expressions of remorse on the part of the wrongdoer. The emphasis in the essay is entirely on the obligation to love one's brother and hence to terminate any quarrel that may arise as quickly as possible. Forgiveness in the modern sense is marginal to the argument.[21]

In a footnote to an article on rape in Ovid, Ralph Johnson refers to several "instances of contrition" in the *Metamorphoses*.[22] One of these is the story of Aesacus, a Trojan youth who falls in love with Hesperie, the daughter of a river god; as she flees his pursuit, she accidentally treads on a serpent and dies of the poisoned bite. Aesacus embraces her dead body and wails, "I am sorry, sorry that I chased you [*piget, piget esse secutum*]; this I failed to fear, nor was it worth this price to conquer you. We have both killed you – the wound was the snake's, but the cause of it was mine. May I be more accursed than it if I do not grant you solace for your death by my death" (11.778–82). With this, he throws himself from a cliff,

---

[21] Grossel (2008: 375) interprets *sungnômê* in this essay as "*un sentiment de solidarité devant la faiblesse de la nature humaine et la dure loi de nécessité*" (375).

[22] Johnson 1996: 22n17.

but Tethys converts him into a seabird called a "diver" (*mergus*), and in this guise he plunges to the depths, as though still seeking death. It is fair enough, I think, to interpret Aesacus's reaction as remorse for the harm he has done to another and not just egoistic regret at not having attained the object of his desire. It is conceivable that he recognizes, as a result of his loss, that his earlier, selfish passion was fundamentally wrong, and his suicidal impulse may be interpreted as a wish to destroy that former self, because he cannot undo the wrong by appealing for forgiveness (Achilles suffers a comparable guilty despair for having caused the death of Patroclus at *Iliad* 18.98–126). The dead cannot forgive, but it is striking that it is just such situations, in which forgiveness is no longer a possibility, that elicit the most credible descriptions of remorse in classical literature.

Johnson alludes also to Pentheus's confession of having erred (*iam se damnantem, iam se peccasse fatentem*, 3.718) in persecuting the followers of Dionysus, as he is being torn apart by Maenads, including his mother, who mistake him for a wild boar; but in the circumstances, this is scarcely a compelling example of other-regarding remorse. Another instance adduced by Johnson is Scylla, who cuts a magic lock from the head of her father, Nisus, thereby betraying him and her country to the enemy king Minos, with whom she is in love. Having been rejected with horror by Minos when he learns of her act, Scylla cries out (8.125–7): "Exact the penalty, Nisus, my father; O city walls that I betrayed, rejoice in my suffering; for I confess it, I have earned them and deserve to die." But this apostrophe is part of a reproach addressed to Minos as he sails off and abandons her (the scene is modeled on Catullus's account of Ariadne deserted by Theseus, in poem 64); and with this, she leaps into the sea in a vain effort to follow him. This is hardly an example of a change of heart, and as usual, forgiveness is immaterial in the episode. In Book 10, Ovid tells how Myrrha disguised herself so as to sleep with her own father; when on one occasion he lit a lamp and discovered her identity, she fled. In her terror and despair she cries out, "I have deserved this nor do I reject this miserable torture" (10.484–5); she prays that she may neither live nor die, so as not to offend the living or the dead. Heeding her petition, the gods turn her into the myrrh tree. Doubtless her exposure and suffering cause her to repent of her incestuous desire, but her sorrow under the circumstances seems a long way from moral remorse, especially because, like Phaedra in Euripides' *Hippolytus* (on which this episode is partly modeled), she knew in advance that her passion was depraved: there has been no alteration of moral perspective. Finally, there is the case of Dryope, turned into a tree, who swears that she is innocent (9.371–2); this, then, is not an example of remorse at all.[23]

There are undoubtedly situations in which something like remorse serves to mollify an offended party, though such displays of contrition are so shot through with deference based on class that they are difficult to evaluate in strictly moral terms. An excellent example is the situation recorded by Pliny in a letter to his friend Sabinianus (*Epistles* 9.21), which I take the liberty of reproducing in full:[24]

> Your freedman, with whom you had said you were irate, came to me and threw himself before me and clung to my feet as though to yours. How he wept, how he begged, how he kept silent, even: in the end, he gave me confidence [*fidem*] that this was true *paenitentia*. I believe that he is reformed [*emendatum*], because he is aware that he did wrong [*deliquisse*]. I know you are angry, indeed I know that you are rightly angry; but gentleness is especially praiseworthy precisely when there is an entirely just reason for anger. You loved this man once, and I hope you will love him again; in the meantime, just let yourself be prevailed upon. If he again gives you cause, you can be angry with him in the future, and all the more justifiably for having been prevailed upon now. Yield to his youth, yield to his tears, yield to your own leniency [*indulgentia*]. Do not torment him, do not torment yourself: for it is a torment when one so gentle as you is angry. I fear that I may seem to coerce you rather than beg you, if I join my pleas to his. Yet I shall join them all the more fully and abundantly, in that I rebuked him so sharply and severely, sternly threatening that I would never plead for him again. This should have

[23] Fulkerson (2006b: 399) argues that on at least a couple of occasions human beings in Ovid, in contrast to Apollo, do feel something like remorse: "Apollo tries and fails to save both Coronis and Hyacinthus [in *Metamorphoses* Book 2]. Yet, in both cases, he quickly finds someone else to blame. Cyparissus [in Book 10], even though the death he causes is equally accidental, accepts full responsibility for his actions. He cannot fix what he has done and is inconsolable; I would suggest that he thereby shows himself to be more fully a moral agent than Apollo." However, there is no question of forgiveness here.

[24] I am grateful to Zsuzsanna Várhelyi for bringing this passage, and a number of others, to my attention and for her many insights on the subject of ancient forgiveness.

frightened him, but not you: for I may well plead with you again and again win your favor, so long as it is something proper for me to beg, and for you to grant. Farewell.

Here is a case of a confessed offense (there is no indication of what it was) and justifiable anger. Pliny offers one of the standard excuses for misconduct, namely the freedman's youth, and he places great emphasis on his tearful display of regret, which is compounded of fear and what appears to be a genuine consciousness of having erred: it is this that convinces Pliny that the offense is not likely to be repeated, although he allows that it might be, in which case there would be no excusing it. Certainly, the man's anguish and subservience, manifested even more by his silence than by his words, contribute to Pliny's willingness to intercede in his behalf, in line with the prescriptions of Aristotle on assuaging anger. But taken as a whole, the letter looks not so much to forgiveness, with the corresponding change of heart in the forgiver, as to Sabinianus's native mildness of temper, which should dispose him to overlook an offense by an inferior, and it advertises, in the process, Pliny's own clement nature, which he clearly regards as a virtue. It is aristocratic forbearance, rather than forgiveness proper, that is Pliny's theme.

I conclude this chapter with a discussion of a rather odd set of texts, commonly called the "Confession Inscriptions": these are a series of pagan inscriptions found in Lydia and Phrygia (today in northwestern Turkey) and dating to the second and third centuries AD, in which there is an unusual emphasis, outside of Christian circles, on the affirmation of prior error; some scholars have perceived a Christian influence here.[25] Before discussing their character, let me provide some examples, because they are little known; I take them from Appendix B of the recent dissertation by Aslak Rostad (the translations are Rostad's, very slightly modified; Rostad labels them "Reconciliation Inscriptions").[26] "In the year 285 on the 30th of the month Panêmos. For the God Tarsios from whom no one may escape. Because Severus hindered cutting of wreaths the god examined the transgression. His foster daughters

---

[25] E.g., Schnabel 2003. For further discussion, see de Hoz 1999; Rostad 2002; Chaniotis 2004.
[26] Rostad 2006.

Asiateikê and Jouliané raised (this stele) in gratitude."[27] The following is longer and more detailed:

> In the year 320, on the 12th of the month Panêmos. In accordance with the fact that I was instructed by the gods, by Zeus and the great Mên Artemidoros: "I have punished Theodoros on his eyes according to the transgressions he committed." I had intercourse with Trophime, the slave of Haplokomas, wife of Eutykhes, in the *praetorium* (?). He removed the first transgression with a sheep, a partridge and a mole. The second transgression: Even though I was a slave of the gods in Nonu, I had intercourse with Ariagne, who was unmarried. He removed the transgression with a piglet and a tuna. At the third transgression I had intercourse with Arethusa, who was unmarried. He removed the transgression with a hen (or cock), a sparrow and a pigeon; with a *kypros* of a blend of wheat and barley and one *prokhos* of wine. Being pure he gave a *kypros* of wheat to the priests and one *prokhos*. I took Zeus as intercessor. (He said): Behold! I hurt his sight because of his deeds, but now he has propitiated [*heilazomenou*] the gods and written down (the events) on a stele and paid for his transgressions. Asked by the council (the god proclaimed): I will be merciful, because my stele is raised on the day I appointed. You can open the prison; I will release the convict when one year and ten months has passed.[28]

This next one records the successful propitiation of the offended deity:

> Polion (dedicates this stele) to Zeus Oreites and Mên Axiottenos, who rules Perkos (or: Perkon) as a king. When (the circumstances) were hidden from me, and I overstepped the border without permission, the gods punished him (= me). In the year 323, on the 30th of the month Dystros. He removed (the transgression) with a triad consisting of a mole, a sparrow and a tuna. He also gave the means of atonement that by habit is due to the gods when the stele was raised: a modius of wheat and one *prokhos* of wine. As a meal to the priests he gave 1½ (?) *kypros* of wheat, 1½ (?) *prokhos* of wine, peas and salt. And I have propitiated the gods for the sake of my grand-children and the descendants of my descendants.[29]

Here again, the dedicator of the inscription records his gratitude:

> Great is Zeus of the Twin Oaks. Stratoneikos son of Euangelos because of ignorance cut down one of the oaks belonging to Zeus Didymeites.

---

[27] Petzl 4 = *SEG* [*Supplementum Epigraphicum Graecum*] 38: 1229; date AD 200/201.
[28] Petzl 5 = *SEG* 38: 1237; date AD 235/236.
[29] Petzl 6 = *SEG* 39: 1279; date AD 238/239.

And the god mobilized his own power because he (i.e. Stratoneikos) did not believe in him, and placed him ... in a deathlike condition. He was saved from great danger and raised the stele in gratitude. I declare that no one shall ever show contempt for his powers and cut down an oak. In the year 279, on the 18th of the month Panêmos.[30]

Likewise in this example, it is the gratitude of the dedicator that is emphasized:

In the year 300, on the 12th day of the month Xandikos. Because of the transgression which they committed towards the god – and they stole ?? as well as other property – Melitê and Makedôn were punished by the god and their parents asked Apollo Axyros on their behalf. Having asked they raised (the ex-voto) in gratitude.[31]

In this last example, the dedicator does not specify that he succeeded in propitiating the god, but it is surely implied by the very act of erecting the inscribed stele:

I, _ _ _ mos, having been punished by the god, raised a stele to Apollôn Labênos (with an account) of how he punished me because of an oath, my awareness (of my guilt), and a defilement. I proclaim to all that nobody shall show contempt for the gods.[32]

These inscriptions are of great interest from a variety of points of view, including cultic practices in the classical world (for an overview, the reader is referred to the excellent thesis by Rostad). Our concern here is with forgiveness, and in this respect these texts are less illuminating. According to Rostad, these inscriptions "offered an opportunity for a person stigmatised by the allegation of impious behaviour to regain his or her former position. Interestingly, this was not achieved by claiming and proving one's innocence, as may be seen in trials of impiety in classical Athens – even if this may have been one of the options tried before raising the reconciliation inscription – but by admitting the transgression and performing rituals of propitiation. Thereby, the transgressor could be redefined within the moral order and claim to be a pious person who was free of the binding spell. Despite the fact that the transgressor admits guilt he or she can no longer be accused of being subjected to divine wrath" (240).

[30] Petzl 10 = *SEG* 28: 914; date AD 194/195.
[31] Petzl 22 = *SEG* 37: 1737; date = AD 215/216.
[32] Petzl 107; date second or third century AD.

Now, it must be noted that on occasion, the infraction indicated in these inscriptions is purely accidental in character, as in the following example: "Great is Mêtêr who gave birth to Mên, great is Meis Uranios, Meis Artemidorou who rules Axiotta and his power. When P(h)osphoros, son of Artemas, a child six years old, was dressed in a garment stained with impurity, the god investigated. A triad took (the transgression) away, and he (i.e. Phosphoros) wrote down the powers of the god on a stele. In the year 245 on the 12th of the month Panêmos."[33] This inscription illustrates not so much an admission of guilt as an acknowledgment of ritual transgression (on the part of a six-year-old). What is more, even where guilt is conceded, it is almost always the case that the punishment has already been administered – it is the god's chastisement and subsequent propitiation that is celebrated in the inscriptions. The offense is not redeemed by the confession because the god has already been appeased by sacrifices and other gestures of atonement. The narrative outline implied by these inscriptions may be represented as (1) offense; (2) punishment; (3) remission of the penalty; and (4) proclamation of the god's conciliation and the consequent reintegration of the dedicator into the sacred community, sometimes (5) accompanied by a warning to others to be wary of committing similar offenses. Thus, the dedicators of these texts are not asking for forgiveness for a transgression through confession or repentance; they are announcing their success in having appeased the god for the infraction to which they are giving public expression. Admission of guilt, not to say remorse and a change of heart, is not the means by which expiation is sought. For genuine instances of repentance before God as a way to achieve forgiveness, we must turn to Jewish and Christian texts; these are the subject of the next two chapters.

---

[33] Petzl 55 = *SEG* 39: 1278; date AD 160/161.

4

Divine Absolution

The Hebrew and Christian Bibles

If one were to consult Philo, or Origen, or any other Jewish or Christian writer of Greco-Roman antiquity about the proper function of mental distress, an answer would be ready to hand: remorse and repentance bring about a change in one's relationship to god, marked by a fuller awareness of one's responsibilities as a moral agent. This explicitly religious conception of remorse ... is not to be found in the secular philosophical tradition.[1]

In this chapter, I consider the nature of guilt, confession, repentance, and absolution in the Hebrew Bible and the Greek New Testament, in which one encounters a moral structure that, if not yet conforming to the complete modern paradigm of interpersonal forgiveness, nevertheless represents a very different pattern from the one that informs the classical Greek and Roman texts examined so far. But before turning to the biblical literature, I should like to consider a text in the Judeo-Christian tradition that exhibits with particular clarity the role of sin, remorse, and redemption. What is more, this work invites comparison with a set of romantic Greek narratives, in which the relationship of suffering mortals to the divine is markedly different. The contrast thus serves to highlight what is distinctive about the attitude toward forgiveness in the Jewish and Christian scriptures and to confirm the absence of such a conception in pagan Greek and Roman culture.

The Judeo-Christian text that I have chosen is a curious work called *The Life of Adam and Eve*, known also, since the first edition in the nineteenth century, under the rather misleading title *The Apocalypse of Moses*; this narrative, like many ancient novelistic

---

[1] Graver 2007: 206.

texts, has only recently become an object of serious scholarly attention. I speak of it as Judeo-Christian, because scholars are unde-
cided as to whether it is Jewish or Christian in origin; at all events,
the Greek version, which appears to be the earliest, contains no
certain allusions to Christian themes. The date of the work is also
in doubt: it has been placed as early as the first century BC (which
would exclude a Christian provenance) and as late as the seventh
century AD. Recensions survive in ancient Greek, which may be the
original language of composition, as well as in Syriac, which also
has a claim to this distinction, and in Latin, Slavonic, Armenian,
Georgian, and Coptic.[2] Greek and Latin manuscripts abound –
the work was clearly very popular throughout the Middle Ages.
There is also considerable variation among the several traditions,
as is to be expected with a work of this kind, which invites abridge-
ment or expansion according to the interests of the copyists (one
thinks in this connection of the multiple versions of the Greek
Alexander Romance or the Latin *Story of Apollonius King of Tyre*, to
which I have applied the label *open text*).[3] The discussion that follows is based on the Greek text.[4]

After the first couple was driven from Eden, Eve gave birth
to Cain and Abel, and after the murder of Abel, to Seth. When
Adam fell ill and was on the point of death, at 930 years of age,
he gathered round him his thirty sons and thirty daughters. Seth
offers to fetch him fruit from Paradise, but Adam explains the
origin of the curse of death, when he, at Eve's instigation, tasted
of the forbidden fruit, with the result that "God became angry at
us" (*orgisthê hêmin ho theos*, 8).[5] At this point Eve laments, "Adam,
my lord, give me half your illness, and let me endure it, because
this has happened to you on account of me, on account of me you

---

[2] The Coptic version is in fragmentary condition. For a handy comparison of the
several versions, in five parallel columns, see Anderson and Stone 1994; for discussion of the date, contents, manuscripts, and related texts, see de Jonge and Tromp
1997; also Tromp 2005. See also Nickelsburg 1984; and especially the important
collection of essays in Anderson, Stone, and Tromp 2000.

[3] Cf. Konstan 1998b.

[4] I follow the recent edition by Tromp 2005, which has an extensive and important
introduction; this represents a major advance over the 1866 edition of the Greek text
by C. von Tischendorf, who had available only 4 of the 25 manuscripts now known,
although the differences between the two are immaterial for my argument.

[5] The Latin version introduces a long interlude here on a vision of Adam: see
Anderson and Stone 1994: 22.

are in such illness and pain" (9). Adam instructs Eve to seek out Paradise together with Seth, bidding them to weep and beg God to have pity on him (*hopôs splankhnisthêi ep' emoi*). This Eve does and groans aloud: "Woe, woe, if I should come to the day of the resurrection, and all who have sinned will curse me, saying that Eve did not observe the commandment of God" (10). When Eve and Seth return to Adam's tent, Adam asks her to relate the story of the fall, and her responsibility for it, to their children (14). Here begins Eve's first great narrative, in which she rehearses how the devil seduced the serpent, and the serpent in turn deceived her, leading her to the forbidden fruit and even threatening to withhold it from her, having changed its mind (*metamelêtheis*, 19), until she promises to give Adam a share as well. When she has tasted the fruit, she becomes aware of her nakedness but nevertheless fulfills her oath to make Adam eat of it. God then pronounces his dread judgment upon the couple, banishing them from Eden. Adam now begs the angels to let him beseech God's pity, because he alone sinned (27), but God is unrelenting. Adam, on his deathbed, begs Eve to rise up and pray to God, and she, falling to the ground, proclaims, "I have sinned [*hêmarton*], God, I have sinned, Father of all, I have sinned against you, I have sinned against your chosen angels, I have sinned against the Cherubim, I have sinned against your unshakable throne, I have sinned, Lord, I have sinned greatly, I have sinned before you, and all sin in creation has arisen through me" (32). At this, an angel approaches her and announces, "Arise, Eve, from your repentance [*metanoias sou*]" (32).[6] He declares to her that Adam is now dead and grants her a vision of a chariot descending to Adam, and the angels beseeching the Lord to yield (*sunkhôrêson*, 33) because Adam is made in His image. God takes pity [*eleêsen*] on his creature (37) and raises him to the third heaven, where he will remain until judgment day. Adam and Cain are then buried together in a secret place, as God declares that he will resurrect Adam on the final day together with all mankind. Eve supplicates the Lord to bury her next to Adam, even though she is unworthy and sinful (*anaxian kai hamartôlon*, 42),[7] and her wish is granted.

---

[6] Much of the narrative from 27–32 is missing in the Latin and Armenian versions.

[7] The last word spelled with smooth breathing in Tromp's edition.

Seth is instructed to mourn for six days, and with this, the story –
which is Eve's story more than anything else – is ended.

In her relation to God, Eve insists upon her own fault and is
obviously remorseful: that she was deceived by the serpent serves
not as an excuse for her sin but rather as a sign that she has now
perceived her error and has repented of it. This profound realization and acknowledgment of their culpability works a change
in Adam and Eve and is the reason why God is prepared to yield
to the petition on the part of his angels and grant the couple
reprieve and resurrection. It would seem safe to call God's mercy
forgiveness here, because all the conditions have been fulfilled –
even a change of heart on the part of God, who had earlier manifested his sternness in expelling the couple from Paradise, despite
the appeals of his angels on their behalf. But divine forgiveness,
which is able to remit or cancel sin, is, as we shall see, in important
respects a thing apart from the mortal sentiment.[8]

The contrast between this novelistic narrative of Adam and
Eve's fall, and the pattern that informs the ancient Greek novels,
is striking. Five long, prose fictions survive from Greek antiquity,
all narrating the fortunes of a young couple who fall in love, are

---

[8] A prose narrative that may originally be as early as the first century BC recounts the
story of Joseph and Aseneth, the name given in this tale to Potiphar's daughter (cf.
Genesis 41:45–52). Broadly, the plot revolves around Aseneth's renunciation of idolatry and conversion to the religion of Israel. As a consequence of her repentance, an
angel appears to her and says, "You will no longer be called Aseneth, but rather City
of Refuge" (15.6); the angel explains, moreover, that Repentance (*Metanoia*) is the
daughter of the Highest God. After a complex ritual, Aseneth is granted immortal-
ity. Later, the Pharaoh's son conspires with Gad and Dan to kidnap Aseneth from
Joseph, but the other brothers of Joseph intercept them and kill all their band
of fighters. Gad and Dan fall on their knees, declare themselves to be Aseneth's
slaves, and beg her to have pity on them; she bids them not to fear and persuades
Joseph's brothers not to return evil for evil (28). This latter is the primary message;
Gad and Dan are motivated by fear rather than remorse, and Aseneth spares them
on principle, not because she perceives a moral transformation on their part. For
further discussion, see von Stemm 1999: 54–103, who concludes, "Die erarbeiteten
Konzeptionen lassen sich insgesamt als 'Vergebungs'-Vorstellungen qualifizieren,
doch es ist deutlich geworden, dass der deutsche Begriff 'Vergebung' in keinem
Falle ausreicht, um die in diesen Texten ausgedrückten Vorgänge und Handlungen
Gottes zu beschreiben und angemessen wiederzugeben" (101). See also Ward 1987
for a discussion of a series of tales, highly popular in the Middle Ages, concerning
women who submitted to lust and acted as prostitutes but later repented and found
forgiveness. The ultimate model is Mary Magdalene, the nature of whose sin, however, is not specified in the Gospels.

separated, and are reunited in the end: Xenophon's *Ephesiaca* or *Ephesian Tale*, Chariton's *Callirhoe*, *Daphnis and Chloe* by Longus, *Clitipho and Leucippe* by Achilles Tatius, and Heliodorus's *Aethiopica* or *Ethiopian Tale*. They are identified in English as romances or, more recently, as novels, because the label *romance* is intended to distinguish them from ostensibly authentic novels that are said to have begun with Samuel Richardson's *Pamela* and were hence invented by the British.[9] They were composed, in all likelihood, sometime between the first and third centuries AD, which is to say, very possibly around the time of the *Life of Adam and Eve*. The two earliest are those that bear the names of Xenophon and Chariton as authors (each of these survives in a single manuscript, discovered in the eighteenth century). The other three, which had a substantial influence on the rise of the modern novel, are those ascribed to Longus, Achilles Tatius, and Heliodorus (it may be worth remarking that ancient tradition indentifies the latter two as Christians).

At the beginning of Xenophon's *Ephesian Tale*, we are told of the extraordinary beauty of the protagonist, Habrocomes, of which he was so proud that he disdained the charms of others and went so far as to deny that Eros was a god (1.1.5). Eros is predictably furious (*mêniâi pros tauta ho Erôs*, 1.2.1) and causes the youth to fall in love with Anthia, whom he marries. The situation would seem to be tailor-made for a plea for forgiveness on Habrocomes's part. Yet the first time either of the two protagonists offers supplication to a deity, it is Anthia, and she appeals to Isis rather than to Eros: she declares that she has remained chaste and kept her marriage to Habrocomes pure and prays that she either be restored to her husband, if he is still alive, or else that she remain faithful to his corpse (4.3.3–4; cf. 5.4.6). When Habrocomes is bound to a cross, as a result of the false testimony of a vicious woman who fell in love with him, he does not hesitate to proclaim his innocence as he prays to the god of the Nile: if he has done any wrong, he declares, let him die a miserable death and endure a punishment even worse than crucifixion (4.2.4), but let the gracious Nile not look on indifferently at the death of a man who has committed no injustice. The god at once takes pity on him (4.2.6) because his

---

[9] Discussion and bibliography in Konstan 1994: 205–6.

suffering is unmerited. Later, Anthia appeals to Apis as the most humane (*philanthrôpotate*) of deities, who takes pity on all strangers, and begs him to pity her as well in her misfortune (5.4.10), again requesting that she either find her husband or else die; she receives the reply that she will soon have Habrocomes. In the end, when the pair is reunited on Rhodes, they give thanks to Isis for their salvation (5.13.4). Nowhere do they suggest that they might be guilty of some offense against the gods; there is no question of repentance or forgiveness. They have proved their mutual fidelity in the course of their sufferings and now express gratitude for their deliverance. The contrast with the story of Eve is manifest, and yet the two narratives have a great deal in common. Each centers upon a couple driven from their birthplace, in part thanks to the anger of a deity; the pair is then forced to wander abroad. In the end they recover one another and return to their original home, though for Eve this will occur after her death and Adam's, with heaven standing in for the earthly paradise. Yet Xenophon's novel, which has certain traits in common with Christian narratives, wholly lacks the dimension of sin and redemption.[10]

The reason for the hostility of the gods toward Chaereas and Callirhoe in Chariton's novel is unclear: she blames her plight upon malicious Fortune (*Tukhê baskane*, 1.14.7; cf. 2.8.3–6, 3.3.8, 4.1.12, 4.4.2, 4.7.4, 5.1.4, 6.8.1, 8.1.2). When she is finally restored to Chaereas, Callirhoe offers thanks to Aphrodite for being reconciled (*diallattêi*) with her (8.4.10), although no indication of a motive for the goddess's hostility is offered. One might have imagined that she was vindictive toward Callirhoe because of her extraordinary beauty, which causes mortals to mistake her for the goddess (2.2.6, 2.3.6, 2.5.7, 3.2.14): this is the motive of Venus's antagonism toward Psyche in Apuleius's *Metamorphoses* (4.29), although Psyche is blameless, so the question of forgiveness is moot. But Chariton never even hints at such a motive. In the end, back home in Syracuse, Callirhoe visits the temple of Aphrodite to give thanks once again and adds, "I do not blame you, mistress, for what I have suffered: it was my fate" (8.8.16). There is clearly no place for forgiveness here.

Turning now to the later novels, Achilles Tatius is not much interested in appeals to the gods; once, Clitopho bids Aphrodite not to

---

[10] For discussion, see Konstan 2009b.

resent it as an insult to her dignity that he and Leucippe preserved their virginity until they might be properly married (8.5.8), hardly an expression of contrition. In Longus's novel, Daphnis and Chloe are under the protection of Pan and the Nymphs, and there is never any suggestion that they may have offended them. When Chloe is carried off in a raid, Daphnis reproaches the Nymphs for betraying them (2.21.3), upon which the Nymphs appear to him in a dream and reply that they are not to blame (2.23.2) and reassure Daphnis that all will be well and that Pan is already coming to Chloe's defense.

When Chariclea and Theagenes are taken prisoner by Thyamis and his bandits at the beginning of Heliodorus's *Aethiopica*, Chariclea in her grief berates Apollo for her sufferings (1.8.2–3): "You are retaliating too much and too harshly for our sins [*hamartêmatôn*], and all that we have gone through does not suffice for your vengeance.... Where will you put an end to these things?" Like other novelistic heroines, she asserts that rather than suffer shame she will slay herself and remain chaste until death. "But," she adds, "there is no judge harsher than you." Theagenes, however, advises her to leave off such reproaches, because lamentations merely irritate the god further: "one must not censure but rather beseech, for the powerful are rendered propitious by prayers, not by reproofs" (1.8.4). Chariclea seems to acknowledge certain faults, but they do not merit such extreme chastisement. Theagenes, for his part, suggests entreaty as opposed to blame, thus finessing the question of guilt. Neither gives any hint of apology or remorse. Much later, when, thanks to the jealous plots of the queen Arsace, Chariclea is condemned to be burnt at the stake, she, like Habrocomes in Xenophon's novel, cries out to the Sun and Earth and the spirits above and below the earth who watch over human injustice (8.9.12): "You are witnesses that I am innocent of the charges brought against me."[11]

---

[11] Compare Encolpius's prayer to Priapus (*Satirica* 133.2):
> *Non sanguine tristi*
> *perfusus venio, non templis impius hostis*
> *admovi dextram, sed inops et rebus egenis*
> *attritus facinus non toto corpore feci.*
> *Quisquis peccat inops minor est reus. Hac prece, quaeso,*
> *exonera mentem culpaeque ignosce minori,*
> *et quandoque mihi fortunae arriserit hora,*
> *non sine honore tuum patiar decus....*

In observing that the heroes and heroines of the Greek romantic novels do not regard themselves as having done wrong or offended the gods, I am not advancing any startlingly new claims. The tribulations to which the protagonists are subject are designed to test their fidelity, not to punish them for their sins (see Konstan 1994). Where there is no sin, there is no place for forgiveness, and so it is unsurprising that the complex of confession, remorse, and change of heart or conversion is absent from the novels, in stark contrast to the story of Adam and Eve, where these motives are central to the narrative. Yet the absence of forgiveness in the Greek novels is notable, especially because the genre might so easily have accommodated this motif. Comparing the pagan and Judeo-Christian texts brings out the difference between the two traditions in this respect.[12]

Encolpius excuses the offense ("Whoever commits a crime out of poverty is less guilty"), and pleads guilty only to a lesser charge. Aldo Setaioli, who called my attention to this passage, notes (in a personal communication): "although in my view the Greek novels are probably earlier than Petronius ..., one cannot deny that in the Greek novels the theme of divine vengeance, though not entirely absent, is not much developed, at least in those that have come down to us." Setaioli adds that "this kind of formula is common in prayers, in which the petitioner, prior to directing his plea to the god, affirms his purity and innocence"; cf. Appel 1909: 150–1, who cites *inter alia* Catullus 76.19 ("if I have led a pure life ..."), and Silius Italicus 17.35 ("if my body has not been contaminated by any crime ..."); also Valerius Maximus 8.1.5; Seneca *Trojan Women* 641, cited in Courtney 1991: 37. For confession of lesser offenses as a way of excusing oneself from more serious ones (as in the case of Encolpius), cf. Tibullus 1.2.81–4, 1.3.51–2, Lygdamus 5.7–14; Raith 1971; Merkelbach 1973: 82–6. I am most grateful to Aldo Setaioli for these references.

[12] As a postscript to the analysis of *sungnômê* and its cognates in Chapter 2, I examine here the few occurrences in the Greek novels. In Achilles Tatius (5.26.2), Melite, who is in love with Clitopho, begs him no longer for marriage but just a brief affair: "Extinguish just a bit of this fire in me; if I seemed urgent and overbold to you, forgive me [*sungnôthi*], my dearest: passion when it fails of its object grows mad." Melite is excusing her forwardness by an appeal to the argument from *pathos*. In Xenophon of Ephesus (5.9.10), Anthia, having fallen into the possession of the pirate Hippothous, seeks his pardon (*sungnômê*) for having killed one of his men, explaining that he had attempted to rape her: she does not believe that her action was wrong. In Heliodorus (1.17.6), Aristippus discovers that his wife, Demaenete, tried to seduce his son and tricked the boy into seeming like the aggressor; after Demaenete commits suicide, Aristippus secures judicial pardon (*sungnômê*) for his innocent son. Later (6.7.6.), Cnemon begs allowance (*sungnômê*) or sympathetic understanding from Calasiris and Chariclea (and of the gods of friendship, *theôn philiôn*) for not accompanying them to find Theagenes. When Theagenes has been brought before Arsace, who has fallen madly in love with him, he greets her in a manner that seems brazen, without prostrating himself; Arsace, however, asks

The Greeks and Romans did propitiate and attempt to concili-
ate their gods, when they had reason to think that they might be
angry at an offense; but placating someone, whether a human
being or a deity, is a different matter from beseeching forgiveness. For the latter, as we have said, one must repudiate the act
of wrongdoing together with the values that permitted it; such a
repudiation "is a step toward showing that one is not simply the
'same person' who did the wrong" (Griswold 2007b: 50). The forgiver too, in turn, must come round, again in Griswold's words,
to "seeing the offender and oneself in a new light" (53). Now, the
sources of the attitude toward repentance and redemption in *The
Life of Adam and Eve* have their origin, clearly, in the Jewish Bible.
But not every instance of what is translated as "forgive" or "forgiveness" in that text necessarily bears the full moral sense of the term
as described in Chapter 1. Consider the following passage from
Leviticus, which deals with unwitting wrongdoing (4:13–20, RSV
translation):

> If the whole congregation of Israel commits a sin unwittingly and the
> thing is hidden from the eyes of the assembly, and they do any one of
> the things which the Lord has commanded not to be done and are
> guilty; 4:14 when the sin which they have committed becomes known,
> the assembly shall offer a young bull for a sin offering and bring it
> before the tent of meeting; 4:15 and the elders of the congregation
> shall lay their hands upon the head of the bull before the Lord, and the
> bull shall be killed before the Lord. 4:16 Then the anointed priest shall
> bring some of the blood of the bull to the tent of meeting, 4:17 and the
> priest shall dip his finger in the blood and sprinkle it seven times before
> the Lord in front of the veil. 4:18 And he shall put some of the blood on
> the horns of the altar which is in the tent of meeting before the Lord;
> and the rest of the blood he shall pour out at the base of the altar of
> burnt offering which is at the door of the tent of meeting. 4:19 And all
> its fat he shall take from it and burn upon the altar. 4:20 Thus shall he

the others to pardon him (*sungnôte*), because he is a stranger and unfamiliar with
their ways and has a Greek's contempt for foreigners (10.16.7): this is the motive of
ignorance, combined with a habitual Greek view for which Theagenes is not indi-
vidually responsible. In the last occurrence of the term in the *Aethiopica* (10.23.3), a
servant refrains from announcing the arrival of the brother of the Ethiopian king
Hydaspes, out of respect for protocol; when Hydaspes explodes, the servant asks
for pardon (*sungôthi*), explaining that his behavior was correct under the circumstances. In no case do the Greek terms involve a response to a confession of guilt
nor is there evidence of remorse or even regret; forgiveness in the modern sense is
beside the point.

do with the bull; as he did with the bull of the sin offering, so shall he do with this; and the priest shall make atonement for them, and they shall be forgiven.

The term employed for *forgive* here is a form of the root *salakh*; in the Hebrew Bible, only God is the subject of this verb.[13] Because the offense is apparently committed in ignorance (there is some question about how to interpret the Hebrew here, but the Greek Septuagint gives *akousiôs*, or involuntarily), it is not a matter of forgiving deliberate or voluntary wrongdoing. The sacrifice of the bull and the rest of the ritual procedure are rather a kind of compensation due for the trespass, irrespective of intention (cf. 4:26 where the unwitting error is that of a ruler; 4:27 where it is that of the common people; 5:1–19 on various apparently unintentional infractions, all earning pardon upon proper acts of propitiation; also Numbers 15:22–9; 30:3–15).

In the case of conscious wrongdoing, Leviticus requires something more than just ritual atonement: one must first compensate the person one has deceived or harmed (6:1–13 = 5.14–26 in the Hebrew Bible), and then one may, by the priest's intercession, receive pardon (*salakh*) from the Lord (6.6 = 5.16 in the Hebrew Bible). Leviticus 19:20–2 considers the case of a man who has had sexual intercourse with a slave woman who is betrothed to another; neither shall be put to death, because the woman was not free (a condition that would seem to exonerate the man also in this case), but an offering is required on his part, and he is then pardoned (the verb is *salakh*). More severe is Numbers 15:30–1, which offers an explicit contrast with unwitting error:

> 15:30 But the person who does anything with a high hand, whether he is native or a sojourner, reviles the Lord, and that person shall be cut off from among his people. 15:31 Because he has despised the word of the Lord, and has broken his commandment, that person shall be utterly cut off; his iniquity shall be upon him.

There is no tolerance for deliberate offenses.[14]

---

[13] The form given (here and elsewhere) is third-person masculine singular, under which it is lemmatized in Hebrew dictionaries. On the usage, cf. Krašovec (1999: 445): "The subject of words denoting mercy is usually God, more rarely humans; while that of words meaning forgiveness is always God…. The terminology of forgiveness is more closely related to guilt and repentance than is that of mercy or compassion."

[14] David Daube (1960) traces what he takes to be an evolution over the course of the Hebrew Bible from punishment for "unwitting trespass" (3) to that based on

When, during the Exodus, the Israelites despair of being able to conquer Palestine and murmur about returning to Egypt, the Lord prepares to punish them, but Moses intercedes on their behalf (Numbers 14:17–20):

14:17 And now, I pray thee, let the power of the Lord be great as thou hast promised, saying, 14:18 "The Lord is slow to anger, and abounding in steadfast love, forgiving [literally, "lifting": *nasa*] iniquity and transgression, but he will by no means clear [or exempt: *nakah*] the guilty, visiting the iniquity of fathers upon children, upon the third and upon the fourth generation." 14:19 Pardon [*salakh*] the iniquity of this people, I pray thee, according to the greatness of thy steadfast love, and according as thou hast forgiven [לָקֶם, i.e., lifted the reproach from] this people, from Egypt even until now. 14:20 Then the Lord said, "I have pardoned [*salakh*], according to your word."

The guilty will be punished along with their descendants, but pardon is granted to the dispirited Israelites, whose offense is evidently more innocent.

At Deuteronomy 29:19 (in the Hebrew text; 29:20 in the RSV), Moses delivers the covenant with God to the people assembled at Moab and threatens any who might turn from the worship of him:

29:20 The Lord would not pardon [*salakh*] him, but rather the anger of the Lord and his jealousy would smoke against that man, and the curses written in this book would settle upon him, and the Lord would blot out his name from under heaven.

In this context, the offense is that of abandoning the covenant, and the consequences are dire. This is a significant moment in the evolution of the idea of divine leniency: for here it is not a matter of ritual infractions, but of the Israelites' fundamental relationship to God, in which a falling away from the faith is conceived of as unpardonable.

When King Solomon prays to God, he bids him (1 Kings 8:30): "hearken thou to the supplication of thy servant and of thy people Israel, when they pray toward this place; yea, hear thou in heaven thy dwelling place; and when thou hearest, forgive [*salakh*]. If a man sins against his neighbor and is made to

"moral fault" (12), a perspective adopted especially by the rabbis. Given the difficulties in dating the various portions of the Bible, it is best to withhold judgment on hypotheses predicated on moral progress.

take an oath, and comes and swears his oath before thine altar in
this house, 8:32 then hear thou in heaven, and act, and judge thy
servants, condemning the guilty by bringing his conduct upon
his own head, and vindicating [literally 'justifying,' *tzadik*] the
righteous [or just] by rewarding him according to his righteousness [*tzidakah*]." Solomon does not petition mercy for those who
have erred, but rather consideration for those who are innocent.
But immediately afterward a new note is sounded, as Solomon
continues,

> 8:33 When thy people Israel are defeated before the enemy because they
> have sinned against thee, if they turn again to thee, and acknowledge
> thy name, and pray and make supplication to thee in this house; 8:34
> then hear thou in heaven, and forgive [or "be propitious toward": cf.
> the Greek *hileôs*] the sin of thy people Israel, and bring them again to
> the land which thou gavest to their fathers. 8:35 When heaven is shut up
> and there is no rain because they have sinned against thee, if they pray
> toward this place, and acknowledge thy name, and turn from their sin,
> when thou dost afflict them, 8:36 then hear thou in heaven, and forgive
> the sin of thy servants, thy people Israel, when thou dost teach them
> the good way in which they should walk; and grant rain upon thy land,
> which thou hast given to thy people as an inheritance [cf. 8:39, 8:50: in
> each case, *forgive* renders *salakh*].

Here it is the forgiveness of a people that is in question – though
the sin is in each case against God, not against another group or
individual, and it is clear that it consists in failure to revere the
true God and his commandments. To be sure, these commandments include a great many ethical precepts, and a violation of
these – for example, the prohibition against murder – counts
as a lapse of faith. But the focus is on fidelity to God as such, a
matter of religious attitude or conviction. This is what must be
demonstrated, if one is to "turn again to thee."[15] As we shall see
shortly, there is a deep disparity between divine and interpersonal forgiveness.

Again, not every sin is overlooked; at 2 Kings 24:3 we read:
"Surely this came upon Judah at the command of the Lord, to

---

[15] Cf. Joshua 24:19: "But Joshua said to the people, 'You cannot serve the Lord; for he
is a holy God; he is a jealous God; he will not forgive [יִשָּׂא] your transgressions or
your sins. 24:20 If you forsake the Lord and serve foreign gods, then he will turn
and do you harm, and consume you, after having done you good.'"

remove them out of his sight, for the sins of Manas'seh, according to all that he had done, 24:4 and also for the innocent blood that he had shed; for he filled Jerusalem with innocent blood, and the Lord would not pardon."

In the beautiful hymn that concludes Isaiah (the so-called Third Isaiah), the emphasis on the compassion of God for those who have abandoned his worship but have returned again is repeated: "55:7 let the wicked forsake his way, and the unrighteous man his thoughts; let him return to the Lord, that he may have mercy on him, and to our God, for he will abundantly pardon [*salakh*]." God continues to reward those who find their way back to him but remains equally stern in respect to unrepentant sinners. So too in Jeremiah, the Lord will accept the just and honest man (5:1) and reject the wicked, above all, those who have forsaken him (5:7); but those who return will find redemption (31:34, 33:38, 36:3, 50:20; 2 Chronicles 6:20–7, 6:39; Amos 7:2; Psalms 25:11, 86:5, 103:3; Lamentations 3:42; Daniel 9:9, 9:19 [always *salakh*]).[16] He will know who is sincere in repenting, "for thou, thou only, knowest the hearts of the children of men" (2 Chronicles 6:30).

There is little doubt that the idea of repentance for abandoning God received a strong boost after the fall of the Davidic kingdom and the consequent exile of a great many Jews from the land of Israel.[17] To explain the catastrophe that befell them, despite the protection of their Lord, the Israelites shifted the blame onto themselves – a form of transference or *metastasis*, as the Greek rhetoricians defined it, in reverse, in which instead of arguing for one's own innocence by transferring responsibility for the offense

---

[16] Cf. Jeremiah 15:19 (on which Origen comments at length): "if you return [*epistrepsêis*], I will restore you [*apokatastêsô*]"; "returning" is a leitmotiv throughout this text. On forgiveness in the Hebrew Bible, see Ramelli 2007.

[17] John Milbank observes (2001: 97): "up until the time of the Babylonian exile, there is little evidence for a strong Hebraic notion of forgiveness, other than ideas of mitigation according to circumstance and for future mutual interest." See also Boda (2006: 27) on "the belief that prayer is an essential component of authentic penitence that will bring an end to the exile and that such prayer must contain a confession of sin." Boda concludes (49), "During the sixth century B.C.E. the state of Judah experienced a blow to its political and religious institutions that would shake it to its sociological and, in turn, theological core. At the same time, however, members of this same community introduced a liturgical transformation that would provide the theological foundation to enable this people to survive the demise of state and temple."

to another, the Israelites were concerned above all not to inculpate their God and assumed the guilt themselves. This necessity came to inform much of the larger narrative of Jewish history, patterned on a turning away from God, followed by a return or "conversion" (in the root sense of the word) after due signs of repentance and an appeal to God's mercy, often on the part of intercessors such as Moses or, later, the several prophets. There was no choice but to admit one's sin, however reluctantly – one cannot deceive God, after all – and count on his loving and gentle disposition to moderate his justifiable anger.[18]

God, in the course of his complicated relationship with his stiff-necked chosen people, had occasion to regret, more than once, the severity of the punishments he had visited on them, and a case can be made that he too came to adopt a less harsh posture, more willing to open his own heart and cancel his own resentment: Jack Miles, for example, has argued for such an evolution in the personality of God, throughout the course of the Hebrew Bible, in his popular book *God: A Biography* (1995). As Jože Krašovec, in an immensely detailed survey of passages concerning sin and forgiveness in the Hebrew Bible, writes (1999): "forgiveness means the overcoming of feelings hostile to the evil-doer – something that is possible only if the injured person condones the wrongdoing: only then is he able to see the wrongdoer in a more favourable light. Condoning the offense implies revising one's judgment of the offender, and in the final analysis, this means a change of heart with respect to him." Thus, many of the elements of *forgiveness* in the rich, modern sense of the term, involving the restoration of a moral relationship between two parties as a consequence of a mutual change of heart, were in place. As Michael Morgan, in a brilliant article about repentance and forgiveness in the Hebrew Bible (2011), observes, "Forgiving is a surplus that includes a change of attitude, a sense of good will, and an overcoming of the sense of being violated, humiliated, or diminished. The Bible does not thematize this surplus, but it does hint in its direction."[19]

---

[18] Moore (1997, vol. 1: 507) observes that Hebrew "has no specific name" for repentance, but uses the word for "turn about, go back" (*shoov*): "By this association the transparent primary sense of repentance in Judaism is always a change in man's attitude toward God."

[19] Muffs 1992 argues that *joy* in the Hebrew Bible and other Near Eastern texts may signify a free and willing decision as the condition for a legal contract; Douglas

These ideas would be developed and systematized by Jewish commentators on the Bible. As Kaufmann Kohler (1901–6) writes in the online *Jewish Encyclopedia*: "Atonement in Jewish theology as developed by the Rabbis of the Talmud, has for its constituent elements: (a) on the part of God, fatherly love and forgiving mercy; (b) on the part of man, repentance and reparation of wrong." Repentance is interpreted as "the expression of self-reproach, shame, and contrition" (ibid.). Kohler quotes the Jewish philosopher Philo (*De Execratione* 8 = *De praemiis et poenis* 163.28): "They must feel shame throughout their whole soul and change their ways; reproaching themselves for their errors and openly confessing all their sins with purified souls and minds, so as to exhibit sincerity of conscience" (on the idea of conscience, cf. Philo *On the Decalogue* 87, who affirms that "native and indwelling in every soul is a cross-examiner [*elenkhos*] ..., which is our accuser and judge"; also the extended discussion at *De specialibus legibus* 1.235–8).[20] Kohler adds that "repentance consists in abandoning the old ways, and in a change of heart." This is just the pattern of remorse and forgiveness that is given such moving narrative expression in *The Life of Adam and Eve*.

Nevertheless, there is a sense in which the representation of forgiveness in the Hebrew Bible falls short of the full modern conception: for the focus on the Jewish people's relationship to God not only has the consequence that it is for the most part God who forgives, rather than human beings, but also that the kind of offense that requires forgiveness is a generalized rejection of the Lord, as opposed to particular wrongs committed against a fellow being. Repentance, correspondingly, takes the form of a return to God, that is, an alteration of religious conviction and commitment, deep and sincere as it must be, rather than of one's moral character per se (cf. Sirach 17.29 [originally in Greek]: "How great is the pity and the mercy [*exilasmos*] of the Lord toward those who turn [*epistrephousin*] to him"). Because much of what constitutes genuine worship in the Jewish tradition is ethical in nature, a return to God's commandments certainly entails moral reform; as Chong-

---

(1999: 44), raises the possibility that negative emotions, such as hate or resentment, might be similarly rewritten as signifying avoidance, rather than an inward feeling.

[20] I am grateful to Zsuzsa Varhelyi for calling my attention to this passage. Cf. Wallis 1974–5; Milgrom 1974–5: 41–5; also Winston 1995.

Hyon Sung concludes, after a survey of forgiveness in the Hebrew Bible and the Gospels: "sin is the violation of God's law, and is thus understood as a breach of justice [Rechtsbruch]."[21] As Morgan puts it: "The Biblical God is a lawgiver; sin is transgression of divine law," and this law dictates relations among human beings as well as those between man and God; nevertheless, "the primary 'victim' of wrong, so to speak, the one who is wronged and the one with whom a relationship has been breached by the wrong, is God." But the emphasis on the orientation to God tends to endow wrongdoing with the quality of sinfulness as a state or spiritual condition, as opposed to a specific act of wrongdoing. As we shall see, this becomes a crucial feature in the Christian tradition.

The Hebrew Bible is not without examples of personal forgiveness, though the term employed in these cases is not *salakh*, which, as we have seen, is reserved for God. Thus, after Joseph's father had died, his brothers, fearful that Joseph would take revenge for their having sold him into slavery, send him a message in which they claim that their father had bade him:

> (Genesis 50:17) "Forgive [*nasa*, literally "lift up"; Greek *aphes*], I pray you, the transgression of your brothers and their sin [*chaṭat*; Greek *hamartia*], because they did evil to you." And now, we pray you, forgive the transgression of the servants of the God of your father. Joseph wept when they spoke to him. 50:18 His brothers also came and fell down before him, and said, "Behold, we are your servants." 50:19 But Joseph said to them, "Fear not, for am I in the place of God? 50:20 As for you, you meant evil against me; but God meant it for good, to bring it about that many people should be kept alive, as they are today."

We have already encountered the idea that a favorable outcome can justify, at least partially, the offense that gave rise to it; besides, it is not clear that Joseph's brothers are truly repentant – they are rather afraid of Joseph's wrath, now that he is in a position of power, and rather than exhibit remorse they fabricate an exhortation to mercy on the part of their father. Finally, they adopt a posture of self-abasement, thus seeking to placate Joseph by acknowledging his superiority, a good Aristotelian technique for assuaging anger.[22]

---

[21] Sung (1993: 182) adds, "At the same time, sin is an infringement of God's rule of life.... To forgive or remain conscious of sin is thus God's job."

[22] Cf. Morgan (2011): "Joseph seems to have justified or at least rationalized what had happened to him; his reconciliation with his brothers may not have been easy for

So too, the Pharaoh's regret at his treatment of the Jews is inspired by a plague:

> Exodus 10:16 Then Pharaoh called Moses and Aaron in haste, and said, "I have sinned against the Lord your God, and against you. 10:17 Now therefore, forgive my sin [literally, lift my sin: שָׂא נָא חַטָּאתִי; in the Greek, προσδέξασθε οὖν μου τὴν ἁμαρτίαν, i.e., "be hospitable toward"], I pray you, only this once, and entreat the Lord your God only to remove this death from me." 10:18 So he went out from Pharaoh, and entreated the Lord. 10:19 And the Lord turned a very strong west wind, which lifted the locusts and drove them into the Red Sea; not a single locust was left in all the country of Egypt.

As opposed to such self-interested petitions for mercy, true contrition in the Hebrew Bible is always felt before God.[23]

Before proceeding to discuss the New Testament, we may pause to consider the ancient rabbinical interpretations of the Hebrew Bible, to see what contributions they may have made to the theme of forgiveness. We have already seen, in Chapter 1, that Moses Maimonides, writing in the twelfth century, produced an account of forgiveness that comes remarkably close to what we have identified as the prevailing modern conception (see Chapters 1 and 6).[24]

---

him but ultimately it was grounded in his commitment to the hegemony of divine agency. Neither he nor his brothers were free agents; they were all instruments of divine will."

[23] Morgan (2011) finds a closer approximation to forgiveness in the story of Jacob and Esau (Genesis 33): "Many years after Jacob had swindled Esau out of his birthright and after Jacob had fled and married Leah and Rachel, the two brothers met once again. Although the text does not use the language of sin, resentment, repentance, and forgiveness, the passage in Genesis does describe their encounter in a way that suggests the propriety of such a vocabulary. It tells us that Jacob feared his brother's anger but bowed before him and drew near to him; in response 'Esau ran to meet him, and embraced him, and fell on his neck, and kissed him; and they wept.' These words suggest an act of remorse and repentance and a request for acceptance, and Esau's response certainly seems like the kind of change of attitude and act of acceptance that is associated with forgiveness." True, but one might also interpret Jacob's behavior as a sign of self-abasement, designed to appease Esau, and Esau's enthusiastic response as a sign both of his love for his brother and his having overcome, with the years, a sense of injury.

[24] Maimonides may also have been influenced by Islamic doctrines; cf. Stern (1979: 590), who observes that "Repentance is touched upon by al-Ghazzali in a number of his works"; for al-Ghazzali, "Repentance is a process of conversion whereby a man corrects his past errors, assures the discontinuance of like action, and strives for future abstention from negatively valued behavior" (591). See also Harvey 1991; Peli 1980 (I am indebted to Noam Zion for bringing this work to my attention).

Maimonides's tract is part of his great work, the Mishneh Torah, a systematization of Jewish law based in part on his reading of the Mishnah, a law code compiled around the second century AD and incorporating much oral lore, and the Tosefta (literally, Supplement), a secondary compilation organized along similar lines to the Mishnah, as well as other rabbinical sources known collectively as the Gemara or, more generally, the Talmud, which exists in two principal versions (one assembled in Jerusalem, the other in Babylonia) and often takes the form of commentaries on the Mishnah and the Tosefta.[25]

There are a few – very few – passages in the Mishnah and Tosefta that refer to interpersonal forgiveness, or more strictly to atonement; this is perhaps unsurprising, given that these texts are concerned primarily with laws and forms of expiation for transgression of them, not with interpersonal relations per se. Penitence, to be sure, receives its due. Thus, in the tractate called Mishnah Yoma, the eighth Mishnah or section explains that "death or the Day of Atonement effects atonement if accompanied with penitence; repentance effects atonement for lesser transgressions against positive commands and against negative commands, whereas for graver sins it suspends punishment until the Day of Atonement arrives and effects atonement."[26] In the Avoth (ch. 4, Mishnah 17), we read: "He [Rabbi Jacob] used to say, Better is one hour of repentance and good action in this world than the whole life of the world to come" (Blackman 1965, vol. 4, 522). But it is the ninth Mishnah of the Yoma that scholars most often cite in connection with forgiveness: "If one says, 'I will sin and repent, I will sin and repent,' he will not be given [from on high] an opportunity to repent. 'I will sin and the Day of Atonement will effect atonement,' then the Day of Atonement does not effect atonement. For transgression from man towards God the Day of Atonement effects atonement; but for transgressions between a man and his fellow man the Day of Atonement does not effect atonement until he shall have first appeased his fellow man" (311–12; this passage is followed by an opinion to the same effect

---

[25] Moore 1997 provides a comprehensive and still valuable introduction to the nature of the sources.

[26] Cited from Blackman 1965, vol. 2: 311.

by Rabbi Elazar). This declaration of the necessity to seek reconciliation with the person you have offended as a precondition for gaining God's mercy on the Day of Atonement is as remarkable as it is isolated in the context of the Mishnah. We may supplement the preceding with the following citation from the Baba Kamma (ch. 8, Mishnah 7): "Even though he [who offers the insult] pays him [the party offended], it is not forgiven him [by God] until he seeks pardon from him" (Blackman 1965, vol. 4, 67). The parallel section of the Tosefta (Bava Kamma 9:1) contains a rather different injunction: "It teaches that the victim of an assault should pray to God to have mercy on his assailant even if the assailant has not requested that he do so."[27]

Louis Newman, in an investigation of "whether and under what circumstances Judaism recognizes a duty to forgive others for the

[27] There is a certain tension between the Mishnah and the Tosefta here; for discussion, see Hauptman 2005: 154–6; also Schimmel 2002: 84–5: "Although the predominant theme in traditional Jewish teaching about forgiveness is that you needn't forgive someone who has sinned against you and who doesn't express remorse, compensate you, and request forgiveness, there appears to have been a debate about this that is reflected in two closely related texts from the second and third centuries C.E. The first is from the Mishnah [citing Bava Kamma 8.7]. The context of this teaching is the law of torts that specified the fines that a person who shamed another was required to pay. After specifying the monetary penalties, the Mishnah goes on to state, 'Even though he (the perpetrator) pays (the victim of his insult), he is not forgiven until he requests from him [forgiveness].' The text continues with an admonition to the victim that it would be cruel for him not to grant forgiveness once the perpetrator has paid the fine and also requested forgiveness. This teaching reflects the predominant attitude of the tradition. However, another rabbinic text takes a different approach [Tosefta, Bava Kamma 9:1]. It teaches that the victim of an assault should pray to God to have mercy on his assailant even if the assailant has not requested that he do so. Later commentators who juxtaposed the two passages either accepted the fact that there were two different views, or tried to harmonize the two texts by explaining the latter to mean that if the perpetrator has requested forgiveness, the victim should not only forgive him himself, but also pray to God on his behalf, even though he did not request that from the victim." Cf. Neusner 1981: 57, from Baba Qamma 9:29: "A. He who injures his fellow, B. even though the one who did the injury did not seek [forgiveness] from the injured party – C. the injured party nonetheless has to seek mercy for him, D. since it says, Then Abraham prayed to God, and God healed Abimelech (Gen. 20:17) [cf. M. B. Q. 8:7 A–D]. E. And so you find in regard to the friends of Job, as it is said [the reference is to Job 42:7–8, supplied by translator.] 9:30 A. R. Judah says in the name of Rabban Gamaliel, 'Lo, it says, [allusion to Deut. 13:18, supplied by translator, on showing mercy and compassion] B. Let this sign be in your hand. C. So long as you are merciful, He will have mercy on you.'"

offenses which they commit against us,"[28] interprets Baba Kamma (or Qamma) 8:7, cited in the preceding text, to mean that there are two kinds of harm, or "two separate offenses" of which one is material, and can be repaid, whereas the "more intangible injury ... can be remedied only through seeking forgiveness."[29] Newman argues further that the Mishnah "never proposes that one has a duty to forgive, so to speak, unilaterally, irrespective of the offender's stance, but only as a response to an appropriate gesture of repentance on the part of the offender" (160). This would seem to approach the modern conception, according to which forgiveness requires signs of a change of heart in the offender and in the party who forgives, and hence forgiveness can never be obligatory in the sense of a simple reflex: it is an active process and must be earned. Nevertheless, Newman observes that, whereas the "interrelationship of these two duties – that of seeking forgiveness and that of granting it – is expressed with characteristic clarity and precision by Maimonides (Mishneh Torah, Laws of Repentance, 2:9–11)," the fact is that "Maimonides emphasizes what the Mishnah passage only implied, that the offender bears primary responsibility for initiating the process of forgiveness." Newman adds that "throughout rabbinic literature one finds repeated admonitions to the effect that any sinner who repents will be met with divine forgiveness" (163), and there is some evidence – though it is exiguous – that the rabbis encouraged their followers to follow this rule: "Just as it is God's way to be merciful and forgiving to sinners, and to receive them in their repentance, so do you be merciful one to another."[30]

---

[28] Newman 1987: 156. Newman is responding in this article to a paper in the same issue by Paul Lauritzen (1987).

[29] Given the difficulty of rendering into English the legal language of the Mishnah, I provide here the translation that Newman (1987) gives in his article: "Even though a person gives [monetary compensation] to one [whom he has shamed] he is not forgiven until he asks [explicitly for forgiveness] from him [whom he has shamed]" (citing Genesis 20:7). One may compare also Danby 1933.

[30] Tanna de bei Eliyahu, cited on p. 164 from Montefiore and Loewe 1938: 468–9; taken from a text consisting of moral advice by Eliyahu Rabba and Eliyahu Zuta, dating originally to the Talmudic period, though the manuscript is considerably later (tenth century). It should be noted that others passages indicate that some sins are unforgivable.

Morgan, in the article cited earlier in this chapter, also finds in rabbinic literature a "continued emphasis on the divine-human relation but also, on occasion, a more nuanced awareness of interpersonal sin and forgiveness," mentioning in particular the Mishnah Baba Kamma 8:7 in the Babylonia Talmud as a "text that seems to come closer to our sense of forgiveness as a change of heart regarding a person who has done wrong to us, without excusing his culpability or reducing his punishment." As Morgan points out:

> Commentators regularly cite this Mishnaic passage as evidence for forgiveness that is more than a merciful or compassionate pardon or mitigating of punishment. Here we are told that forgiveness does not excuse the sin or cancel the punishment, that what elicits the forgiveness from the victim (and from God) is a request for forgiveness – which many identify with repentance, and finally that the human victim should not withhold forgiveness once it is requested. If we take the text at face value, then human forgiveness is valuable, dependent upon prior request, and yet conditionally obligatory, i.e., due the sinner who asks for it.

But the passage may not be as transparent as it seems. The proof text to which the Mishnah alludes is the story of Abraham and Abimelech. Abraham has falsely identified Sarah as his sister rather than wife, and this has led Abimelech to take her as his own (Genesis 20:2). God reveals the truth to Abimelech in a dream, and tells him: "Now then restore the man's wife; for he is a prophet, and he will pray for you, and you shall live" (20:7). And so it transpires. Abimelech declares to Sarah: "'Behold, I have given your brother a thousand pieces of silver; it is your vindication in the eyes of all who are with you; and before every one you are righted.' Then Abraham prayed to God; and God healed Abimelech, and also healed his wife and female slaves so that they bore children" (20:16–17). As Morgan observes, "In a sense, it is Abraham here who both receives Abimelech's compensation and transmits to God Abimelech's request for forgiveness. The human victim, in this case of doubling, acts as both the recipient of compensation and repentance and as the deputy of repentance, and it is God who ultimately dispenses forgiveness to the sinner by mercifully cancelling any punishment of him." After a close comparison between this text and the parallel passage in the Tosefta (cited in the preceding text), which refers to the same episode in Genesis, Morgan concludes that in both versions, "Abraham, the human victim, acts as a mediator between the sinner and God. To be sure, Abraham's role in the exchange is not incidental, but it is none-theless not that of an independent agent. Interpersonal sin and forgiveness occur only within the background framework of the covenantal relationship between God and Israel." Morgan finds the same focus on the role of God in forgiving transgressions in the Yoma tractate dealing with repentance and the Day of Atonement, in which we are told that, for transgressions between two people, there is atonement only if the one appeases the other:

> here as there, the focus is on God's acceptance of the ritual acts and the repentance. The human victim of the wrongdoing, while he or she must be compensated first, is nonetheless an incidental factor in the sinner's effort to reconcile with God and to be forgiven by God. In short, the text ... is not introduced into the Mishnah in order to single out and highlight the importance of interpersonal forgiveness. Its purpose is to clear away a possible objection to the efficacy of the rituals of the Day of Atonement and to accommodate a potential obstacle to divine mercy.

Although it is true that the Talmudic texts recognize the culpabil-ity of the offender and the moral duty of the victim to make peace if there is evidence of contrition (or, in the Tosefta passage, even without this condition), interpersonal forgiveness is still set in the context of the relationship with the divine. This having been said, one must again insist on how rare any such discussions of forgiveness are in this corpus and on the corresponding danger of falsifying their significance by excerpting them from their nar-rowly legal context and treating them as independent reflections on human ethics.

It was Hannah Arendt who made the controversial, and to my mind mistaken, claim that the idea of forgiveness as a human capacity began with Jesus,[31] and it is to the New Testament that we may now turn. The reader is doubtless aware that the quantity of modern interpretative commentary on every passage in the New Testament, and no less on those concerning remission of sin, is

---

[31] Arendt 1998: 239, citing Luke 5:21–4, Matthew 9:4–6, and Mark 12:7–10 (the last evidently a misprint for 2:7–10); these passages are discussed in the following text in fuller context.

vast, and a great deal of it is subtle and profound. I do not hope to contribute substantially to the understanding of Jesus's doctrines or of Christian thought in general. My purpose is rather to evaluate the relation between mentions of forgiveness in the New Testament and the views on repentance and forgiveness expressed in the Hebrew Bible, and also to place the teachings of Jesus in the context of attitudes toward reconciliation current in the Greco-Roman world at the time. More especially, I am concerned to see the extent to which forgiveness in the New Testament corresponds to what I have described as the full or rich modern sense of the term.

Perhaps the best known passage on forgiveness in the Gospels is Jesus's Sermon on the Mount, in which he enjoins the people (Matthew 6:9–15):

> 6:9 Pray then like this: "Our Father who art in heaven, hallowed be thy name. 6:10 Thy kingdom come. Thy will be done, on earth as it is in heaven. 6:11 Give us this day our daily bread; 6:12 and forgive [*aphes*] us our debts [*opheilêmata*], as we also have forgiven our debtors [*aphêkamen tois opheiletais*]; 6:13 and lead us not into temptation, but deliver us from evil." 6:14 For if you forgive [*aphête*] men their trespasses [*paraptômata*], your heavenly Father also will forgive [*aphêsei*] you; 6:15 but if you do not forgive men their trespasses, neither will your Father forgive your trespasses (trans. RSV).

The word for *debt* here is *opheilêma*, meaning "what is owed"; the word for *forgive* (the dictionary form of the verb is *aphiêmi*), moreover, is a standard term for the remission of a debt.[32] *Trespass*, in turn, renders the Greek *paraptôma*, literally a "misstep" or "slip." In the version of the Lord's prayer in Luke, the language is slightly different, for there Jesus bids us pray that God "forgive [*aphes*] us

---

[32] Arendt was fully aware of the problems of translation posed by the Hebrew and Greek terminologies: "It is important to keep in mind that the three key words of the text – *aphienai*, *metanoein*, and *hamartanein*, carry certain connotations even in New Testament Greek which the translations fail to render fully. The original meaning of *aphienai* is 'dismiss' and 'release' rather than 'forgive'; *metanoein* means 'change of mind' and – since it serves also to render the Hebrew *shuv* – 'return,' 'trace back one's steps,' rather than 'repentance' with its psychological emotional overtones; what is required is: change your mind and 'sin no more,' which is also the opposite of doing penance. *Hamartanein*, finally, is indeed very well rendered by 'trespassing' in so far as it means rather 'to miss,' 'fail and go astray,' than 'to sin'" (239); cf. Friedland 2004: 28–34 on Arendt.

our sins" or faults (*hamartias*; cf. Matthew 9:2, on the healing of the paralytic, discussed in the following text), "for we ourselves forgive [*aphiomen*] everyone who is indebted to us" (11:4): the second term (indebted, or *opheilonti*) recalls the language of borrowing and owing. Formally, Jesus's injunction has the character of a pact or reciprocal commitment: to receive the indulgence of others, in this case God's, it is good practice to be similarly gracious toward those who are obliged to you, whether for money borrowed or for some other thing that is due. So too, Luke 6:37 affirms that those who forgive (the verb here is *apoluô*) will be forgiven (cf. 18:32–4, the parable of the wicked servant). Such advice to treat others as you would be treated is familiar enough: the Greek orator Lysias (13.53), as we have seen, states that people are more inclined to grant *sungnômê* to those who grant it willingly themselves (Chapter 3, with further references), and Dio Cassius has Livia assert "people love those who are *sungnômones*" (compare Seneca *Epistles* 9.6.6: "Love if you would be loved [*si vis amari, ama*]").[33]

---

[33] Caputo, Dooley, and Scanlon 2001a summarize Derrida's argument on forgiveness as follows: "Like the gift, forgiveness must resist becoming a system of exchange. In classical philosophy and theology, forgiveness is inscribed precisely within an economic order according to which it can be 'given' only under certain conditions. If the offender admits that he is wrong and asks to be forgiven, expresses sorrow, means to make amends as far as possible, and promises to avoid repeating his offense in the future, then he is forgiven. The deal is struck, the exchange is made, and the reconciliation follows.... The offender meets the conditions, pays off the debt, and thus is *owed* forgiveness. Anything else would be unfair." For Derrida, however, this symmetry violates the essentially asymmetrical nature of forgiveness: "Reconciliation and redemption ... belong to an economy that ought not to be confused with forgiveness.... For forgiveness in itself, if there is such a thing, is a gift, not a deal, good or bad, which means that to 'give' or grant pardon to the other, is to do so unconditionally, apart from any economic considerations, even if the other does not ask for forgiveness, does not repent or plan to make amends or promise to sin no more. There is forgiveness as such just when there is no hint of a deal, no sign from the other side that they intend to keep the peace, no sign of equilibrium" (4). All this seems to me wide of the mark: forgiveness is not like paying a debt; rather, when the other meets certain conditions involving repentance and a change of heart, forgiveness becomes an option – never a requirement. The real mystery of forgiveness, if we are speak of paradoxes, is that one must recognize the wrong committed and yet not allow this to disrupt the restoration of a moral relationship with the offender; this seems to me to be an inherently unstable state (on Derrida, see further Chapter 6). De Lange (2004: 163) worries on the contrary that today, "no one is *obliged* to maintain or to restore a relationship with someone who is in debt towards him or her. Forgive one another? That is possible, and it may do one credit. But there is no obligation to do it, and one cannot expect it from anybody, let alone demand it."

The difference is that God, in Jesus's sermon, is merciful toward those who treat not him but others well: he rewards generosity as a virtue. (The argument can also be reversed, as at Colossians 3:13: "as the Lord has forgiven you, so you also must forgive.") It is a significant shift and raises a series of questions concerning the relationship between human and divine forgiveness.

We have seen that, at least according to some scholars, the injunction to grant forgiveness to an offender in the Mishnah and the Gemara portions of the Talmud has a double aspect: as an interpersonal gesture, it involves giving over anger in return for suitable compensation, at the same time that the offended party petitions God's forgiveness for the offender. The Gospel of Matthew (9:2–7) makes it clear that, in the Jewish tradition (at least as perceived through the lens of early Christianity), forgiveness in the deepest sense – that is, the lifting of sin – pertains not to mankind but to God: for when Jesus miraculously heals a paralytic man, the scribes protest at Jesus's affirmation: "Take heart, my son; your sins are forgiven," regarding it as a form of blasphemy (9:2–3). Jesus first offers the evasive, or at all events ironic, reply: "For which is easier, to say, 'Your sins are forgiven,' or to say, 'Rise and walk'?" (9:5), but he immediately addresses the substance of the scribes' objection: "'But that you may know that the Son of man has authority on earth to forgive sins' – he then said to the paralytic – 'Rise, take up your bed and go home'" (9:6). So too, after the parable of the debtors (to which we shall return in a moment), Jesus says of the woman who has anointed his feet: "'Therefore I tell you, her sins [*hamartiai*], which are many, are forgiven [*apheôntai*], for she loved much; but he who is forgiven [*aphietai*] little, loves little.' And he said to her, 'Your sins are forgiven [*apheôntai sou hai harmartiai*]'" (Luke 7:47–8). Jesus, however, is not arguing here that forgiveness of sin lies within the competence of ordinary human beings; rather, he is demonstrating the legitimacy of his claim to be God's son, and hence his regent on earth, with authority to act in behalf of his father.

Let us return to the imagery of debt, which figures so prominently in the Sermon on the Mount. In the parable of the two debtors, Jesus explains (Luke 7:40–3): "'Simon, I have something to say to you.' And he answered, 'What is it, Teacher?' 7:41 'A certain creditor had two debtors [*khreopheiletai*]; one owed [*ôpheilen*]

five hundred denarii, and the other fifty. 7:42 When they could
not pay, he forgave [*ekharisato*] them both. Now which of them
will love him more?' 7:43 Simon answered, 'The one, I suppose,
to whom he forgave [*ekharisato*] more.' And he said to him, 'You
have judged rightly.'" In classical Greek, the word *kharizomai*
means "grant a favor," and its use here to mean acquit someone
of a debt is consistent with this sense (it can be used of overlooking or pardoning a wrong [*adikia*] as well, as in 2 Corinthians
12.13). However, the term most employed for forgiveness or remission of sin in the New Testament is *aphesis*, from the verb *aphiêmi*,
which has the basic sense of "let go" or "dismiss" – "cast away"
or "cast forth" would be a literal rendering of the compound,
from the root verb *hiêmi*, "to throw" or "toss," and the prefix *apo-*,
"away." *Sungnômê* is found only once in the New Testament, at
1 Corinthians 7:6, where Paul advises married couples: "7:5 Do not
refuse one another except perhaps by agreement for a season, that
you may devote yourselves to prayer; but then come together again,
lest Satan tempt you through lack of self-control. 7:6 I say this by
way of concession [*sungnômê*], not of command [*epitagê*]. 7:7 I wish
that all were as I myself am. But each has his own special gift from
God, one of one kind and one of another" (RSV). For *sungnômê*
here, the Authorized Version and the Webster Bible give "permission," whereas the God's Word Bible renders it as "suggestion"; the
Bible in Basic English, in turn, has "as my opinion," although the
American Standard Version and New Revised Standard Version
keep the RSV rendering "concession": all of these translations
capture the fact that Paul is not assuming the power to forgive
in his own right but merely indicating that he understands and
grants a certain allowance to sexual relations within marriage.
Paul recognizes that not all people can abstain permanently from
sex, and his concession is in accord with Aristotle's view that *sungnômê* is due "when someone does things one ought not to do on
account of circumstances that are beyond human nature and
which no one could endure" (*Nicomachean Ethics* 3.1, 1110a23–6,
cited more fully in Chapter 2). So too, Paul acknowledges that a
virgin who marries does not sin, and though she will subsequently
suffer in the flesh, Paul is gracious enough to affirm (7:18): "I
spare you" (RSV, etc.); the Greek verb here is *pheidomai* (cf. 2
Corinthians 1:23, 12:16), which in this connection means "release"

from punishment or reproach (the Latin Vulgate gives *parco,* which bears the same sense).

In the Septuagint, that is, the Greek translation of the Hebrew Bible composed sometime after 300 BC, the term *sungnômê* and its cognates are again relatively rare; what is more, all six occurrences are found in texts composed originally in Greek, and all are among the latest to be included in what became, for Christians, the Old Testament. At 4 Maccabees 5:13 we read: "For consider this, that if there is some power watching over this religion of yours, it will excuse [*sungnômoneô*] you from any transgression that arises out of compulsion [*di'anankên*]." The use of the term here is clearly in line with classical Greek notion that pardon is due to offenses committed under duress. So too, 4 Maccabees 8:22 explains (the translation is again that of the RSV): "Also, divine justice will excuse [*sungignôskô*] us for fearing the king when we are under compulsion [*di'anankên*]."[34] Wisdom 6:6 affirms, "For the lowliest man may be pardoned [*sungnôstos,* literally "is pardonable"] in mercy [or pity: *eleos*], but mighty men will be mightily tested"; the point is that those of humble station are less likely to be guilty of offenses. At Wisdom 13:8, it is affirmed that pagan religious thinkers are not "to be excused" [*sungnôstoi*], because they ought to have been able to discover the truth; only those faults that are unavoidable are strictly speaking blameless.[35] Finally, in the prologue to Sirach (18) the author begs the reader's indulgence [*sungnômê*] if some Greek word or phrase does not correspond exactly to the Hebrew, because the meanings of terms in the two languages do not precisely overlap; and at 3:13, the author admonishes: 3:12 "O son, help your father in his old age, and do not grieve him as long as he lives; 3:13 even if he is lacking in understanding, show forbearance [*sungnômê*]; in all your strength do not despise him." The passage emphasizes the duty to honor one's parents, even when they reach an age at which their mental abilities are waning; there is no question here of forgiving deliberate wrongdoing.

---

[34] See De Silva 1998, who argues that the fourth book of Maccabees arose in the Greek-speaking Jewish diaspora and shows a knowledge of Greek rhetorical conventions; also Klauck 1989; Renehan 1972; Seim 2001.

[35] Wisdom may have been composed as late as texts of the New Testament; see Scarpat 1989–99. For general background and theology, see Reese 1970; Bizzeti 1984; Calduch-Benages and Vermeylen 1999; Bellia and Passaro 2004; Hübner 2004.

We shall return to the significance of *sungnômê* in scripture in connection with the discussion of the church fathers in the following chapter, in which it will become clear that they were aware of a distinction between God's forgiveness, for which the most common term is, as we have said, *aphiêmi*, and *sungnômê*, which refers to an ostensible offense that is excusable, either on the grounds that it was unintentional or involuntary, or that the action is allowable under the circumstances. But it is now time to resume the analysis of *aphiêmi* and the language associated with the remission of debts; the principal point to note is that the cancellation of a debt is not normally an instance at all of forgiveness in the sense under investigation here. At the most elementary level, remitting a debt does not imply any wrongdoing on the part of the debtor: it is simply an act of generosity on the part of the lender, equivalent to a gift. Put differently, when one annuls a debt, the slate is wiped clean: it is as though there had been no loan in the first place. Although the former debtor, like the recipient of any benefaction, may and perhaps should feel gratitude, this does not constitute a continuing obligation but rather a response to a favor freely awarded. As Aristotle puts in the *Rhetoric* (2.7, 1385a17–19): "Let a favor [*kharis*, the root of the verb *kharizomai*] … be a service to one who needs it, not in return for anything, nor so that the one who performs the service may gain something, but so that the other may." The liberated debtor makes no apologies, feels no remorse, and undergoes no change of heart in respect to the benefactor, for there has been no offense at all, whether voluntary or involuntary.

The logic of foregoing return on a debt thus differs fundamentally from that of forgiveness in the moral sense of the term (despite the fact that we sometimes speak of forgiving a debt). But in the context of the Gospels and the actions of Jesus, the difference runs deeper. The scribes and pharisees would not have made a fuss about Jesus cancelling a paralytic's loan or a debt due him by the woman who washed his feet. But wiping away sin is another matter: it is this that God alone can do. The language of debt remission is ambiguous, in that, in the case of human beings, it may be taken literally, but with respect to Jesus's actions it acquires the broader metaphorical meaning of rendering a person free of sin. But although moral forgiveness, unlike the remission of a debt and unlike exoneration, is granted only in the case of an inexcusable wrong, the vocabulary of debts and the cancelling of debts – *opheilêmata* and *aphiêmi* – employed in the Sermon on the Mount points to an important discrepancy between human forgiveness, in the sense defined in Chapter 1, and Jesus's actions as recorded in the Gospels of Matthew and Luke. For Jesus, we understand, can eradicate a fault or state of sinfulness in the way we mortals can abolish a debt or a doctor can heal a sick man: he requires no change of heart nor does he need evidence of remorse. He may demand it: but whereas human forgiveness "cannot be forgetting," as Griswold puts it (see Chapter 1), in the sense that one continues to recognize the wrong that was done, with divine forgiveness the offense or fault is abolished, and there is nothing to remember. This distinction has much to do, as I shall argue in the following chapter, with the reason why a fully developed concept of interpersonal forgiveness failed to emerge in the ancient and medieval Christian tradition.

If repentance is not emphasized in the Sermon on the Mount and in the other passages involving debt language analyzed so far, it certainly receives its due elsewhere in the New Testament, and very particularly in the Gospel of Mark. Thus John the Baptist is described as having appeared in the wilderness, "preaching a baptism of repentance for the forgiveness of sins [*metanoia eis aphesin hamartiôn*]" (1:4; cf. the same expression in Luke 3:3). So too, Luke 24:47 insists that "repentance for the forgiveness of sins should be preached in his [Jesus's] name to all nations" (cf. Acts 2:38, 5:31, 8:22). At 1 John 1:9 there is in addition notice of the importance of confessing one's sins [*homologômen tas hamartias*].[36]

In Acts, and again in the epistles of Paul, the conditions for receiving God's grace and forgiveness take on still another dimension, with what seems to be a new emphasis on belief or faith (*pistis*, verb *pisteuô*). Thus, "every one who believes in him receives

---

[36] Cf. Nave 2002; but Nave examines only instances of the term *metanoia* and not *metameleia*, which bears much the same sense. Jones (1995: 150) states that "one of the crucial differences between Jesus and the Judaism of his day was Jesus' willingness to forgive in God's name without requiring prior repentance and, more determinately, his authorization for his disciples to do likewise." But the parables in the Gospels cannot be taken as a complete statement of the process of forgiveness, and I believe the idea of unconditional forgiveness, without prior remorse, rests on a mistaken view of the New Testament passages; see especially Ramelli 2010.

forgiveness of sins through his name" (Acts 10:43; cf. 13:38–9, 26:18; Ephesians 1:7; Colossians 1:14).[37] The idea is not in principle distinct from that of turning to the Lord, which we have discussed in relation to the Hebrew Bible,[38] but there is perhaps a special stress in the New Testament texts on an inner credence as opposed to observance of the law. If so, it is in line with Jesus's own admonitions on pureness of heart, as in the Sermon on the Mount (Matthew 5:21–2): "You have heard that it was said to the men of old, 'You shall not kill; and whoever kills shall be liable to judgment.' But I say to you that every one who is angry with his brother shall be liable to judgment." Or again (5:27–8): "You have heard that it was said, 'You shall not commit adultery.' But I say to you that every one who looks at a woman lustfully has already committed adultery with her in his heart." These injunctions are not necessarily to be seen as a radical departure from the prescriptions of the Hebrew Bible. There too, confession and repentance were understood as manifestations of an inward change, involving a return to a proper regard for God and his commandments. But in drawing a contrast between the old code and the new, Jesus makes the distinction between inner disposition and outer behavior more conspicuous, with the result that the profession of faith can be seen as laying bare the depths of the soul.

There is one particular instance of forgiveness on the part of Jesus that deserves special attention. At the moment of the crucifixion, Jesus exclaims, "Father, forgive [*aphes*] them; for they know not [*ou gar oidasin*] what they do" (Luke 23:34). The text here is highly controversial, because these words do not appear in all manuscripts of the Gospel. The Nestle-Aland edition of the New Testament, for example, maintains that they are an interpolation (27th ed., published by the Institute for New Testament Textual

---

[37] Bash (2007: 87) writes, "In Jesus' teaching, repentance and faith go together (e.g., Mark 1:15)"; but this connection seems to me to be stronger outside the Gospels proper.

[38] The role of turning to God is evident in the following negative example from the Gospel of Mark: "4:11 And he said to them, 'To you has been given the secret of the kingdom of God, but for those outside everything is in parables; 4:12 so that they may indeed see but not perceive, and may indeed hear but not understand; lest they should turn again [*epistrepsôsin*], and be forgiven [*aphethêi*].'"

Research). Ilaria Ramelli, however, points to the close correspondence between this appeal and the passage in Luke Acts in which Peter declares (3:17): "And now, brethren, I know that you acted in ignorance [*kata agnoian*], as did also your rulers."[39] It may be that, rather than interpolation, we do better to see an instance of expurgation at the hands of scribes who found unpalatable what they regarded as a potential exculpation of those who condemned their Lord to death. For Jesus's words can be interpreted as a version of the excuse of ignorance, which, as Aristotle and the classical rhetoricians observed, effectively absolves the offender of the crime (see Chapter 2). The problem was noted by Peter Abelard in his treatise, *Ethics or "Know Yourself,"* where he wonders, "if such people's ignorance is hardly to be counted as a sin at all, then why does the Lord himself pray for those crucifying him, saying 'Father, forgive them, for they do not know what they are doing' ...? For where no fault preceded, there doesn't appear to be anything to be excused."[40] Carl Reinhold Bråkenhielm invokes a distinction between "exculpative forgiveness," where moral criticism is withdrawn, and "admissive forgiveness," where it is not.[41] The former has to do with instances in which the offender is not "morally responsible" as a consequence, for example, of madness, youth, and the like, or else "on the basis of extenuating circumstances" (17), such as ignorance, and Bråkenhielm cites as an example precisely Jesus's words in Luke 23:34. Although Bråkenhielm does not mention it, the Aristotelian provenience of "exculpative forgiveness" is evident – save that I should prefer not to apply the term *forgiveness* to this motive for dismissing resentment but rather "exoneration" (see Chapter 2). We may observe that not all offenses are pardonable. Thus, sins "against the Spirit" are given a special weight, for they are excluded from the dispensation of forgiveness (Matthew 12:31–2). In this, Jesus would seem to be in accord with the conception of sin and forgiveness in the

---

[39] See Ramelli 2008 for a detailed discussion of the textual question.

[40] Abelard, sec. 112; translation in Spade 1995: 24. The argument presumably is that those who condemned Jesus thought that he was a mortal claiming to be the son of God and thus blasphemous; what they did not know is that he really was God's son. The case is thus comparable to Aristotle's reference to Oedipus's slaying of his father to illustrate an act committed in ignorance (see Chapter 1).

[41] Bråkenhielm 1993: 16.

Hebrew Bible, in which repudiation of the Lord is the predominant concern.[42]

I do not wish to leave the impression that New Testament has nothing at all to say about interpersonal forgiveness. Thus Jesus admonishes his disciples (Luke 17:3): "if your brother sins, rebuke him, and if he repents, forgive [*aphes*] him." And in the Gospel of Matthew (18:21–2), Peter asks, "Lord, how often shall my brother sin against me, and I forgive [*aphêsô*] him? As many as seven times?" and Jesus replies, "I do not say to you seven times, but seventy times seven." The latter injunction encourages a posture of general charitableness, without reference to the attitude of the offender (the parable that follows deals with debt). But Jesus's admonition in the Gospel of Luke specifies the requirement of repentance (*metanoia*), and here we may perhaps see at least the germ of the modern conception of forgiveness. Nevertheless, there is no further elaboration of the idea, and the emphasis here too would appear to be more on the moral requirement for the victim to be reconciled with the wrongdoer than on a change of heart on the part of the offender.

Although much has been written on Christian forgiveness, the passages discussed in the preceding text come near to exhausting explicit mentions of it in the Bible. As Anthony Bash observes, "the astonishing fact is that there is relatively little about forgiveness in the New Testament."[43] The scarcity of such references, together with their sometimes enigmatic brevity, might lead one to conclude, with Bash (99): "In the New Testament, as in the popular mind, there is undoubtedly a degree of confusion about forgiveness." Certainly, there is nothing like a systematic philosophical

---

[42] Gibbs (2001: 76) cites a passage in the Mishnah 8–9: "Transgressions between a human and God – the Day of Atonement atones. Transgressions between a human and his companion – the Day of Atonement does not atone until he has satisfied his companion." Gibbs writes, "Human forgiveness has been identified and indeed elevated here" (77): "What is novel here is that the Day alone cannot atone for the sins between people.... The other person is clearly in control: He must be satisfied" (78). Gibbs quotes (82) Levinas 1990 (trans. Gibbs): "It is thus very serious to have offended a human. Forgiveness depends on him, one finds oneself in his hands. There is no forgiveness that has not been requested by the guilty. The guilty must recognize his sin; the offended one must want to welcome the supplications of the offender." Gibbs goes so far as to affirm: "The sages dispatched God from the central role: The other person is in control.... We must save each other, for until then, even God cannot save us" (91).

[43] Bash 2007: 79.

interrogation of the concept and seeking one is likely to be a frustrating exercise. Nevertheless, some broad themes emerge. First, the primary emphasis is on God's forgiveness of human faults, rather than on interpersonal relations. Second, insofar as divine forgiveness is analogous to human generosity in cancelling debts, it is distinct from ordinary forgiveness: for human beings cannot wipe away the sins of others – only God, and Jesus as a part of the Godhead, are capable of doing that. Third, repentance is an important condition for forgiveness: there is no evidence in the New Testament that forgiveness is understood to be unconditional, although this is not always stated explicitly.[44] Finally, repentance is perceived, especially outside the Gospels, as a function of faith, not just regret over harm done to other human beings; in this, it assumes a peculiarly spiritual or inward character, even as it looks back to the unique focus on God's forgiveness in the Hebrew Bible, with its almost obsessive concern with a fall from God's grace because of a failure to observe his commandments. Absent in the New Testament, however, is the Hebrew Bible's preoccupation with the transgressions of an entire people. The emphasis is rather on individuals, and their particular sins and faults.

Taken as a whole, the entire Bible, the Hebrew and the Greek, treats error or sin as the major cause of a disruption in the relationship between human beings and God. This is not a fault that can be excused by projecting the blame onto others (what the Greek and Roman rhetoricians call "transference," *metastasis* or *transferentia*) or by other exculpating factors, save perhaps for a sympathetic recognition of human weakness and ignorance generally ("they know not what they do"). The protagonists of the biblical narrative, unlike those of the ancient Greek novels, are not innocent. Sinners, accordingly, have no choice but to confess their delinquencies frankly and commit themselves to reforming their natures, sincerely and with deep remorse, in the hope of obtaining a remission of God's anger. God is stern, but also kindly toward his creatures and mercifully disposed toward honest repentance or a

---

[44] For full discussion, see Ramelli 2010. The idea that "tout comprendre, c'est tout pardoner" (cited in Toltoy's *War and Peace*, etc.) is not precisely equivalent to unconditional forgiveness, as it suggests that a complete understanding of the conditions of a deed would acquit the offender of malicious intent, and hence there would be nothing to forgive.

change of ways. But God is not an ordinary person: he does not go through a process of overcoming his resentment at mistreatment, or work through doubts about the authenticity of apologies and promises. If it is true, as Bash maintains (2007: 157), that "Restoration presupposes the willing and voluntary participation of wrongdoer and victim in a process where the hoped-for result will be mutual reconciliation," there is something decidedly one-sided in the establishment or reestablishment of a moral relationship with God. Despite the judgment of Arendt, a fully developed conception of forgiveness as an interpersonal, human process is not yet present, I believe, in the Judeo-Christian scriptures. We shall see in the following chapter that, apart perhaps from some possible, and mostly vague, intimations, it was equally lacking in the early Christian tradition. It is the task of the last chapter to investigate how and when the modern idea finally came into being.

5

Humility and Repentance

The Church Fathers

"pardonner; c'est son métier" ("to forgive, that's [God's] job") Voltaire[1]

"But, dear, all that is forgiven now. Is it not?" "There is a forgiveness which it is rather hard to get," said Alice.[2]

Among early Christian writers, the theme of repentance plays an enormous role, and whole treatises and sermons are devoted to it. Thus Tertullian (late second and early third century), for example, affirms (*On Penitence* 4.1): "God has promised his pardon [*venia*] through repentence [*per paenitentiam*], declaring to the people: 'repent [*paenitere*] and I shall save you.'" So too Saint Ambrose (fourth century), in his treatise *On Penitence: Against the Novatians* (1.90–1), insists that a person who has committed sins in secret, if he repents sincerely, will be reintegrated into the congregation of the church: "I wish that the guilty person hope for pardon [*venia*], beg for it with tears, beg for it with groans, beg with the tears of all the people, entreat that he be pardoned [*ignoscatur*] … I have people who, during penitence, have made rivulets of tears in their faces, hollowed their cheeks with continual weeping, prostrated their bodies so that they might be trampled by all, and with their faces forever pale with fasting, presented the appearance of death in a breathing body." This is the way to demonstrate sincere repentance and to earn forgiveness from God and the church.

Here again is Saint John Chrysostom, who preached nine homilies on the theme of repentance in Antioch in the years 386–7. In

---

[1] Cited in de Lange 2004: 165.
[2] Trollope 1989: 709.

the first, he admonishes his flock: "To commit sin is frightening; however, it is much more painful to be exceedingly proud [*mega phronein*] with respect to sin" (1.2.19 = *Patrologia Graeca* 49.280.41–3; tr. 7); and he adds, "be mindful of this; if you become lazy and indifferent, sin [sc. *hamartia*] will seize [*katalêpsetai*] you at one time or another" (1.3.22 = 49.281.26–7; tr. 9).[3] For John, sin is all but personified (it is, after all, a manifestation of the devil), lying in wait and ready to attack us as soon as we lower our guard; it is not just something one commits, but a thing one falls victim to. In the next sermon, John asks, "Are you a sinner [*hamartôlos*]? Do not become discouraged, and come to Church to put forward repentance. Have you sinned? Then tell God, 'I have sinned....' Admit the sin in order to annul it" (2.1.2 = 49.285.11–19; tr. 16–17). One has not just sinned: one is a sinner. The noun *hamartôlos* is not part of the classical Greek vocabulary, but entered the language with so-called pseudepigraphical Jewish texts composed in the second and first centuries before Christ and occurs frequently in the New Testament and subsequently in the works of Christian writers.[4] With it there is created a new category, as it were: a person is now qualified as an evildoer, not just one who has done wrong. It is the difference between having committed a crime and being a criminal: it touches on one's very nature, as being in a state of sin.[5]

In the third homily, which takes as its text the parable of the ten virgins (cf. Matthew 25) and expatiates upon the virtue of

---

[3] Translations (slightly modified) are taken from Christo 1998.

[4] It was apparently employed by Chrysippus once, as the scholia to Homer *Iliad* 4.295 = *Stoicorum veterum fragmenta* 156 and a couple of other ancient sources testify (cf. *Etym. Magn.* s.v. *alastôr* = *SVF* 158; Lexicon ap. Bekker *Anecd. Gr.* I 374 = *SVF* 157); there are several occurrences in the *Apocalypse of Esdra*, more than two dozen in the *Book of Enoch*, and the word turns up as well in the *Sybilline Oracles* and the *Testaments of the Twelve Patriarchs*, the *Prayer of Manasseh*, and *The Life of Adam and Eve*. Plutarch employs it just once but as an adjective. There are more than 40 instances in the New Testament, and it is common in early and late Christian sources, e.g., in the *Letter of Barnabas*, Clement of Alexandria, Justin Martyr, Origen (more than 500 occurrences), etc. John Chrysostom seems to hold the record with something like 800 examples.

[5] As Dominik Perler reminds me, the Greeks and Romans recognized that some individuals had vicious characters (the Greek terms are *tropos*, *êthê*, or, in Aristotle, *hexis*; in Latin, *habitus*), which might even, as a result of bad education and behavior, become inveterate; but it was never imagined that such base or corrupt individuals would petition for forgiveness, and the expected reaction to them was anger or odium.

almsgiving, John explains that "virginity engages in an endless war every day, one worse than that against the barbarians" (3.3.12 = 49.296.17–19; tr. 35). Why so? Because it is the devil himself who is the enemy (49.296.23), and the virgin "carries the tumult and the warrior around inside of herself" (3.3.12 = 49.296.28–29; tr. 36). Repentance is not just a response to wrongdoing but a defense against the vulnerability of the subject on all fronts and within; it is our nature, not just a single act, that demands repentance in the hope of gaining forgiveness.

John affirms further that "the Church is a hospital, not a court of justice. Here, the priests do not hold you responsible for your sins, but grant you forgiveness. Tell your sin solely to God – '*Against you only have I sinned, and done evil before you*' [Ps. 50:6] – and your sin is forgiven [*sunkhôreitai*]" (3.4.19 = 49.297.58–298.3; tr. 39). Clearly, the issue for John is not interpersonal forgiveness but the restoration of a proper relationship with the deity, as a consequence of a generalized sense of remorse for the evil that each individual contains inside. In the fourth sermon he makes the point emphatically, again employing the image of healing rather than judging: "do not look to human beings for refuge and do not seek mortal help; rather, disregard all of them, and run quickly with your thoughts toward the physician of the soul. For only He can cure our hearts" (4.3.17 = 49.304.15–18; tr. 51; for the metaphor of repentance as healing, cf., among many texts, Ephraim *On Repentance* 362–3: "approach, O sinner, the good doctor, bearing tears, which are the finest medicine").

Repentance must result in a change of heart. Thus, in explaining why God relented toward Ahab for having murdered a man whose property he wished to possess (1 Kings 20), John paraphrases God's train of thought: "'Do not think,' He said, 'that I forgave him without any reason [*haplôs sunekhôrêsa autôi*]. He reformed his manner of living [*tropos*], and I changed my wrath and dissolved it.... If he had not changed his character, he would have suffered the consequences of the decision'" (Homily 2.3.20 = 49.289.27–30; tr. 24). Forgiveness is not granted unconditionally or on the basis of mere remorse; this must be accompanied by a reform of one's nature.[6]

---

[6] Cf. Plumer 1864: 214: "The following is probably as good a definition as has yet been given. 'Repentance unto life is an evangelical grace ... [whereby] a sinner, out

Although God can see into the soul of a person, an external sign of a change of heart is weeping, which is itself a cure – and a pleasant one – for sin (Homily 3.4.20–3 = 49.298.3–5).[7] Remorse is a kind of perpetual mourning, and one of the terms commonly employed in this context is *penthos*, which signifies grief or sorrow: thus, "mourning [*to penthêsai*] wipes away sins" (49.289.36).[8] Another method is fasting (the subject of Homilies 5 and 6); for the purpose is to cleanse the heart and purge not just the action but also the cause of the action, that is, the sinful state that corrupts our nature: "Fasting eradicates not only the disease but also the root of the disease, and the root of adultery is wanton desire. For this reason, Scripture punishes not only the adultery but also the desire, the mother of adultery" (6.2.8 = 49.316.26–9; tr. 73; cf. Basil's two homilies *On Fasting* 31.164–97).

There are many roads to repentance (*metanoia*), according to John, and one of these is humility (*tapeinophrosunê*) (2.4.21 = 49.289.38–41). Here again we have a concept that is characteristically Christian: the abstract noun does not occur in classical texts, and when cognates of it do appear they invariably suggest lowliness or inferior status rather than meekness as a virtue. But this humility has nothing to do with the classical strategy of humbling oneself before a peer or a superior whom one has insulted, so as to appease their anger, as in Aristotle's observation, cited in Chapter 2, that "we feel calm towards those who humble themselves [*tois tapeinomenois*] before us and do not gainsay us; we feel

of the sight and sense not only of the danger, but also of the filthiness and odiousness of his sins, as contrary to the holy nature and righteous Law of God, and upon the apprehension of His mercy in Christ to such as are penitent, so grieves for and hates his sins as to turn from them all unto God, purposing and endeavoring to walk with Him in all the ways of His commandments.'"

7 Hunt 2004 surveys the function of grief or remorse (*penthos* in Greek) for the state of sin, and how tears manifest this grief: "repentance and *penthos* ... describe a continual process in which individuals become aware of their sins, regret them, and know that they cause a division and distance from God" (14). Hunt defines *katanuxis*, or "compunction," as "that pricking of the heart, or conscience, which acts as a catalyst to repentant thoughts and deeds" (16).

8 Cf. Chryssavgis 2004: "It is clear that what is at stake here is not particular acts of contrition, but an attitude, a state of mind. 'For this life,' states John Chrysostom, 'is in truth wholly devoted to repentance, *penthos* and wailing. This is why it is necessary to repent, not merely for one or two days, but throughout one's whole life'" (citing *On Compunction* 1.1 = 4.7.395 and 1.9 = 4.7.408).

that they thus admit themselves our inferiors, and inferiors feel fear, and nobody can slight any one so long as he feels afraid of him."[9] Christian *tapeinophrosunê*, or humbleness of mind, signifies rather self-doubt as opposed to pride in one's own wisdom or virtue or innocence.[10] For we are all stained by sin, and the only thing we can truly boast of is God, which happens when a person "is not exalted by his own righteousness but recognizes that he is wanting in true righteousness" (Basil, *On Humility* 31.525–40; quotation from 529.38–40; cf. Gregory of Nyssa, *Five Orations on the Lord's Prayer* 298.15–300.9; John Cassian, *Conference* 23, ch. 18).

There is no way for a human being to deny, evade, or extenuate guilt before God: any gesture of remorse must involve a confession of culpability or rather of sinfulness. God, in turn, if he should accept repentance and reform as genuine, grants remission (*aphesis*) from sin, acknowledging that alteration of self which is the condition for the new or restored relationship with the divine. This conception is at a considerable remove from the traditional Greco-Roman idea of *sungnômê*, which depended, as we have seen, precisely on one's ability to excuse one's act or shift blame for away from oneself. What is more, the Christian writers in antiquity were aware of the difference.

Gregory of Nyssa, in his treatise *Against Eunomius* (1.1.69), an attack on a follower of Arian who denied the independent divinity of Jesus as son of God, begins by picking holes in the logic of his opponent's self-defense or apology, insisting that it represents not so much the correction of his sins as a confirmation of the charge. He goes on to say:

> Who does not know that every legal defense looks to the removal of the charge that has been brought? For example, a person who is under accusation of theft or murder or some other wrongdoing either denies the deed altogether or transfers [*metatithêsi*] responsibility for the evil onto another or else, if he can do neither of these things, he asks for pity and *sungnômê* from those charged with delivering the verdict. But his argument here [i.e., in the book being refuted] neither contains a

---

[9] Compare Plutarch's *Life of Nicias* (2.6): "for the many, the greatest honor they can receive from their betters is not to be despised by them"; cf. Alexiou 1999.

[10] Cf. Chryssavgis 2004: "The motive for repentance is at all times humility, unselfsufficiency.... In repentance it is man's total limitation and insufficiency that is placed before God, not simply particular wrongdoings or transgressions."

denial of the charges brought nor a transfer [*metastasis*, i.e., of blame]
toward another nor even seeks refuge in pity or promises a good attitude [*eugnômosunê*] for the future, but instead he strengthens the very
charge laid against him by his exceedingly labored argument. For the
charge, as he himself says, is an indictment for impiety, nor does it introduce an ill-defined accusation against him, but specifies the kind of
impiety. But his defense argues for the necessity of being impious, and
so does not remove the accusation, but rather confirms the charge.

Gregory clearly has an expert command of the types of argument
or "issue" (*stasis*) that the rhetoricians classified in relation to judicial procedures. Thus, he specifies denial of the deed, which is
the first line of defense.[11] He then takes up *metastasis*, or the transfer of blame to another party or external cause. Finally, Gregory
adduces the appeal to pity and *sungnômê*, in the event that one is
obliged to admit to the deed, and there is no way to evade responsibility for it. Here, Gregory departs somewhat from the classical
Greek manuals on argumentation, for by pairing *sungnômê* with
pity he subsumes it under what the Roman rhetoricians called *deprecatio*, which according to Cicero is employed "when the defendant
admits that he has committed a wrong and done so deliberately,
and yet nevertheless asks that he be granted pardon" (*On Invention*
1.15), whereas in the traditional handbooks on *staseis* ("issues")
sungnômê was granted precisely to involuntary offenses, in which
the blame could be assigned to an outside agency. As we saw in
Chapter 2, *deprecatio* was a strategy that Cicero and Quintilian
strongly discouraged, or, if they allowed it at all, it was only as a
last resort; what is more, Cicero advised that the defendant seek to
dissimulate this kind of argument so as to make it appear that he
was making a case for his innocence (Cicero *On Invention* 2.106;
for further references and citations, see Chapter 2). We may note
that even the appeal to pity requires a demonstration that the penalty is undeserved, inasmuch as pity is elicited not by suffering as
such but by unmerited misfortune (see Konstan 2001a: 34–44).
Gregory is thus stripping his opponent of every kind of justification, according to classical precepts.

---

[11] There is also a suggestion, toward the end of the paragraph, of the argument from
definition, according to which the offense is not prohibited by law (a demonstration that the charge was poorly framed would come under this head).

Later in the same tract, however, Gregory explicitly endorses the classical usage, when he writes, "a misfortune is pardonable [*sungnôston*] when it is involuntary" (3.2.80; cf. 1.1.213, 1.1.238, 1.1.659, 3.10.45; for old age as an excuse, see *De infantibus* 70.12). Gregory of Nazianzus, in turn, who was steeped in classical Greek literature, affirms that *sungnômê* may be granted on account of *agnoia* or ignorance (*Against the Emperor Julian* 1, 35.608–26), and in his eulogy of Athanasius (*Oration* 21, 35.1109.24–37 Migne), he avers that one may pardon (*sungignôskô*) ordinary people (or laymen) for their errors, but "how can we grant this to the teachers, who are supposed to correct the ignorance of others?" (cf. Origen *Extracts from the Commentary on Proverbs* 17.172; Clement of Alexandria *Protrepticus* 10.100.2, in which the ignorance in question is that of the Word). Basil, the great friend of Gregory of Nazianzus and brother of Gregory of Nyssa, speaks of the *sungnômê* that may be granted by God to one who errs involuntarily (*On How to Profit from Pagan Literature* 8; cf. *On the Beginning of Proverbs* 31.404; *Ethical Homilies* 6, "On Sin," 32.1197), while in *On the Holy Spirit* (6.13) he warns that "it is impossible to take refuge in the *sungnômê* based on ignorance," and later in the same paragraph denies his opponents the excuse of inexperience (*apeiria*). In a letter to Amphilochius (188.7), Basil states that one must not reject those who have long repented of what they did in ignorance, for "their ignorance makes them worthy of *sungnômê*," and a little later in the same epistle (188.10) he urges that we leave judgment to the Lord, who can see into our hearts, and grant *sungnômê* to forgetfulness, which is a human failing (*pathos*). So too, the weak are deemed worthy of *sungnômê* (*Commentary on Isaiah* [perhaps not by Basil] 1.54, 2.84). John Chrysostom, in his tract *On Fate and Foreknowledge* (1 = 50.755.76), exclaims, "this is why I groan, this is why I weep and lament, for those sins are truly worthy of lamentations, when they are sins that are not even worthy of *sungnômê*. For tell me, what kind of *sungnômê* can there be, when God speaks out?"

We observed in the previous chapter that the principal term for forgiveness in the New Testament is *aphesis* (verb *aphiêmi*), and that *sungnômê* occurs just once, in the sense of "concession" or "permission"; what is more, in the Greek version of the Hebrew Bible, which includes some additional texts originally composed

in Greek, the term and its cognates are used in the classical sense
of pardon due to involuntary acts. Thus, there was ample basis
in scripture for the church fathers to draw a distinction between
God's forgiveness, which consists in the remission or cancellation
of sin, as of a debt, and *sungnômê*, which suggests rather that an
ostensible offense is excusable on the grounds that it was unintentional or in some other way free of blame. In his *Commentary
on the Song of Songs* (6.24), Gregory of Nyssa provides something
like a definition of *aphesis* that is revealing of its special character,
when he says of the gifts that the worthy suitors bring to the virgin
bride: "these are *aphesis* of trespasses [*paraptômata*], the forgetting
of evils, the abolition of sin [*hamartias anairesis*], the transformation [*metastoikheiôsis*] of nature, the alteration of the perishable
into the imperishable." The association of *aphesis* with the eradica-
tion of sin and the transcendence of mortal nature suggests not
human exculpation, which requires reasons and excuses, but the
divine capacity to cancel even the memory of evil. In the same
vein, Gregory declares in *On the Day of Lights* (9.224): "For baptism
is the purification [*katharsis*] of sins, the *aphesis* of errors, the cause
of renovation and rebirth." In his *Stromata*, Clement of Alexandria
(second century AD) devotes a section (2.15) to sin and voluntary
actions, in which he explains how the psalmist allegorized the
various kinds of fault or *hamartia*, when he called those people
"blessed" for whom God has "wiped away their iniquities, concealed their sins, did not reckon others, and remitted [*aphêke*] the
rest" (2.15.65). Clement specifies that it is the "illuminating word
[*logos*]" that remits sins. After reaffirming that transgressions and
errors are up to us, that is, within our own power (2.15.69), and
that the Lord provides cures for each kind, Clement asks with a
rhetorical flourish: "What then? After the *sungnômê* granted to
Cain, did not God correspondingly introduce, shortly afterwards,
Enoch, who had repented, thereby signifying that *sungnômê* is
such as to generate repentance? But *sungnômê* comes about not
according to *aphesis*, but according to cure" (ibid.). The passage is
rather obscure, but the sense, I take it, is that *sungnômê* or pardon
is granted with a view to healing sinfulness, and this therapy in
turn leads to repentance; it is repentance, finally, that is the basis
for the divine redemption from sin and consequent salvation.

It was possible, no doubt, to employ *sungnômê* as a synonym or near synonym for God's pardon or *aphesis*. Thus, Origen, in his commentary on the Gospel of John (2.11.80), explains why Jesus held that offenses against himself are pardonable, but not those against the Holy Spirit (cf. Matthew 12:31, and Chapter 4): "Perhaps it is not strictly the case that there is no remission [*aphesis*] toward one who has sinned against the holy spirit of Christ because it is too precious [*timiôteron*], but rather because all rational beings partake of Christ, and to them there is granted *sungnômê* when they turn away from their sins, whereas it is not reasonable that those who have once esteemed the Holy Spirit should receive any *sungnômê* at all, if they still fall away and reject the counsels of the Spirit within them after receiving so great and such an inspiration toward the good."[12] Jesus had said simply that all blasphemy would be indulged or pardoned (*aphethêsetai*, future passive of *aphiêmi*) save that against the Holy Spirit, which would not be pardoned (same verb: *aphethêsetai*). Origen apparently has no hesitation about substituting *sungnômê* for the biblical expression. Yet even here it may be that Origen shifts naturally to the language of *sungnômê* when he considers what are, or are not, reasonable grounds for pardon, his point being that those who ignore the spirit cannot appeal to ignorance as an excuse for their offense. So too, in his commentary on the Lord's Prayer, Origen explains that "it is not possible for one who prays to obtain remission [*aphesis*] for his sins unless he has remitted [*aphienta*] from his very heart those of his brother who has erred but is worthy of obtaining *sungnômê*" (8.1); one speaks more readily of desert in respect to *sungnômê*, insofar as it rests on motives that justify pardon (cf. 14.6; for the juxtaposition of both terms, see also Clement of Alexandria *Stromata* 2.13.58.1; Didymus the Blind 21.281.4–9, from the *Commentary on Psalm 31* [in *Commentary on Psalms* 29–34]; Ephraim *Confession* [1] 83).

By and large, however, the semantic spheres of the two terms remain distinct. To take a commonplace example, as a formula for begging the indulgence of one's readers, the petition for *sungnômê* (often in the imperative) is frequent enough at the beginning or

---

[12] Contrast Ambrose *On the Holy Spirit* 3, in which he argues that the dignity of the Holy Spirit is demonstrated precisely by the fact that blasphemy against it is unpardonable.

end of a treatise (e.g., Origen *Against Celsus* Prologue 6.18, 21; Gregory of Nyssa *Against Usurers* 9.196.8; at the end: *Commentary on Matthew* 15.37.66; Gregory of Nazianzus *On the Holy Spirit* 11.11). But for this polite expression one cannot substitute *aphesis* ("remission") or the imperative *aphes*, which would not sound like a plea to the reader or dedicatee for the toleration of some excusable oversight but rather like a request to cleanse the text of errors.

It might seem that, with the Christian emphasis on repentance, the elements of what we have called the modern conception of forgiveness were now available: it would simply be a matter of expanding the classical methods of assuaging anger, whether through compensation, self-abasement, or, most relevant to forgiveness, the denial of full responsibility for the offense and an appeal to *sungnômê*, so as to include confession of guilt and the manifestation of sincere remorse as the condition for reconciliation. Instead of seeking to excuse or camouflage the offense, the wrongdoer would beg forgiveness in all humility, and the injured party would acknowledge the spiritual transformation in the offender and be moved to grant him or her full moral recognition. But no such development occurs, or at least not in any systematic way, and the preceding discussion of divine forgiveness or mercy suggests why. There is a deep gulf, reflected even at the level of vocabulary, between God's ability to cancel or obliterate sin, in the way that one can abolish a debt, and human or interpersonal forgiveness, in which the reality of the offense – always a particular act – must in some sense persist into the present, neither abolished nor forgotten.

To earn God's consideration, one must show that one has returned to his path, and this involves a profound conversion or alteration of the self, signaled by such expressions of grief as weeping, fasting, and mortification of the flesh. Such an attitude certainly resembles the remorse that a wrongdoer may feel upon accepting moral responsibility for the harm done to another person, but its function is different: one petitions God to free one from a state of sinfulness, which he does by his grace or favor (*kharis*), a freely offered gift, something no human being can do for another.[13] Even

---

[13] Cf. Hobbes's *Leviathan* (Hobbes 1966, ch. 38) ("Of the Signification in Scripture of Eternal Life, Hell, Salvation, the World to Come, and Redemption"): "the damage

if the ordained ministers of the church have the surrogate authority to absolve the confessor of sin, as some authorities maintain, they do so in the name of God, not in their own right.[14] When we manifest remorse before another human being, we are seeking to effect a change of disposition in the victim – the foregoing of resentment and the desire for revenge – predicated on a complex awareness that we are no longer the same person (in some sense) we were before, so that there is now a basis for a restored moral relation.

Unlike the divine dispensation of mercy, such an alteration in the injured party requires a great effort and may be all but impossible to achieve. As John Macquarrie writes, "True forgiveness is always costly. Damage has been done. Someone has suffered an injury, it might be a physical injury, or just as likely an injury to the soul.... The person who is determined to forgive has to swallow a bitter pill and remain steadfast in his love, even when it has been spurned. And what is perhaps a still greater demand is that he must bring himself to forgive many times when the offence is repeated ... perhaps 'seventy times seven.'"[15] Macquarrie goes on to state, "God's forgiveness is, of course, unique and very different from ours. His very nature is love.... But this does not mean that his forgiveness costs him nothing, or that it is merely automatic." Automatic it is not, because it generally is thought to require repentance on the part of the sinner; as to how costly it is for God to grant remission of sin, it is perhaps safest to reserve judgment.

It is not the case that the church fathers neglected interpersonal forgiveness entirely. Jesus's injunction, in the Lord's Prayer

a man does to another he may make amends for by restitution or recompense, but sin cannot be taken away by recompense; for that were to make the liberty to sin a thing vendible. But sins may be pardoned to the repentant, either gratis or upon such penalty as God is pleased to accept."

[14] See Hanna 1907, where *absolution* is defined as "the remission of sin, or of the punishment due to sin, granted by the Church." The article, from *The New Advent Encyclopedia*, affirms that from the time of Pope Callistus I, who died c. 223, "the power to absolve sins committed after baptism is recognized as vested in the priests of the Church in virtue of the command of Christ to bind and loose, and of the power of the keys.... After the middle of the fourth century, the universal practice of public penance precludes any denial of a belief in the Church's power to pardon the sinner, though the doctrine and the practice of penance were destined to have a still further expansion. Following the golden age of the Fathers, the assertion of the right to absolve and the extension of the power of the keys are even more marked." Full documentation is provided in the article.

[15] Macquarrie 1998.

(Matthew 6:12), to release our debtors from obligation as a condition for God's remitting our debts could serve as a springboard for consideration of the topic, especially if taken in conjunction with passages in the New Testament that refer specifically to offenses against human beings, such as Jesus's exhortation to Peter to forgive even multiple wrongs (Matthew 18:21–2; Luke 17:3–4), and his counsel to his disciples to rebuke one's brother, should he sin, even up to seven times in a day, but "if he repents, forgive [*aphes*] him" (Luke 17:3; cf. Chapter 4). Thus Origen, in his *Commentary on the Lord's Prayer*, observes in connection with the entreaty, "forgive us our debts, as we also have forgiven our debtors," that we are all debtors in respect to Jesus (28.3), who "purchased us with his blood." He then encourages his readers to be mild and humane toward others and to recall that many are unable to repay what they owe, and that we have often failed to repay our own debts, not just to our fellow human beings but also to God (28.6). Origen cites the parable of the slave who would not forgive the debt of his fellow slave, though his master had forgiven his (Matthew 18: 23–35), and continues, "One must forgive [*apheteon*] those who have sinned against us but say that they have repented, even if our debtor does this repeatedly; for he says, 'If your brother should sin against you seven times in a day, and turn to you seven times and say, "I repent," you must forgive him.' It is not we who are harsh toward those who do not repent, but rather such people are wicked toward themselves" (28.7). There is, then, a clear requirement for repentance, along with a parallel obligation on the part of the creditor – that is, the person who has been wronged – to pardon the offense if the offender does repent. The emphasis, here as in other Christian treatments, is on the need for the offended party to forego vengeance so that she or he may in turn be shown mercy by God. Origen proceeds to affirm that there are some "sins unto death," such as adultery and idolatry, that are too grave for priests to pardon (28.10). This is as far as Origen goes in discussing the human obligation to forgive the sins of others.

Gregory of Nyssa devotes the last of his five orations on the Lord's Prayer to Matthew 6:12–13, which Gregory calls "the highpoint of virtue" (290.19–20 Oehler): "And forgive us our debts, as we also have forgiven our debtors; and lead us not into temptation, but deliver us from evil." Gregory affirms that one who forgives scarcely remains within the limits of human nature but approaches that of God: "for the remission of debts is the specific and exceptional characteristic of God" (290.25–6; cf. 292.27–30). Gregory understands the instruction to forgive as Jesus does to mean that we are to be imitators (*mimêtai*, 294.22) of God. He goes on to inquire more exactly into "what are the debts to which human nature is obligated, and what are those, in turn, over the remission of which we ourselves are masters" (296.19–21), and he notes that we are first and foremost in debt to our creator for having deserted him originally (296.25–8), and for all the missteps that followed upon this original sin – a debt that is unrequitable in human terms. But though he broaches the issue, Gregory does not examine in more detail what human forgiveness involves, as distinct from divine, nor does he make any mention of remorse or reform on the part of the debtor whose debts or sin we, as human beings, are to remit. The assimilation of human forgiveness to divine precludes a closer examination of interpersonal apology and reconciliation.[16]

The Syrian deacon Ephraim (fourth century) also contemplates Jesus's pronouncement on the entailment between human and divine pardon, and he concludes that human beings have been given the better part of the bargain. As he puts it (*On the Second Coming of the Lord and On Repentance* 213.7–10): "Listen to the one great yet light command: for our humane God said, 'My burden is light.' For how much of a weight is it to remit [*aphienai*] the faults of your brother, and for your own faults [*paraptômata*] to be acquiesced in by God?" (cf. *On Prayer* 42–7). But just because pardoning the debts and slips of our brother is said to be so easy, at least for the sake of the argument in this passage, it does not require a closer look at what the process of forgiving another might involve. Once again, a promising line of inquiry is foreclosed by the exclusive focus on God's power to release mankind from sin (cf. John Cassian, *Conference* 9, ch. 22).

Moving over to the Latin fathers, in his 114th sermon on the New Testament, Augustine expatiates upon the question of human

---

[16] Meredith 2002 offers a brief comparison of Origen's and Gregory's exegeses of the Lord's Prayer, discussing the forgiving of debts on p. 353; he concludes that, although Gregory very likely knew Origen's treatise, his own discussion is largely

forgiveness in considerable detail. He begins (1): "The Holy Gospel
which we heard just now as it was being read, has admonished us
concerning the remission of sins."[17] After citing the words of Jesus,
with which he urges forgiveness even up to seven times in a day
(Luke 17:3), Augustine goes on to explain (2): "Whosoever then you
are that have your thoughts on Christ, and desire to receive what He
has promised, be not slow to do that which He has enjoined. Now
what has He promised? Eternal life. And what has He enjoined? That
pardon [*venia*] be given to your brother." Augustine then puts to rest
a potential qualm in his congregation (3): "You are just on the point
of saying to me, But I am not God, I am a man, a sinner"; and to this
Augustine replies, "God be thanked that you confess that you have
sins. Forgive [*ignosce*] then, that they may be forgiven [*dimittantur*]
you. Yet the Lord Himself our God exhorts us to imitate Him.... But
since we are speaking of the remission of sins, lest you should think
it too high a thing to imitate Christ, hear the Apostle saying, 'Be
kind [*donantes*; Greek *kharizomenoi*] to one another, even as God in
Christ has been kind [*donavit*; Greek *ekharisato*] to you [Ephesians
4:32; Colossians 3:13]. Be therefore' – these are the Apostle's words,
not mine – 'imitators of God [Ephesians 5:1].'" Once again, the
focus is on the imperative to forgive, and to the extent that such
behavior is godlike, it is legitimate to imitate Jesus in this regard.
Augustine has little to say of repentance in this sermon nor in his discourse on the Sermon on the Mount, in which he observes (Book 2,
ch. 8): "The fifth petition follows: 'And forgive us our debts, as we
also forgive our debtors.' It is manifest that by debts are meant
sins."[18] He affirms, "Here, therefore, it is not a money claim that one
is pressed to remit, but whatever sins another may have committed
against him," though as he points out at once, such sins may be "in
reference to money also." Augustine goes to some lengths to show
that the remission of a debt is a work of charity; for the debtor's

---

independent of it. On the need for repentance, see also Gregory of Nazianzus,
Oration 39.18 (*On the Holy Lights*).
[17] The translation is adapted from that of R. G. MacMullen in Schaff 1888. The translation has been slightly modified, above all in substituting "be kind to" and "has
been kind to" for "forgive" and "has forgiven" (as in the Revised Standard Version).
The Latin text may be found in *Patrologia Latina*, vol. 38.
[18] Trans. Rev. William Findlay in Schaff 1888.

"unwillingness to pay will arise from one of two causes, either that he has it not, or that he is avaricious and covetous of the property of another; and both of these belong to a state of poverty: for the former is poverty of substance, the latter poverty of disposition." One will attempt to rescue the reluctant debtor from sinning by virtue of his refusal to pay back the sum that is due. This too is a reflex of Christian charity. But the entire emphasis is on the disposition of the forgiver: the debtor has virtually been excused in advance.

Pope Leo the Great (fifth century), in chapter 5 of *Sermon* 39, offers the following counsel on forgiveness (*Patrologia Latina* 54, col. 267): "If any one, therefore, has been so fired by the desire for vengeance against another, that he has given him up to prison or bound him with chains, let him make haste to give absolution [*absolutio*] not only to the innocent, but also to one who seems worthy of punishment, that he may with confidence make use of the clause in the Lord's prayer and say, 'Forgive [*dimitte*] us our debts [*debita*], as we also forgive our debtors.' Which petition the Lord marks with peculiar emphasis, as if the efficacy of the whole rested on this condition, by saying, 'For if ye forgive [*dimiseritis*] men their sins [*peccata*], your Father which is in heaven also will forgive you: but if ye forgive not men, neither will your Father forgive you your sins.'"[19] But by joining together offenses that are innocent – and here it is not entirely appropriate to speak of forgiving – with those that are deserving of castigation, without any demand for remorse, apology, or a request for pardon on the part of the offender, Leo continues to show that neglect of the conditions for human forgiveness that is characteristic, I believe, of all fathers of the church.

In emphasizing the appeasement of anger as the route to reconciliation, pagan Greek and Roman writers concentrated on the offended party's injured sense of dignity, and what the offender might do to repair it, rather than on a change of heart in the wrongdoer, as represented by repentance, and the struggle of the injured person to alter her or his moral evaluation of the offender.

[19] Trans. Charles Lett Feltoe (slightly modified) in Schaff and Wace 1895. In respect to repentance, Leo was primarily concerned with its public and collective manifestation; thus Salzman (2010: 2) observes, "Communal penance was important for, in Leo's view, the barbarian invasions were the result of Roman sins."

They thus evaded the dilemma posed by the paradoxical nature
of forgiveness, which requires that one continue to recognize that
real harm was done and still forgive it on the basis of a moral
transformation in the wrongdoer. The Christian thinkers, in turn,
were so focused on the trials of penitence that they too paid relatively little attention to what it might mean to forego resentment in
the case of harm that is done intentionally; the injunction in the
Gospels to forgive all debtors glosses over the question of voluntary and involuntary forfeiture and encourages a posture of loving
consideration that is similar to God's and wins God's grace.

There are, to be sure, many points of contact between Christian
ethics and that promoted by pagan thinkers. For example, Christian writers discouraged anger, though they found themselves
obliged to justify righteous anger, to which God was susceptible
(see Lactantius, *On the Anger of God*). Basil, in his treatise, *Against
Those Who Are Angry* (31.353–72), follows in the footsteps of the
Stoic of Seneca (*brevis insania*: *On Anger*, 1.1.2) in defining anger as
a "brief insanity [*mania oligokhronios*]," 31.356.18).[20] Like the Greek
and Roman thinkers, the Christians did not in general mention
forgiveness as a remedy for umbrage, whether justified or not.
More often, they offered the injunction not to answer evil with
evil, that is, not to respond angrily to harm, emphasizing, as did
pagan writers, especially in the time of the Roman Empire, the
negative effects of giving way to anger, irrespective of contrition
on the part of the offender. Thus Basil writes (*Against Those Who
Are Angry* 31.357.24–7), "Do not cure evil with evil.… For in vicious
competitions the winner is the worse off, since he comes away
bearing more sin." The object is to root anger out of the soul: "He
reviled you? Praise him. He struck you? Endure it. He spit at you
and thinks you are nothing? Then you bear in mind that you are
made of earth, and into earth you will again be dissolved" (ibid.,
31.360.7–10). Where Basil's counsel departs from that of the Stoics
and other ancient authorities, like Galen, who also condemned
anger in any form (*On the Medical Art* 1.371 Kühn; *On the Diagnosis
and Cure of the Several Passions of the Mind* 5.7, 17 Kühn), is in the
emphasis placed on lowliness of spirit – the acknowledgment of
one's nothingness as a consequence of one's state of sinfulness.

---

[20] Basil warns against fear in much the same spirit, as a kind of drunkenness of the
soul (*On Fasting* 1, 31.181.25–39).

This kind of meekness might manifest itself in keeping silent, in acknowledgment of the moral diffidence that befits a soul conscious of its sins. But such silence, insofar as it was a sign of righteousness, could also represent and confer power. Thus, Ignatius of Antioch (latter half of the first century), in his *Epistle to the Ephesians* (6.1), affirms, "the more, therefore, someone sees the bishop keeping silent [*sigônta*], the more ought one to one fear him."[21] So too, in his *Epistle to the Philadelphians* (1.1), Ignatius praises a bishop "at whose meekness [*epieikeia*] I am struck with admiration, and who by his silence [*sigôn*] is able to accomplish more than those who speak vainly." Ambrose, in his tract *On the Duties of Priests* (1.1.5), writes, "I have seen many who have incurred sin by speaking, but scarcely anyone who did so by keeping silent [*tacendo*]." Silence here, in the sense of as modesty or humility, is simply good policy. But John Chrysostom, in his discourse *On the Priesthood* (4.6), answers those who criticize St. Paul's lack of learning: "he had a greater power by far than that of speech, and which was capable of accomplishing more: for merely by appearing, though he kept silent [*sigôn*], he was terrible to the demons."

In the year 387, the citizens of Antioch rioted against a new tax and tore down statues of the Emperor Theodosius. To assuage Theodosius's wrath, the bishop, named Flavian, who was eighty years old, traveled to Constantinople and successfully appealed to the emperor's mercy. During Flavian's absence, John Chrysostom delivered a series of twenty-one homilies called "On the Statues" to encourage the people, reminding them of the Lord's Prayer as a way of reassuring them that their trespasses would be forgiven, at the same time as he denounced their vices. In the last of these (*On the Statues* or *To the People of Antioch* 21 = *PG* 49.213–14), John speaks with particular clarity on the theme of assuaging anger. He recounts how Flavian imitated the noble spirit (*megalopsukhia*) of Saint Paul, and "to those who everywhere asked him what he said to the emperor, and how he persuaded him, and how he cast out all his anger [*orgê*], he replied in these words: 'I contributed

---

[21] I owe this and the following references to the virtue of silence to Alberto Quiroga, of the University of Granada, who noted them in a talk delivered at a conference on "*Homo Romanus Graeca Oratione*: From 2nd to 4th Centuries, 300 Years of Greek Culture in the Roman Empire," held on March 12–14, 2009 at the University of Barcelona. See now Quiroga (forthcoming).

nothing to the matter, for it was God who softened his heart, and
by means of my words abated [*aphêke*] his anger and dissolved
his wrath [*thumos*].' But what Flavian concealed out of humility
[*tapeinophrosunê*]," John explains, "God made public" (213.39–49).
John continues, "As he entered the imperial court, he stopped at
a distance from the emperor, silent [*aphônos*], weeping, eyes downcast, concealing his face, as if he himself were the one who had
done all those terrible things. He did this with his posture, his
look, his groans, because he wished first to incline him to pity
[*eleos*], and only then begin his defense [*apologia*] in our behalf.
For the one absolution [*sungnômê*] that remains for those who sin
is to be silent [*sigân*] and say nothing in defense of what was done"
(214.11–19). Finally, John reports that "the emperor, upon seeing him weep, with eyes downcast, approached him himself, and
what he felt as a result of the bishop's tears, he made manifest in
the words he addressed to him; for his words were not those of a
wrathful or irritated man, but of a man in pain – not those of an
angry man, but rather of one who is saddened and in the grip of
anguish" (214.28–33).

This passage presents a fascinating mix of classical attitudes
to placating the ire of a superior (such as we find in the section
on "calming down" in Aristotle's *Rhetoric*) and the Christian ideal
of humility. Clearly, Flavian's self-abasement is in part a strategy
for manifesting the reverence due the emperor, thereby making
it clear that the actions of the citizens of Antioch, whom he represents by acting their part, must have been an aberration, not a
sign of deliberate disrespect but more like a temporary bout of
insanity and hence all but involuntary – like the madness or *atê* to
which Agamemon, in the *Iliad*, attributes his insulting behavior
toward Achilles (see Chapter 2). It is just this manner of shifting
of blame to another agency (what the rhetoricians call *metastasis*
or *transferentia*) that may win pardon (*sungnômê*), in the sense of an
acknowledgment that the offense in question was in some sense
accidental. We recall, in particular, that Aristotle specifically recommended that slaves who have provoked the ire of their masters
not "talk back and deny what they have done" but simply confess
that they are in the wrong. But Flavian's humility or *tapeinophrosunê* is not Aristotle's humbleness (*tapeinoumenoi*), designed to
make manifest one's inferiority and dread of the offended party,

but rather a Christian virtue that is compatible with the dignity of a "great-souled" man (*megalopsukhos*), which for Aristotle was the virtue associated with the justifiable pride and self-esteem of a born aristocrat (see *Nicomachean Ethics*, 4.3, 1123a34–1125a35). Nothing could be further from such a figure than servility or cowardice. To be sure, Flavian adopts a posture of the most profound sorrow for the errors of his compatriots, and this has the appearance of an almost craven deference. But his silence is not that of the cowed slave, but rather – or also – a sign of the bishop's power, like that which Ignatius of Antioch so admired and which John Chrysostom lauded in Saint Paul as more potent than speech. Christian humility, as manifested in speechlessness and tears, succeeds in gaining the pity or mercy of the emperor, by causing him to feel pain at the misfortune of his repentant subjects: for pity is a response, as we have seen (Chapter 2), not to suffering as such but to undeserved affliction. Flavian's ability to induce the pain of compunction in the emperor by his silence and demeanor is a sign, in Christian terms, not of weakness but of strength. John's account represents a sublimely canny cross between the pagan and Christian values.

If the ancient church fathers have relatively little to say about interpersonal forgiveness, one might have expected that the medieval schoolmen would have granted it more attention; after all, we have seen that Maimonides begins to bring together the need for repentance and the duty to forgive, and this might have led to a more detailed investigation of human forgiveness. Yet, so far as I can judge, the major scholastic thinkers largely ignored the topic. I have found no systematic commentary in Abelard or Anselm, for example, or in Thomas Aquinas. Eric Luijten, in a detailed study of forgiveness and repentance in Thomas, notes that "when compared to Thomas's approach, the question about forgiveness is asked differently in our times.... Words like sin, guilt and forgiveness no longer function primarily within the context of the relationship between the sinner and God.... Similarly, the forgiveness that is sought is not primarily God's forgiveness, or divine forgiveness, but instead the forgiveness of the victim."[22] Luijten goes on to observe: "One of the striking features of Thomas's theology of

[22] Luijten 2003: 41.

the sacrament of penance is the near absence of the notion of
interpersonal forgiveness"; for in principle, "forgiveness of guilt is
the restoration of the relationship of grace with God" (43). Like
the church fathers who preceded him, Thomas does take the
opportunity to reflect on interpersonal forgiveness in his commentary on the Lord's Prayer, in which, as we have seen, forgiveness is a precondition for being forgiven. But even here, as Luijten
points out, "the emphasis is placed on the relationship with God"
(44). As Luijten summarizes Thomas's account, "The only thing
that is said with respect to interpersonal forgiveness is that it must
be given. Nothing is said about what we may expect from those
whom we forgive, except that he or she asks to be forgiven (and
for those who are perfect, not even that).... And nothing is said,
with respect to interpersonal forgiveness, about the need to admit
what one has done wrong, or the need to pay for the hurt one has
caused" (44).

Luijten concludes that "divine forgiveness differs radically from
interpersonal forgiveness" (46). "Forgiveness of sin (*remissio peccati*)," he writes, "is put in terms of conversion of the mind to
God" (50–1) and involves a reunion with Christ (55): it is achieved
by removing the "stain of guilt" (*macula culpae*; cf. 58). In sum,
"Thomas understands the transmutation of the state of guilt to the
state of grace as the *generatio* of grace and the *corruptio* of the state
of guilt" (76). In this respect, Thomas's analysis of forgiveness follows in the footsteps of the earliest Christian exegetes, who treated
the divine remission of sin as the annulment of sinfulness, rather
than as the human process of overcoming resentment through
the acknowledgment of a moral reform in the offender.

We have remarked that the difference between divine forgiveness, which purges sin in the way one cancels a debt, and the
human decision to forsake vengeance because the offender has
had a change of heart, tended to inhibit the development of a fully
formed notion of interpersonal forgiveness. If we look at the same
distinction from the angle of the offender, and the requirement
of ever more intense forms of repentance to gain release from sin
and the favor of God, we may discover another reason why the
barrier between divine and human forgiveness was so durable. For
repentance before God took, as we have seen, the form of a spiritual conversion, a turning or return to God's way. Expressions of

remorse before a fellow human being might be loosely modeled on conversion, but this was scarcely tantamount to the fully secular conception of the moral transformation of the self that would become the cornerstone of modern forgiveness.

In the main Christian traditions, Western and Eastern, the conception of repentance and release from sin have remained much the same as that developed by the early church fathers writing in Greek and Latin. John Chryssavgis, professor of theology and former dean at the Holy Cross Greek Orthodox School of Theology, has recently written: "Christianity testifies that the past can be undone. It knows the mystery of obliterating or rather renewing memory, of forgiveness and regeneration.... One repents not because one is virtuous, but because human nature can change, because what is impossible for man is possible for God.... Forgiveness, absolution is the culmination of repentance, in response to sincerely felt compunction.... It is a freely given grace of Christ and the Holy Spirit within the Church as the Body of Christ."[23] It would take a new conception of the self, predicated on a secularized sense of the possibility of conversion, before the modern conception of human forgiveness would come into being.

[23] Chryssavgis 2004.

6

Enter Forgiveness

The Self Transformed

All major religious traditions and wisdoms extol the value of forgiveness. Forgiveness has been advocated for centuries as a balm for hurt and angry feelings. Yet effective means for engendering forgiveness as a way of dealing with life's problems has often been lacking.[1]

In the year 1671, Molière produced a short, three-act farce entitled *Les Fourberies de Scapin* (The Ruses of Scapin), loosely modeled on Terence's comedy, *Phormio*, which was based on a Greek original, now lost, by Apollodorus of Carystus, a somewhat younger contemporary of Menander (Apollodorus's play was called *Epidikazomenos*). The story is as follows. Two young men, Octave and Léandre, have married without the permission of their fathers, who have been journeying abroad. Octave has wedded Hyacinte, a poor orphan whose mother has just died, while Léandre has bound himself to the Gypsy girl Zerbinette. As the play opens, news arrives that the fathers have just returned, and in this bind, they appeal for help to Scapin, a wily fellow who had been appointed to look after Léandre (in this, he differs from his prototype, the "parasite" Phormio, who intervenes to help the two youths in Terence's comedy out of friendship and high-spiritedness). The fathers are furious with their sons, in part because they have made such dubious alliances, but also because Argante, Octave's father, has promised to wed his son to the daughter of Léandre's father, Géronte: this is a daughter that Géronte had by a second wife, in Tarentum (the scene of the play is Naples); he

---

[1] From "The Stanford Forgiveness Project," at http://www.hawaiiforgivenessproject .org/Stanford.htm (accessed March 7, 2010).

has kept this liaison a secret until now, but the wife and daughter have embarked for Naples for the sake of the intended marriage. It will turn out, as the reader may have guessed, that Hyacinte is none other than Géronte's daughter, and that, for good measure, Zerbinette is the daughter of Argante.

In the meantime, there occur various complications, one of which is set in motion when Léandre concludes, erroneously, that Scapin spilled the beans about his marrying Zerbinette to his father. In a fury, Léandre threatens to run him through with his sword, as Scapin confesses to various peccadilloes in an effort to fend off Léandre's rage. In the end, he convinces Léandre of his innocence in the matter of Zerbinette, but at this point word arrives that the Gypsies are about to break camp and carry Zerbinette off with them, unless Léandre pays them the money he promised for her. In desperation, Léandre begs Scapin for help, but Scapin is mortally offended. Léandre pleads with him: "Come, I pardon you [*je te pardonne*] all that you've just told me, and even worse, if you've done it," but Scapin is implacable: "Don't pardon me a thing [*ne me pardonnez rien*], run my body through with your sword." Léandre begs him to forget (*oublier*) his conduct just now, and Octave joins his pleas to those of Léandre, but Scapin replies, "This insult has touched me to the quick!" Octave insists: "You must give over your resentment," and Léandre chimes in: "I was wrong, I admit it [*J'ai tort, je le confesse*] ..., I'm as sorry as can be [*J'en ai tous les regrets du monde*] ..., I beg your pardon with all my heart [*Je t'en demande pardon de tout mon cœur*]," and he offers to throw himself at Scapin's feet. At this, Scapin finally yields, warning the lad not to be so hasty next time around.[2]

The preceding scene has no parallel in Terence's comedy and is Molière's own invention (it may be worth observing that Molière played the part of Scapin in the original production). Molière has dramatized a situation that includes many if not most of the elements of modern forgiveness, and a case could be made for rendering "pardon" and "pardonner" here as "forgiveness" and "forgive," rather than by the English "pardon," at least in respect to Léandre's plea to Scapin (his earlier offer to overlook Scapin's

---

[2] There is perhaps an echo here of the last scene of Plautus's *Epidicus*, discussed in Chapter 2, in which the slave Epidicus refuses to be pardoned by his master and must be begged to consent to his own manumission.

minor offenses is more like mere pardoning, inasmuch as it is granted not because of Scapin's remorse but because Léandre is now desperately in need of his services). On the plus side, we have a character who has wronged another by falsely accusing him of a betrayal of trust; he confesses his guilt, begs for pardon, and expresses remorse. The offended party at first cannot abandon his resentment but finally accepts the other's contrition as sincere, warning that he must change his behavior in the future. On the minus side, it is true that Léandre had some reason to be suspicious, though he was wrong to jump to conclusions about Scapin's role: this is Scapin's point in telling him not to be so rash (*prompt*), and we could see in this concession something of an excuse for Léandre's conduct. Beyond this, we have no reason to imagine that Léandre is about to undergo a deep moral transformation; he is in need of Scapin at this point and promises everything, without necessarily recognizing his impulsiveness as a genuine moral fault. This is comedy, after all, and the tone remains light. Still, the exchange would seem to reflect certain expectations about how forgiveness in the modern sense (or something like it) typically works – a kind of behind-the-scenes paradigm – that differentiate this episode from anything that we have seen in the literature of classical antiquity.

Scapin first tricks Argante, Octave's father, out of money for Hyacinte, and then proceeds to swindle the miserly Géronte, by pretending that his son, Léandre, has been abducted by pirates. Having extracted the necessary sum from him, Scapin is not content but seeks revenge for the way Géronte maligned him in hinting that he had betrayed Léandre's confidence. To this end, he fabricates the story that Hyacinte's brother, a violent cutthroat, has got wind of Géronte's desire to break off the match between Octave and Hyacinte and is out to kill him. Scapin induces Géronte to hide in a sack and, mimicking the voice of foreign brigands, gives Géronte a thorough beating, all the while pretending that it is he who is receiving the blows for defending his master's integrity. Finally, Géronte peeks out from the sack and perceives the trick, upon which Scapin flees the scene. Immediately thereafter, Zerbinette accidentally reveals to Géronte the ruse about the pirates, redoubling the old man's ire. He and Argante, who has also cottoned to Scapin's treachery, plot their revenge, but in the meantime they learn that Hyacinte is Géronte's daughter, and soon after Argante recognizes Zerbinette as his. This leads to the final scene, in which Scapin is carried in, head bandaged and to all appearances on the point of death, and groans: "I did not want to die without coming to beg pardon [*pardon*] of all those whom I may have offended. Yes, gentlemen, before giving up my last breath, I implore you with all my heart to pardon me willingly [*vouloir me pardonner*] all that I may have done to you, and above all Mr. Argante and Mr. Géronte." Argante is prompt to oblige and bids him die in peace, but when Scapin tactlessly (but deliberately) reminds Géronte of the beating for which he is now apologizing, insisting that he feels "an inconceivable grief [*douleur*] for the cudgel blows that he ...," Géronte interrupts him: "Shut up! All is forgotten [*j'oublie tout*]." Scapin, nothing daunted, continues, "But is it really willingly [*de bon cœur*], Sir, that you pardon [*pardonnez*] me for those cudgel blows that ...," to which Géronte replies, "Yes, not another word about it – I pardon [*pardonne*] you everything, there, all done." Scapin exclaims, "Ah, Sir, I feel better for your saying that," to which Géronte answers, "Okay, but I forgive you on condition that you die" and adds that he withdraws his promise if he recovers.[3] As Scapin pretends to faint once more, Argante intercedes and asks Géronte to pardon him unconditionally (*pardonner sans condition*), in light of their present happiness. "So be it," says Géronte, and all go in for dinner, with Scapin requesting a place at the end of the table, as he awaits his death.

Here again, we have a scene that seems to bear the earmarks of authentic forgiveness, which might justify translating the French *pardonner* as *forgive*: a contrite wrongdoer who professes his profound pain at the realization of the harm he has caused others, together with the demand for a sincere and willing forgiveness and not just a remission of the penalty. To top it off, Molière has

---

[3] I cannot resist citing here some words of Heinrich Heine, as quoted by Sigmund Freud (1972: 47), and that I found, in turn, in Janover (2005: 221–2): "Mine is a most peaceable disposition. My wishes are a humble cottage with a thatched roof, but a good bed, good food, the freshest of milk and butter, flowers before my window, and a few fine trees before my door; and, if God wants to make my happiness complete, he will grant me the joy of seeing some six or seven of my enemies hanging from those trees. Before their death I shall, moved in my heart, forgive them all the wrong they did me in their lifetime. One must, it is true, forgive one's enemies – but not before they have been hanged."

staged the episode as a deathbed repentance, albeit a fake one, in which a conscience-stricken sinner seeks the pardon of his victims before passing to the other world. The religious overtones lend to Scapin's confession a note of genuine conversion, the more hilarious in that it is entirely phony.

It would appear, then, that interpersonal forgiveness, in a form at least resembling the modern idea, was available as a theme at the time when Molière was writing, in the middle of the seventeenth century. It may have had a function in drama even earlier, in the works of Shakespeare, for example, although it seems to be illustrated there in rather a perfunctory way, and perhaps scarcely counts as true forgiveness. Thus, in *Two Gentlemen of Verona*, Proteus apologizes to Valentine for a series of deceptions, culminating in an attempt to rape Silvia, Valentine's beloved (5.4.73–7):

> My shame and guilt confounds me.
> Forgive me, Valentine: if hearty sorrow
> Be a sufficient ransom for offence,
> I tender't here; I do as truly suffer,
> As e'er I did commit.

Michael Friedman, in a study of forgiveness in Shakespeare's comedies, observes, "Like the expressions of contrition provided by the other Forgiven Comic Heroes, Proteus' speech of 'shame and guilt' is brief, but apparently sincere. Thus, the objections of readers and audiences to this sequence usually stem from the ease and hastiness with which Valentine accepts this apology: 'Then I am paid;/And once again I do receive thee honest' (5.4.77–8)";[4] Valentine continues,

> Who by repentance is not satisfied
> Is nor of heaven nor earth, for these are pleased.
> By penitence the Eternal's wrath's appeased.

Friedman goes on to discuss how difficult it is to make Proteus seem forgivable in modern performances, given his opprobrious behavior. In the finale, the Duke, who has appeared on the scene, dispenses pardon liberally, first of all to the banished Valentine, granting him the hand of his daughter Silvia, who had loved and eloped with him against her father's wishes:

---

4 Friedman 2002: 47.

> Now, by the honour of my ancestry,
> I do applaud thy spirit, Valentine,
> And think thee worthy of an empress' love:
> Know then, I here forget all former griefs,
> Cancel all grudge, repeal thee home again,
> Plead a new state in thy unrivall'd merit,
> To which I thus subscribe: Sir Valentine,
> Thou art a gentleman and well derived;
> Take thou thy Silvia, for thou hast deserved her.

Valentine, in turn, begs pardon for his band of outlaws:

> These banish'd men that I have kept withal
> Are men endued with worthy qualities:
> Forgive them what they have committed here
> And let them be recall'd from their exile:
> They are reformed, civil, full of good
> And fit for great employment, worthy lord.

To this, the Duke replies,

> Thou hast prevail'd; I pardon them and thee:
> Dispose of them as thou know'st their deserts.
> Come, let us go: we will include all jars
> With triumphs, mirth and rare solemnity.

Though Valentine's men are said to have reformed, the Duke's action is not so much forgiveness as clemency or amnesty, the right, inherent in the office, to revoke a sentence that he had imposed. In this, the conclusion to *Two Gentlemen of Verona* resembles the finales of *A Comedy of Errors* and *A Midsummer Night's Dream*, in which a prince cancels a harsh law or ruling that would, if enforced, have conflicted with a higher sense of justice. The modern derivative of this practice is executive pardon.[5] If there is an anticipation of modern forgiveness – and it is more in evidence in Molière than in the Shakespearean plays we have examined – it still seems to fall short of the fully evolved notion, as described in Chapter 1.

It is well beyond the scope of this book, and of my own competence, to trace the emergence of forgiveness as a theme in early

---

[5] For a discussion of forgiveness in *The Merchant of Venice*, together with a fascinating reading of the Korean film, *Miryang/Secret Sunshine* (directed by Lee Chang-dong, 2007), which exhibits the trauma associated with the will to unconditional forgiveness in the context of modern globalized Christian evangelism, see Chow 2009.

modern literature. Doubtless, there are many passages that would repay analysis, and it is conceivable that there lurks in one of them testimony to the originary moment of the modern concept. It is remarkable, nonetheless, that interpersonal forgiveness remains marginal to philosophical and theological writings for at least two centuries following Molière's *Les Fourberies de Scapin* and begins to receive systematic treatment, so far as I have been able to determine, only in the nineteenth century and above all in the twentieth.[6] Certainly, the great ethical thinkers of the seventeenth and eighteenth centuries, such as Thomas Hobbes, John Locke, René Descartes, David Hume, Adam Smith, and Jean-Jacques Rousseau, appear to have paid little attention to it.[7] Bishop Butler did pronounce two sermons (no. 8 and 9 in the "Fifteen Sermons Preached at the Rolls Chapel," delivered in 1729) on the topic, "Upon Resentment and Forgiveness of Injuries – Matt. v. 43, 44," which have had a large influence on modern treatments of the subject.[8] But Butler concentrates less on the nature of forgiveness

---

[6] See Pagani (2007: 6): "Whereas it is true that it was only in the twentieth century that forgiveness as a secular concept moved to the forefront of philosophical and political discourse, many of the same issues and problems had been raised – though not satisfactorily resolved – centuries before"; forgiveness "was a concept that proved to be at the limits of Enlightenment moral discourse" (12), which was never fully able to free itself from the influence of Christian theology.

[7] See Miller (2006: 155): "In Hobbes's scheme, killing your victim is a sign of hatred and not of what he calls vengefulness, which aims at humiliation and domination"; cf. Hobbes, *On Human Nature* 9.6: "Revenge aimeth not at the death, but at the captivity and subjection of an enemy.... To kill is the aim of them that hate, to rid themselves of fear; revenge aimeth at triumph, which over the dead is not" (Aristotle makes the same distinction at *Rhetoric* 2.4, 1382a8–15). Pettigrove (2007: 448) observes that "Hume does not speak of forgiveness at any length in any of his published works in moral philosophy. The word 'forgive' appears only once in the *Enquiry Concerning the Principles of Morals* and not at all in the *Treatise* or the *Essays*. But he speaks of forgiveness quite often in his *History of England*"; what is more, "Hume ordinarily uses 'forgiveness,' 'mercy' and 'pardon' as synonyms" (451). Pettigrove attempts to piece together from Hume's remarks on hatred, contempt, anger, repentance, and mercy "a Humean account of forgiveness."

[8] Newberry (2001: 233) writes, "Forgiveness has been defined in a multitude of ways: among others, as the overcoming of resentment, the overcoming of moral hatred, as a speech act, and as forbearance. Of these definitions the one that enjoys anything close to a kind of consensus is that forgiveness is the overcoming of resentment.... The progenitor of this view is widely acknowledged to be Joseph Butler, who wrote sermons on both resentment and forgiveness nearly three hundred years ago." Newberry argues that "the attribution of this definition of forgiveness to Butler is in error: he did not define forgiveness as the overcoming

and far more on that of resentment and revenge, both of which he justifies as appropriate when not taken to excess. He begins the eighth sermon by inquiring: "since general benevolence is the great law of the whole moral creation; it is a question which immediately occurs, 'Why had man implanted in him a principle, which appears the direct contrary to benevolence?'" To find the answer, one must investigate "Why, or for what end, such a passion was given us." Butler goes on to explain that "Resentment is of two kinds: Hasty and sudden, or settled and deliberate." The first type he identifies as anger, which is sudden and momentary. This sentiment "stands in our nature for self-defence, and not for the administration of justice," and thus it has a positive, practical function. We may think of it as an instinctive reaction. Deliberate resentment, on the contrary, has a moral basis, and is akin to the indignation we feel in the presence of injustice against another. If such an injury "be done against ourselves, or those whom we consider as ourselves: it is plain, the way in which we should be affected, would be exactly the same in kind; but it would certainly be in a higher degree, and less transient." Butler affirms that "this seems to be the whole of this passion which is, properly speaking, natural to mankind." There is room for error in such resentment: we may "imagine an injury done us, when there is none" or react with disproportionate indignation. But these are abuses of the sentiment, not a valid reason for regarding such resentment as invariably wrong. "The good influence which this passion, has, in fact, upon the affairs of the world, is obvious to every one's notice. Men are plainly restrained from injuring their fellow-creatures by fear of their resentment."

This is not to say that the expression of such resentment is harmless: where it leads to automatic retaliation, as in conflicts over honor, it is plainly dangerous, as Butler makes clear in the ninth sermon. Worse still, resentment, inasmuch as it has as its object

---

of resentment but rather as the checking of revenge, or forbearance." Newberry maintains that Butler's theory rests on an implicit "feeling theory of the emotions" (234), as opposed to the cognitive theory of emotion that is presupposed in modern approaches. Cf. also Griswold (2007b: 20): "Butler is regularly misquoted as defining forgiveness as the 'forswearing of resentment.' Butler actually claims that forgiveness is the forswearing of *revenge*"; Griswold's detailed discussion of Butler is worth consulting in its entirely.

the inflicting of harm on another, is suspect in itself: "Other vices
eventually do mischief; this alone aims at it as an end." Yet according to Butler, "Resentment is not inconsistent with good will.... We
may therefore love our enemy, and yet have resentment against
him for his injurious behaviour towards us. But when this resentment entirely destroys our natural benevolence towards him, it is
excessive, and becomes malice or revenge." In this way, resentment
is compatible with the biblical injunction to love one's enemies.
What is it, then, that inclines us to forgiveness? Butler first offers
some reflections in a Socratic vein: "Though injury, injustice and
oppression, the baseness of ingratitude, are the natural objects of
indignation, or, if you please, of resentment, as before explained;
yet they are likewise the objects of compassion, as they are their
own punishment, and without repentance will for ever be so. No
one ever did a designed injury to another, but at the same time he
did a much greater [injury] to himself." All very well, but this kind
of suffering is clearly not enough to inhibit wrongdoing, and so
resentment retains its social value and hence its justification. Butler
then offers a second motive for compassion and the forswearing
of revenge: "offences committed by others against ourselves, and
the manner in which we are apt to be affected with them, give a
real occasion for calling to mind our own sins against God." Mere
prudence, consequently, would advise us to be moderate in the
resentment we bear toward others, if it is true that "there is an
apprehension and presentiment natural to mankind, that we ourselves shall one time or other be dealt with, as we deal with others."
For Butler, this is the meaning of Ecclesiasticus 28:1–4: "Forgive thy
neighbor the hurt he hath done unto thee, so shall thy sins also be
forgiven when thou prayest" and again of Jesus's own injunctions.
As he puts it: "these natural apprehensions are authorized by our
Saviour's application of the parable; 'So likewise shall my heavenly
Father do also unto you, if ye from your hearts forgive not every
one his brother their trespasses.'" Butler thus concludes his sermon
with the words: "A forgiving spirit is therefore absolutely necessary,
as ever we hope for pardon of our own sins, as ever we hope for
peace of mind in our dying moments, or for the divine mercy at
that day when we shall most stand in need of it."

Butler's contribution to forgiveness would seem to be comparable to what Socrates did for early philosophy: as Cicero put it, he

brought it down from the heavens – that is, from the cosmological concerns of the so-called pre-Socratic thinkers, introduced it into cities and homes, and obliged it to inquire about human behavior and the nature of good and evil (*Tusculan Disputations* 5.10; cf. *Academica* 1.15). So too, Butler located forgiveness, to the extent that he spoke of it, in the context of the human trait of resentment and the desire for revenge, as opposed to God's mercy and grace. That said, however, it is remarkable how little he has to say about repentance or a change of heart in the offender as a condition for forgiveness. Nor is this surprising: in these sermons, Butler is concerned to limit the desire for vengeance – and this is where forgiveness enters in – as part of his project to demonstrate that moral resentment is a natural and legitimate sentiment among us fallen creatures. To be sure, such a sentiment, which arises from a sense of personal injury, is subject to error and exaggeration, and it thus behooves us to temper it with compassion. A deeper analysis of the conditions for forgiveness was not on Butler's agenda.

It may seem paradoxical to bring up the name of Immanuel Kant in connection with the origins of modern forgiveness, because, as David Sussman has recently written, "Although Kant's moral philosophy is often presented as a kind of secularized Christianity, Kant seems to have very little to say about forgiveness." Sussman adds, "This reticence is particularly striking when we consider the central role in Kant's thought played by ideas of obligation, responsibility and guilt."[9] Sussman notes that, in the *The Metaphysics of Morals*, Kant affirms, "It is therefore a duty of human beings to be forgiving [Daher ist *Versöhnlichkeit* (*placabilitas*) Menschenpflicht] ... because a human being has enough guilt of his own to be greatly in need of pardon," and in part too because "no punishment ... may be inflicted out of hatred."[10] But, as Sussman points out, "Kant tells us here that we have a duty to be forgiving, but does not further specify the content of this duty." Moreover, as Sussman goes on to note: "Although Kant does not tell us much about ordinary human forgiveness, he does have a great deal to say about God's grace, how we are in moral need of it, and how such grace

---

[9] Sussman 2005: 85.
[10] Trans. Gregor 1997: 208 = vol. 6, 461 in the Akademie numeration.

might profoundly transform us as moral subjects." This is all the less promising, insofar as it is just such a concentration on divine mercy that, I have suggested (Chapter 5), served to inhibit the development of a systematic doctrine concerning interpersonal forgiveness: human beings ought not to arrogate to themselves a function that, as Jesus declared (Matthew 9.2–7), properly pertains to God or his ministers on earth. Now, Sussman turns this problem on its head when he states, "Yet we should note that for Kant, God serves as a kind of moral archetype – the personification of the law-giver and judge that has its real basis in our own rational nature. If so, then perhaps the grace of God similarly serves as the kind of moral archetype for the kinds of morally transformative and restorative relations that might, in various imperfect ways, be within the realm of human possibility." But if this is the case, then this move is, as we have come to see, far more radical than it might seem at first blush.

Let us recall some of the conditions that forgiveness has to meet in order to count as such. Sussman's own enumeration will serve as an outline (86):

> By forgiveness I understand, roughly, those attitudes and responses to a wrongdoing that
> (1) can alleviate or at least mitigate guilt and restore morally damaged relationships – in particular, which can repair significant violations of trust
> (2) that do not require the exacting of punishment or some other form of just retribution or expiation
> (3) that do not involve reevaluating the nature or magnitude of the offense, the culpability of the offender, or the sort of punishment that is appropriate (i.e., that remain distinct from wholly or partially *excusing* the offender)
> (4) that do not involve neglecting or misrepresenting any morally important features of the transgression or of the parties involved.

Sussman adds that the offender has no automatic right to forgiveness; it is freely granted and may be freely withheld. What is more, "sincere repentance and attempts at compensation are, if not necessary preconditions of proper forgiveness, at least circumstances that make forgiveness particularly appropriate, and the absence of which makes forgiveness at least morally problematic" (87). This is the ample description of forgiveness to which Sussman holds Kant accountable.

Now, for Kant, the requirement to punish a wrong does not derive from hatred or a personal desire for revenge but from the nature of justice, which the individual simply administers. If the demand to right a wrong is in this sense objective, personal forgiveness would seem to be irrelevant, save perhaps insofar as a disposition to leniency may help us to achieve a more impartial viewpoint (90). But if "Kant's conception of human nature is deeply informed by the idea of original sin," then "attaining our true nature becomes not so much a matter of self-development, but of radical self-transformation" (96). In Kant's words, "a 'new man' can come about only through a kind of rebirth, as it were a new creation."[11] Sussman goes on to argue that the appeal to God's grace is consistent with Kant's view that moral improvement must depend on human effort alone (182) and to explain how human forgiveness may operate on such premises. I wish to lay aside Sussman's explication of Kant's position at this point, however, in order to remark that Kant's insistence on the moral autonomy of human beings, combined with his belief in the practical incompleteness of our virtue, may be seen as paving the way for an understanding of conversion or moral transformation as the precondition for earning forgiveness and for the capacity to forgive in interpersonal relations.[12] Repentance and the concomitant achievement of a new self are now to be judged not by God but by the person who has been wronged, who must make the almost superhuman effort to see the offender as newly virtuous and hence worthy of forgiveness. With this, forgiveness is on the way to attaining the central position in moral thought that it will occupy in the late twentieth century.

Forgiveness plays a role in Hegel's thought, too, but as might be expected, it is integrated into his larger conception of the evolution of the human spirit. Thus, Amos Friedland observes that for Hegel, forgiveness represents the transcendence of evil in

---

[11] Trans. Wood and Di Giovanni 1998 (= RGV AA 06: 47); quoted in Sussman 2005: 97.

[12] See Schneewind (1998: 513): "The invention of autonomy gave Kant what he thought was the only morally satisfactory theory of the status of human beings in a universe shared with God." I am grateful to Dominik Perler for this reference.

history: "The wounds of Spirit heal, and leave no scars behind."[13]
So too, in his *Lectures on the Philosophy of Religion*, delivered shortly
before his death in 1831, Hegel affirms, "Spirit can undo what has
been done. The action certainly remains in memory, but spirit
strips it away.... [T]he finitude of humanity has been put to death
in the death of Christ.... Thus the world has been reconciled; by
this death it has been implicitly delivered from evil."[14] Friedland
argues that this vision of ultimate communion, although rejected
by many modern thinkers, continues to be influential in the ideas
of Bishop Desmond Tutu and other apostles of reconciliation. So
transcendent a conception, however, goes beyond ordinary interpersonal forgiveness and clearly reflects the Christian millenarian
ideal of the final cancellation of sin.

Joanna North has argued that "Neither Kant nor Hegel gives a
coherent account of forgiveness.... For both of them, forgiveness
involves a wiping out of the crime, a making undone what has been
done."[15] From one point of view, then, "the extending of forgiveness to the wrongdoer is a matter of relinquishing the demands
of justice, and perhaps even condoning the crime," especially if,
as Kant maintained, "forgiveness always involves the foregoing of
punishment" (ibid.). North goes on to affirm that, "In fact, Kant
regards forgiveness not merely as problematic but as literally
impossible: for once wrong has been done it cannot be undone even
by God" (499–500). In Christian thought, however, God does not
eliminate the wrong as such – it will never be true that Adam and
Eve did not eat the forbidden apple in Eden – but rather, as we have
seen, absolves mankind from the state of sin that ensued upon this
originary transgression: it is the sin that is cancelled, not the act.[16]

---

[13] Friedland 2004: 25, citing G. W. F. Hegel 1977: 407, para. 669 (*Phenomenology of Spirit*).
[14] Hegel 1987: 324–5; cited according to Friedland 2004: 15.
[15] North 1987: 499.
[16] Cf. Jones (1995: 63): "sin and forgiveness have to do with more than pride and with more than my 'individual' guilt. They have to do with the pervasive brokenness for which we are all, in some measure, culpable and with specific instances and habits of culpable wrongdoing that undermine not only my communion but *our* commu- nion with God, with one another, and with the whole Creation. Hence, forgiveness must involve an unlearning of the habits of sin as we seek to become holy people capable of living in communion." But contrast Elizondo (1986: 72): "humanly speaking, true and unconditional forgiveness seems beyond our natural possibili- ties.... For to forgive means to uncreate, but as only God can create out of nothing

But such a resolution of sinfulness cannot occur in human interactions. As North puts it (500): "Kant's account offers no hope to
those who try to escape punishment by appealing to God's mercy....
Our only hope lies in our positive endeavours to make amends for
our sins and in our decision to act rightly in future."

This is promising as an entrée into the question of human reconciliation, though it would seem to focus on compensation and
a guarantee of security rather than on forgiveness proper. But
North identifies another, more fundamental, difficulty in Kant's
account: "Kant seems to think that through such a positive change
of heart a person can become a 'new man.' The sinful person he
once was will be punished while the new person he has become
will not." How the former incarnation of the offender might suffer retribution is not at all clear, but North puts her finger on the
heart of the matter when she states, "This ingenious solution cre-
ates many problems of personal identity, and makes forgiveness
redundant. If I repent, and in so doing, become a new man, asking for forgiveness seems to be a matter of asking for a response
aimed at a person who no longer exists. But if this is really so, then
there can be no point in asking for forgiveness, and the person
who is asked for forgiveness can only aim his response at a meta-
physical shadow."[17]

North concludes that, "If forgiveness is to be coherent we should
reject this account of repentance" – that is, the account implicit
in Kant's notion of a "new man." To evade the conundrum, she
interprets the idea of a transformation of the self in a way that is
presupposed by what I have been calling the *modern conception of
forgiveness.* Thus, North writes (500):

> The person who repents fully recognizes that the crime committed was
> his own, and that his responsibility for it continues over time, just as he
> does. In asking for forgiveness he wants this very same person to be for-
> given, and the forgiver is required to recognize him as such. When we
> do speak of a person as "becoming a new man" through his repentance
> we must remember that this phrase is used metaphorically, suggesting a

only God can return to nothing what has already come into existence. So it is only
God who can uncreate, it is only God who can truly forgive."
[17] Derrida also noted the paradox of the "reformed criminal," who was in some sense
a "new person" and hence no longer the one who committed the crime; see Derrida
2002: 58, and Rubenstein 2008: 81.

> spiritual transformation from bad to good, but not implying his literal
> re-creation.... I suggest that far from removing the fact of wrongdoing,
> forgiveness actually relies upon the recognition of this fact for its very
> possibility. What is annulled in the act of forgiveness is not the crime
> itself but the distorting effect that this wrong has upon one's relations
> with the wrongdoer and perhaps with others.

It is true that no modern thinker – I daresay, not even Kant –
conceived of the moral transformation in the offender who petitions forgiveness as a "literal re-creation" of the person. But the
appeal to metaphor does not entirely remove the paradoxical
quality of the change of self that is implied in the modern conception of forgiveness.

Meir Dan-Cohen has recently taken a close look at the notion of
"revising the past" as a premise of forgiveness.[18] Dan-Cohen notes
that "the standard account" of forgiveness "gives priority to repentance," and he adds, "Though there are a number of variants, the
basic idea is the same. Repentance involves a change of heart in the
wrongdoer" (118). Dan-Cohen identifies one version of this view,
which derives ultimately from Kant, in Jeffrie Murphie's claim that
wrongdoing "is an expression of disrespect toward the victim"; the
repentant wrongdoer no longer holds the offended party in contempt and so merits forgiveness.[19] Another view, however, "makes
a more radical claim: The change wrought by repentance may
be so profound as to count as a change of identity." Dan-Cohen
goes on to point out the paradox that North discovered in Kant's
analysis: "Since the repentant individual is not the same one as
the wrongdoer to whom we bore a grudge, the offender's transformation deprives the reactive attitudes of their object" (119). If
there is no one left to forgive, what is left of forgiveness? Dan-
Cohen suggests, accordingly, that we speak rather of a change of
the boundaries of the self: "Revisionary practices give rise to a new
version of the self from which the wrongful act is excluded. When
this version is inhabited and enacted, it replaces the older one as
superior or more authoritative" (129). But does this new description succeed in resolving the paradox of forgiveness?

The question is crucial, because the idea of an alteration of the
self is, as we have seen, central to the modern idea of forgiveness

---

[18] Dan-Cohen 2007.
[19] Ibid., 118, citing Murphie and Hampton 1988: 26.

(deriving, as I argue, from the religious conception of conversion). Thus, Richard Swinburne, in an important study, argues that, for the complete removal of guilt, "the wrongdoer must make atonement for his wrong act, and the victim must forgive him." Swinburne explains that atonement "involves four components – repentance, apology, reparation, and what, for want of a better word, I shall call penance."[20] It is possible to compensate for some wrongs, at least, but not for the fact that "the wrongdoer has by doing the act made himself someone who has harmed the victim. He cannot change that past fact, but he can distance himself from it by privately and publicly disowning the act" (82). In so doing, "the wrongdoer makes the sharp contrast between the attitude behind the past act and his present attitude" (82–3). To be sure, "The final act belongs to the victim – to forgive," which results, we are told, in having the "guilt removed" (84–5). Forgiving, for its part, "is a performative act" (85) achieved by the very declaration. Such a description, however, bypasses the complex internal process that is the precondition for the act and renders it sincere: in short, why should a new attitude in the offender suffice to eliminate resentment for a past wrong?

There has been some discussion recently of the paradox of forgiveness in connection with the question of whether there are wrongs that are by nature unforgivable. We saw in Chapter 4 that, according to the Gospel of Matthew (12:31–2), sins against the Spirit are not forgiven.[21] The issue acquired a particular salience in the aftermath of the Nazi extermination camps, when there was perpetrated what many have considered to be the ultimate offense against humanity. With his customary flair for the paradoxical, Jacques Derrida pronounced that "forgiveness forgives only the

---

[20] Swinburne 1989: 81. Jones (1995: 150) criticizes Swinburne's view from a Christian theological perspective, arguing that repentance is not necessary for God's forgiveness: he observes, for example, that Jesus was willing "to forgive in God's name without requiring prior repentance," and he affirms that people "distort a Christian understanding of forgiveness by making repentance a prerequisite for forgiveness" (151). A prime instance of this misconception, according to Jones, is Kant, and he avers that "Richard Swinburne has extended the logic of Kant's argument for the prior requirement of repentance to forgiveness" (ibid., citing the passage in Swinburne quoted in the preceding text). On the much debated question of unconditional forgiveness in Christian thought, see Chapter 4, with nn. 36 and 44, and especially Ramelli 2010.

[21] For unforgivable offenses in the Jewish rabbinical tradition, Newman 1987: 164.

unforgivable."²² Derrida observes that the insistence on repentance places the victim in a position of sovereignty and reduces
forgiveness to a kind of economic exchange; thus, as Mary-Jane
Rubenstein observes, "A strictly conditional 'forgiveness,' even if
it were possible, would merely reverse and repeat the original
violence."²³ Only if an apology were not required could forgiveness "disrupt the specular economy that conditional forgiveness
can only affirm" (Rubenstein 2008: 82).²⁴ Such a model of forgiveness, for Derrida, is more a dream than a reality, and Derrida
hesitates to spell out the lineaments of such an ideal vision. The
closest he came to it, according to Rubenstein, was at a seminar
he gave (together with Avital Ronell) at New York University in
October 2001, the proceedings of which were not published; there,
Rubenstein reports, Derrida "offered his audience a sketch of
what he called an 'authentic scene of forgiveness'" (83). In this
fantasy, Derrida said, according to Rubenstein, that "one criminal would continually commit the same crime against one victim, and the victim would continually forgive him, knowing he
would never apologize and never change. In such a scene, Derrida
explained, there could be no possibility of forgetting or of reconciliation; rather, the two parties would exist in a perpetual and
'reciprocal fascination' with one another, the criminal remaining
the criminal and the victim remaining the victim" (84). For all the
apparent violence of this picture, to which Rubenstein duly calls
attention, it is not entirely dissonant with Griswold's requirement
that the forgiver must "commit to giving up resentment, or at least,
to giving up the judgment that the wrong-doer warrants continued resentment" (2007b: 49; cited more fully in Chapter 1). My

²² Derrida 2002: 32, cited in Janover 2005: 22. Cf. Friedland 2004: 338–47.
²³ Rubenstein 2008: 81.
²⁴ Arendt (1998: 241) describes forgiving as "the only reaction which does not merely
re-act but acts anew and unexpectedly, unconditioned by the act which provoked
it and therefore freeing from its consequences both the one who forgives and the
one who is forgiven." It thus has something of the free and generous character that
Aristotle ascribes to an act of kindness or *kharis* in the *Rhetoric* (2.7): "Let *kharis* ...
be a service to one who needs it, not in return for anything, nor so that the one who
performs the service may gain something, but so that the other may." Such a gesture, in turn, invites gratitude, which must not be construed as a debt or a requirement to return the favor, for this would deprive the original act of its altruism (see
Konstan 2006: 156–68).

emphasis here is on the idea of committing, which requires that one retain at least a trace of the sense of injury caused by the original offense, even as one seeks to overcome it: it is what Griswold characterizes as forgiveness in the "present participle" sense, in which it is not completed but still "under way" (2007b: 17, 45, 70, 86). Forgiveness, so conceived, is an ongoing act – "forgiving" in the progressive or imperfective aspect, to use the grammatical terms – rather than the completed or perfective state of "having forgiven." Forgiving seems to lock the agent and recipient of forgiveness in a strange reciprocal dependency, like that which Hegel, in a famous chapter of *The Phenomenology of Mind*, described as obtaining between master and slave.

Apart, however, from the aporia raised by Derrida's dream of "pure forgiveness" and of the limits of the forgivable, there is the paradox inherent in predicating a self that is new, and so deserves to be forgiven, even as it remains the same, as the author of the offense. It is this stipulation that renders forgiveness so elusive an idea. Mona Gustafson Affinito, for example, seeks to define it by contrast with related notions: "forgiveness is *not* excusing, forgetting, condoning negative and inappropriate behavior, absolution, a form of self-sacrifice, a clear-cut one-time decision, approval of injustice, pretending everything is just fine when you feel it is not,"[25] nor is it a matter of accepting compensation or taking satisfaction in the punishment and suffering of the other. Instead, she offers the following definition (93): "Forgiveness is the decision to forgo the personal pursuit of punishment for the perpetrator(s) of a perceived injustice, taking action on that decision, and experiencing the emotional relief that follows." But this therapeutic conception, with its emphasis on overcoming subjective tension, ignores the interpersonal dimension of forgiveness. As Janet Landman states in the same volume, "Certainly, forgiveness is an inherently *interpersonal*, or relational matter.... It is a change of heart on the part of one person, the one harmed, directed at another person, the one who has done the harm"[26] – a change that is in turn motivated by a series of steps in which "the wrongdoer 'recognizes that he

[25] Gustafson Affinito 2002: 91. For a similar set of contrasts, see Rodrigues 2006: 35–55.
[26] Landman 2002: 235.

has done wrong ...,' experiences other-oriented regret or remorse
for the wrong ..., resolves to reform," and so forth.[27] The premise
of identity in renewal is intrinsic to forgiveness, and it is an enigmatic basis for a moral relation.

Even assuming that a radical change of self is possible, it is a pre-
carious kind of reconciliation that depends on fathoming another
person's sincerity. As William Miller observes in his delightful
book, *Faking It,* "it is rarer to be really remorseful when we meant
to harm someone than when we didn't." Miller allows that "people can and do feel genuine remorse for the wrongs they have
intentionally done. Minds can change." Still, as he points out,
the problem remains: "how does the wronged person know that
the wrongdoer is not feigning his remorse, faking his change of
mind? Or that his sorriness is not of a less noble kind than true
remorse?" – that is, simply the regret that "we got caught."[28] Miller
goes further in reducing the significance of what we think of as
remorse: "Apology is a ritual, pure and simple, of humiliation. The
humiliation is the true compensation" (88). Despite the apparent
cynicism of this description, it accords well with Aristotle's views on
how to appease anger, as we saw in Chapter 2; as Aristotle put it, we
are placated by those who humble themselves before us, because
this proves that they are our inferiors and that they fear us (*Rhetoric*
1380a24). Miller goes on to say (90), "Apology ceremonies, indeed
many reconciliation ceremonies, don't disguise the fact that they
are humiliation rituals; only in America could we think otherwise.
In ancient Israel you rent your clothes, and fasted, and lay in sack-
cloth, and went softly" – and not just in Israel, as Miller points out.
In light of these practices, Miller concludes (94), "We will never
properly understand apology rituals and their requirement of
humiliation and compensation if we do not understand that the
ritual form is largely necessitated by how easy it is to fake remorse,
and by how hard it is to distinguish genuine remorse that arises as

[27] Ibid., 238–40; Landman bases her nine-stage process of forgiveness (foreshort-
ened in my description) on North 1998: 230. Schimmel (2002: 162), observes that
"Another focus of repentance is an even deeper and broader transformation of self
that goes beyond changing a specific character trait. Sometimes, for example, a
heretofore incorrigible sinner or criminal undergoes a conversion experience in
which he becomes a new and different person, so to speak."

[28] Miller 2003: 81, in the chapter "Say it Like You Mean it: Mandatory Faking and
Apology."

a moral response to the harm done to the other from the equally genuine amoral regret that arises from the discomfort the whole fiasco is causing the wrongdoer."[29]

The danger of hypocrisy is perhaps one motive for such rituals of contrition, but the role of self-abasement in various ancient practices of conciliation, and more particularly in Aristotle's advice on how to assuage anger, suggests that it may have a more basic function, namely that of restoring due respect for the status of the other where a slight or other offense has called it into question. In modern societies imbued with a democratic ideology, there is a tendency to disguise such marks of deference, but the ancient Greeks and Romans had fewer such inhibitions. They did not feel so great a need to verify the remorse of the offender, because repentance was not the principal condition for restoring a moral relationship with the wrongdoer. Their attitude in this was not only more candid, it was also, as I am inclined to believe, more coherent, in that it did not postulate the paradoxical notion of self-reform that lies at the heart of the modern understanding of forgiveness.[30]

I have been arguing in this book that forgiveness, in the modern acceptation of the word, did not exist in classical antiquity or in the early Judeo-Christian tradition, despite a new vision of divine absolution that was predicated on the repentance of the sinner and a turning, or returning, to the ways of the Lord. Rather, I have sought to show that the modern conception, which involves a moral transformation in the offender and a corresponding change of heart in the forgiver, is of relatively recent vintage as a moral idea and has its roots in large part in the revolution in ethical thinking heralded by Immanuel Kant. This new conception of the moral autonomy of the individual, and the requirement

---

[29] Ure 2007 applies a Nietzschean critique to Arendt's defense of forgiveness as a means of social reconciliation and concludes (68): "Christian *agape* defeats resentment only at the price of a radical denial of our own need for recognition."

[30] It is not necessary to conceive of remorse or a change of heart as constituting so radical a transformation of self; one may, for example, regard the self in a postmodern vein as a product of multiple, criss-crossing identities, which combine and recombine in response to different circumstances (I am grateful to Ellen Rooney for suggesting this alternative). Such a view, however, is not the basis of modern discussions of forgiveness, which are implicitly indebted to a tradition of repentance and conversion.

to treat human beings as ends in themselves, created the conditions for a secular notion of interpersonal forgiveness, in which remorse, and the inner change it presupposed, were directed not to God but, in a way that might have seemed blasphemous in an earlier age, to the fellow human whom one had wronged. However, the original, religious conception of conversion continued to inform this notion of a moral transformation, which, once secularized and rendered the basis for forgiveness, assumed a new and potentially contradictory form. For now it was no longer a matter of becoming "a new man" in the eyes of God, who was under no obligation to recall the disobedience of the old Adam; forgiveness, as we have seen, is not equivalent to forgetting or to a cancellation of the wrong that was committed. And here, precisely, is the rub.

To quote Chryssavgis once again, repentance "is an invitation to new life, an opening up of new horizons, the gaining of a new vision. Christianity testifies that the past can be undone. It knows the mystery of obliterating or rather renewing memory, of forgiveness and regeneration, eschewing the fixed division between the 'good' and the 'wicked,' the pious and the rebellious, the believers and the unbelievers. Indeed, 'the last' can be 'the first,' the sinner can reach out to holiness.... One repents not because one is virtuous, but because human nature can change, because what is impossible for man is possible for God."[31] Although the notion of a change of character so deep as to render us different from what we were sounds particularly Christian, however, it was not entirely foreign to classical thought. Plato, in the *Phaedrus* (241A), explains that when a lover has accepted reason and moderation as his masters, in place of passion and madness, he becomes "another person" (*allos gegonôs*). In Plato's *Euthydemus*, the sophistical Dionysodorus insists that for Cleinias to become wise rather than ignorant, it is necessary for him to become a different person: "Surely," he says to Socrates, "who he is not, you wish him to become, and who he now is, no longer to be" (283C–D). As Mary Margaret McCabe observes in a subtle study of the dialogue, the debate "focuses attention on the issue of personal identity. It invites Socrates to agree that who Cleinias is, is delimited by the character and properties that he

[31] Chryssavgis 2004.

has at some particular time; when once one of those may change, he is no longer *who* he was before."[32] The dilemma, as McCabe points out, is that "if identity is episodic, *I* cannot become wise; but if it is persistent, I cannot *change*" (122–3). The question of continuity of the self was evidently in the air but was regarded as a clever conundrum rather than a serious ethical possibility.[33]

Glenn Most has recently remarked upon a sharp contrast between modern and ancient ways of explaining character formation.[34] He illustrates the modern approach by way of Salman Rushdie's novel *Fury*, in which the uncontrollable rages to which the protagonist is prone are traced to the sexual abuse to which he was subjected in his childhood. Most writes, "no one in antiquity ever even hinted that Achilles' notoriously excessive anger might have been the result of his having had an unhappy childhood." Although there was ample material in Greek mythology that might have lent itself to such an explanation, such as the early separation of Achilles's parents or his disguise as a girl on the island of Scyrus, nevertheless, when the Greeks and Romans "imagined Achilles as a child, they imagined him as being just like the adult Achilles, only rather smaller." In general this is how the ancients understood the process of character formation – marked not by ruptures but by continuity, in which traits visible in childhood persist or become accentuated over time. Thus, in Plutarch's *Lives*, there is little attention paid to childhood experiences: "Already as a child, Philopoemen is the consummate soldier" (*Life* 3.2), whereas "Themistocles is already the perfect politician" (*Life* 2.1), Cato "the stern Stoic sage" (*Life* 1.2), and Alcibiades the same charming cad (*Life* 2.1–2).

---

[32] McCabe 2008: 118.

[33] Simplicius, in his *Commentary on Aristotle's Physics* 10.1066.3–4 and following (on *Physics* 7.3), discusses whether a change from vice to virtue means that a person has fundamentally changed (I owe this reference to Orna Harari). Sissa (2006: 48) argues that, on Aristotle's view of suffering and remorse (*lupê* and *metameleia*: cf. *Nicomachean Ethics* 3.1110b17–22), "the agent does take responsibility and yet does not endorse the act, here and now, by a retrospective approval (or a careless indifference), which would create a sort of continuity – and thus complicity – between his present self and 'the one who did that.' Through a feeling of repulsion (*duscherainein*) the agent has become somehow another, as the compound *metameleia* suggests, because he now detaches himself from an act which he has, however, *done*." But Aristotle does not cast the recognition of a past error as a change of self, and the agent, in the case of a nonvoluntary action, remains morally self-identical.

[34] Most 2008; English taken from Most's original manuscript, by permission (see now Most 2009).

This is not to say that childhood character traits were regarded
as incorrigible. It was the function of education to moderate native
dispositions. But this is more like behavior modification than a
deep transformation in the self.[35] Thus, Timothy Duff argues that
Plutarch's *Life of Themistocles* "contains within it a tension between
two models for understanding the relationship of education to
adult character. The first approach sees character as in the process of being formed in childhood, and education as affecting
the way in which character develops; the second approach sees
character as constant and unchanging, and as revealed in childhood behaviour and in attitude to education."[36] But the former
"developmental model" rests on habituation or training, not on
a sudden alteration, much less on bringing repressed traumatic
experiences to consciousness. This is why the two models "are not
as contradictory as they first appear" (20): one has "certain innate
leanings," which however may be corrected or improved by education.[37] The idea of a moral transformation in the adult, along the
lines of Christian conversion narratives, is foreign to classical biography and to the classical conception of the person in general.[38]

[35] Gill (2006: 419) sees Plutarch's approach to biography as reflecting a specifically
Platonic and Aristotelian model of the self, wherein "Stability of character is a product of the interplay of inborn nature, education, and environmental influences."

[36] Duff 2008: 1.

[37] Duff concludes (2008: 21) that the "static/illustrative model of character is ... the
norm in the Lives," and the developmental model occurs "in contexts where philosophical modes of thinking are dominant," especially when there is reference or
clear allusion to Plato (22).

[38] See Konstan 2009a and Konstan 2011. I have deliberately side-stepped the larger
question of whether the self, as it was understood or experienced in classical antiquity, was fundamentally different from the modern idea, in that the ancients lacked
a full sense of interiority, subjectivity, or personal autonomy (sometimes associated with the sentiment of guilt as opposed to shame). An extreme formulation
is that of Veyne 1987–91, vol. 1: 231: "No ancient ... is capable of talking about
himself. Nothing is more misleading than the use of 'I' in Greco-Roman poetry."
This approach owes much to the neo-Kantian view of psychological evolution developed by Ernst Cassirer and Bruno Snell. For an excellent overview of the issue, see
Thumiger 2007: 3–57; Thumiger sees (rightly, in my view) the distinction between
the "public" and the "modern subjective-individualist" conception (6) as a function as much of genre as of historical development; cf. Farenga 2006: 178, who
argues that "In performing Odysseus' wanderings, homecoming, and vengeance
on Penelope's suitors, the Homeric poet reenacts in the hero a personality transformation which he intends his audiences to share intersubjectively" and adds (190): "I
don't think we can separate Odysseus' moral mandate to recreate himself as a person from the inclination of some scholars to identify him as a 'new man.'" Bartsch

Various stories of sudden conversions to philosophy did circulate in antiquity and might even be thought to constitute a motif.[39] But these tales never became the model for a change of character precipitated by remorse over wrongdoing, as happened in nineteenth-century and later constructions of forgiveness. Although Dionysodorus's sophism, to the effect that any change of qualities in an individual threatens the principle of self-identity, is not without a certain philosophical salience, it does not pose the kind of conceptual puzzle that forgiveness specifically entails. As Lucy Allais writes, "The first difficulty is simply to *make sense* of what is involved in ceasing to hold an action against someone while continuing to regard it as wrong and as attributed to the perpetrator in the way which is necessary for there to be something to forgive. Forgiving seems to mean ceasing to blame, but if blaming means holding the perpetrator responsible, then forgiveness requires *not* ceasing to blame, or else there will be nothing to forgive."[40] Allais

(2006: 233) cites Alasdair MacIntyre, Bernard Williams, and Christopher Gill among those who "have suggested that a more appropriate way of understanding the normative ancient self [than the models proposed by Snell and Adkins] (and its anticipation of new, non-Cartesian descriptions of selfhood in the present day) is to recognize the role of interpersonal and communal relationships in its formation and its moral judgments." For a more general discussion of the nature of the self, see Sorabji 2006: 17–22; on the postmodern dissolution of the traditional self, see Holstein and Gubrium 2000, who conclude, "Far from being a grand narrative settled at or near the center of personal experience, the self now materializes in myriad nooks and crannies of everyday life." On the problematic contrast between guilt and shame in classical antiquity, see Konstan 2006: 91–3.

39 See Arieti and Gibson 2005: 277n4: "Perhaps there was a motif in ancient literature of the instantaneous or near-instantaneous adoption of a new course of life. The stories of Polemon, Plato, Antisthenes, Zeno, and many others tell of people whose souls are ignited by an inspirational moment." On Polemon, see Diogenes Laertius 4.16. Also Finn (1997: 85): "To enter a philosophical school required conversion. The language of conversion studded the language of philosophy." One may also compare the effect on Socrates of the Delphic oracle's response to Chaerophon's question concerning the wisest of Athenians, which set Socrates on his mission of cross-questioning his fellow citizens; cf. Czachesz 2007: 10–13, who compares Socrates' mission to that of Saint Paul. In Plutarch's essay, *On Those Who Are Punished Slowly by the Divinity*, Thespesius dies, witnesses the punishments in the afterlife, and returns a reformed man: Plutarch calls it "an unbelievable transformation" (*apiston tina tou biou metabolēn*, 563D), but it is clearly a special case. Achilles Tatius (8.17.5) notes a similarly sudden and wonderous change (*exaiphnēs ... thaumastē metabolē*) in the character of Callisthenes, but his youthful excesses are then chalked up to high spirits rather than to a congenital lack of self-control.

40 Allais 2008: 34. On the paradoxical simultaneity of blame and forgiveness, see also Derrida 2002, with comments in the preceding text.

further recognizes that there may not even be a need for such a problematic concept: "Since we can rid ourselves of consuming resentment without forgiving, and we can justifiably undermine the grounds for resentment where there are reasons to excuse, justify and/or accept, it needs to be shown that there remains a coherent and justifiable role for forgiveness" (35). But does it? Does forgiveness do some significant moral work that ancient methods of reconciliation were incapable of achieving?

There is no doubt that forgiveness is widely perceived as an urgent matter these days, not to say much in vogue.[41] From the legal movement known as *restorative justice*, which seeks to overcome the resentment between criminal and victim as a way of healing both,[42] and the truth and reconciliation commissions that attempt to sublimate the deep resentments resulting from violent social oppression, to the more individualistic psychotherapies and religious counsels that promise peace with oneself or with God, forgiveness has recommended itself as a specially profound, moral, and effective way of rising above bitterness and resolving conflict.[43] That the demand to grant forgiveness may be coercive, the preconditions for eliciting it may be faked, its efficacy in assuaging rage may be overestimated, and, finally, the very concept may depend on assumptions that are philosophically incoherent – all this is reasonably well-known, and points to the possibility that we are dealing here with a notion that serves a particular ideological function in today's world. It is not the purpose of this book to contribute to an indictment of forgiveness or to identify the social conditions that may have made it seem so indispensable in our time. Rather, I have sought to show that the notion of interpersonal forgiveness, as it is basically understood today, is not only

[41] The currency of forgiveness is noted emphatically by Derrida 2002: 28–31.

[42] On restorative justice, see, e.g., Braithwaite 1999; Garvey 2003; also Chapter 1, n. 25. For a powerful critique of the movement, see Acorn 2004.

[43] One domain in which forgiveness seems especially to be invoked is in relation to marital infidelity, which seems to cast the offender as a person forever undeserving of trust, and hence unreformable. The implicit assumption is that there are two types of people, faithful and unfaithful, and that it takes a profound conversion to transform the sinner into a righteous and trustworthy individual. One could argue, however, that the repentant adulterer is more reliable than one who has never strayed, because he or she has experienced the moral damage that such behavior entails and rejects it, whereas the one who has never tried, or been tried, might yet succumb to temptation.

not universal but also is of relatively recent coinage, and that the ancient societies to which we often look as models for our ethical concepts – whether classical Greece and Rome, or the Jewish and Christian traditions that emerged within and alongside them – seem to have done perfectly well without it. I do not mean to suggest that they were in any way morally inferior for this absence; my object is simply to have set the record straight about their strategies of reconciliation, as a way of understanding their practices in their own terms. If, in the process, I have stimulated some doubts about the very concept of forgiveness in a way that invites further inquiry, the intention of this book will have been fulfilled.

Bibliography

Acorn, Annalise. 2007. "'Sumimasen, I'm Sorry': Apology in Dispute Resolution in North America and Japan." *Aichigakuin Law Review* 48: 131–61.

——— 2004. *Compulsory Compassion: A Critique of Restorative Justice*. Vancouver: University of British Columbia Press.

Adrados, Francisco R., and Juan Rodríguez Somolinos, eds. 1989–. *Diccionario Griego-Español*. Madrid: Instituto de Lenguas y Culturas del Mediterráneo Oriente Próximo and Centro de Humanidades y Ciencias Sociales, Consejo Superior de Investigaciones Científicas (CSIC).

Alexiou, Evangelos. 1999. "Zur Darstellung der ὀργή in Plutarchs βίοι." *Philologus* 143: 101–13.

Allais, Lucy. 2008. "Wiping the Slate Clean: The Heart of Forgiveness." *Philosophy and Public Affairs* 36: 33–68.

Allen, Danielle. 2000. *The World of Prometheus: The Politics of Punishing in Democratic Athens*. Princeton, NJ: Princeton University Press.

Anderson, G. E., and M. E. Stone, eds. 1994. *A Synopsis of the Books of Adam and Eve*. Atlanta, GA: Scholars Press.

Anderson, Gary, M. E. Stone, and Johannes Tromp, eds. 2000. *Literature on Adam and Eve: Collected Essays*. Leiden, the Netherlands: E. J. Brill.

Appel, Georg. 1909. *De Romanorum Precationibus*. Giessen, Germany: A. Töpelmann (repr., New York: Arno Press, 1975).

Arendt, Hannah. 1998. *The Human Condition: A Study of the Central Condition Facing Modern Man*. 2nd ed. Chicago: University of Chicago Press.

Arieti, James A., and David M. Gibson. 2005. *Philosophy in the Ancient World: An Introduction*. Lanham, MD: Rowman and Littlefield.

Arnim, Hans Friedrich August von. 1964. *Stoicorum veterum fragmenta*. 2nd ed. 4 vols. Stuttgart, Germany: Teubner.

Aubert, Sophie. 2011. "Réflexions sur une μῆτις stoïcienne à travers les témoignages de Stobée." In *Deciding Culture: Stobaeus' Collection of Excerpts*, ed. Carlos Lévy, Gretchen Reydams-Schils, and Emmanuele Vimercato. Turnhout, Belgium: Brepols.

Aubriot, Danièle. 1987. "Quelques refléxions sur le pardon en Grèce anci-
    enne." In *Le pardon*, ed. Michel Perrin. Paris: Beauchesne, 11–27.
Bartsch, Shadi. 2006. *The Mirror of the Self: Sexuality, Self-Knowledge, and the
    Gaze in the Early Roman Empire*. Chicago: University of Chicago Press.
Bash, Anthony. 2007. *Forgiveness and Christian Ethics*. Cambridge: Cambridge
    University Press.
Beal, John P., James A. Coriden, and Thomas J. Green, eds. 2000. *New
    Commentary on the Code of Canon Law*. New York: Paulist Press.
Bellia, Giuseppe, and Angelo Passaro, eds. 2004. *Il Libro della Sapienza:
    Tradizione, redazione, teologia*. Rome: Città Nuova.
Bioy Casares, Adolfo. 2006. *Borges*. Barcelona: Destino ("Imago Mundi").
Bizzeti, P. 1984. *Il Libro della Sapienza: Struttura e genere letterario*. Brescia,
    Italy: Paideia.
Blackman, Philip, trans. 1965. *Mishnayoth*. 6 vols. 3rd ed. New York: The
    Judaica Press.
Blumoff, Theodore Y. 2006. "An Essay on Vengeance and Forgiveness." *bepress
    Legal Series* 1427: 12–13. Available at http://law.bepress.com/expresso/
    eps/1427.
Boda, Mark J. 2006. "Confession as Theological Expression: Ideological
    Origins of Penitential Prayer." In *Seeking the Favor of God: The Origins
    of Penitential Prayer in Second Temple Judaism*, vol. 1, ed. Mark J. Boda,
    Daniel K. Falk, and Rodney A. Werline. Atlanta, GA: Society of Biblical
    Literature, 21–50.
Borgeaud, Michael and Caroline Cox. 1999. "'The Most Dreadful Sentiment':
    A Sociological Commentary." In *Remorse and Reparation*, ed. Murray
    Cox. London: Jessica Kingsley Publishers, 135–44.
Borges, Jorge Luis. 1985. *Obra poética 1923/1977*. Madrid: Alianza.
Braithwaite, John. 1999. "Restorative Justice: Assessing Optimistic and
    Pessimistic Accounts." *Crime and Justice* 25: 1–127.
Bråkenhielm, Carl Reinhold. 1993 (orig. Swedish version 1987). *Forgiveness*.
    Trans. Thor Hall. Minneapolis, MN: Fortress Press.
Cairns, Douglas. 1999. "Representations of Remorse and Reparation in
    Classical Greece." In *Remorse and Reparation*, ed. Murray Cox. London:
    Jessica Kingsley Publishers, 171–8.
Calduch-Benages, Nuria, and J. Vermeylen, eds. 1999. *Treasures of Wisdom:
    Studies in Ben Sira and the Book of Wisdom: Festschrift M. Gilbert*. Leuven,
    Belgium: Peeters.
Caputo, John D., Mark Dooley, and Michael J. Scanlon. 2001.
    "Introduction: God Forgive." In *Questioning God*, ed. Caputo, Dooley,
    and Scanlon. Bloomington: University of Indiana Press, 1–20.
Chaniotis, Angelos. 2004. "Von Ehre, Schande und kleinen Verbrechen unter
    Nachbarn: Konfliktbewältigung und Götterjustiz in Gemeinden des
    antiken Anatolien." In *Konflikt*, ed. Frank R. Pfetsch. Berlin: Springer,
    233–54.
Chavalas, Mark W., ed. 2006. *The Ancient Near East: Historical Sources in
    Translation*. Oxford: Blackwell.

Chow, Rey. 2009. "'I insist on the Christian dimension': On Forgiveness ... and the Outside of the Human." *differences* 20: 2–3 (double issue on "The Future of the Human").

Christo, Gus George, trans. 1998. *St. John Chrysostom on Repentance and Almsgiving.* Washington, DC: The Catholic University of America Press.

Chryssavgis, John. 2004. *Repentance and Confession in the Orthodox Church.* Brooklyne, MA: The Holy Cross Orthodox Press. "Introduction" available at http://ad-orientem.blogspot.com/2007/11/repentanceconfession.html.

Courtney, Edward, ed. 1991. *The Poems of Petronius.* Atlanta, GA: Scholars Press.

Cox, Murray, ed. 1999. *Remorse and Reparation.* London: Jessica Kingsley Publishers.

Czachesz, István. 2007. *Commission Narratives: A Comparative Study of the Canonical and Apocryphal Acts.* Leuven, Belgium: Peeters.

Dan-Cohen, Meir. 2007. "Revising the Past: On the Metaphysics of Repentance, Forgiveness, and Pardon." In *Forgiveness, Mercy, and Clemency,* ed. Austin Sarat and Nasser Hussain. Stanford, CA: Stanford University Press,117–37.

Danby, Herbert, trans. 1933. *The Mishnah.* Oxford: Oxford University Press.

Daube, David. 1960. *Sin, Ignorance and Forgiveness in the Bible.* London: The Liberal Jewish Synagogue.

Davis, Paul. November 3, 2007. "Shaking the Family Tree." *Providence Journal,* A: 1, 4.

Derrida, Jacques. 2002. "On Forgiveness." In *On Cosmopolitanism and Forgiveness,* trans. Mark Dooley and Michael Hughes. London and New York: Routledge, 25–60.

Douglas, Mary. 1999. *Leviticus as Literature.* Oxford: Oxford University Press.

Dover, Kenneth J. 1994. *Greek Popular Morality in the Time of Plato and Aristotle.* Oxford: Blackwell.

Downie, R. S. 1965. "Forgiveness." *The Philosophical Quarterly* 15: 128–34.

Duff, Timothy E. 2008. "Models of Education in Plutarch," *Journal of Hellenic Studies* 128: 1–26.

Elizondo, Virgil. 1986. "I Forgive but I Do Not Forget." In *Forgiveness,* ed. Casiano Floristán and Christian Duquoc. Edinburgh: T. and T. Clark, 69–79.

Farenga, Vincent. 2006. *Citizen and Self in Ancient Greece: Individuals Performing Justice and the Law.* Cambridge: Cambridge University Press.

Fingarette, Herbert, and Ann Fingarette Hasse. 1979. *Mental Disabilities and Criminal Responsibility.* Berkeley: University of California.

Finn, Thomas Macy. 1997. *From Death to Rebirth: Ritual and Conversion in Antiquity.* Mahwah, NJ: Paulist Press.

Freud, Sigmund. 1972. *Civilization and Its Discontents.* Trans. Joan Riviere, ed. James Strachey. London: Hogarth.

Friedland, Amos. 2004. "Evil and Forgiveness: Transitions." *Perspectives on Evil and Human Wickedness* 1: 24–47.

Friedman, Michael. 2002. *"The World Must Be Peopled": Shakespeare's Comedies of Forgiveness*. Madison, NJ: Fairleigh Dickinson University Press.

Fulkerson, Laurel. 2006a. "Neoptolemus Grows Up? 'Moral Development' and the Interpretation of Sophocles' *Philoctetes*." *Proceedings of the Cambridge Philological Society* 52: 49–61.

— 2006b. "Apollo, *paenitentia*, and Ovid's Metamorphoses." *Mnemosyne* 59: 388–402.

— 2004. *"Metameleia*: Remorse and Repentance in 5th and 4th Century Athenian Oratory." *Phoenix* 58: 241–59.

Gaiser, Konrad. 1977. "Griechisches und christliches Verzeihen: Xenophon, Kyrupädie 3, 1, 38–40 und Lukas 23, 34a," *Latinität und Alte Kirche* (Festschrift für Rudolf Hanslik) (supplement), *Wiener Studien Beiheft* 8: 78–100.

Garvey, Stephen P. 2003. "Restorative Justice, Punishment, and Atonement." *Utah Law Review* 303: 303–17.

Gibbs, Robert. 2001. "Returning/Forgiving: Ethics and Theology." In *Questioning God*, ed. John Caputo, Mark Dooley, and Michael J. Scanlon. Bloomington: University of Indiana Press, 73–91.

Gill, Christopher. 2006. *The Structured Self in Hellenistic and Roman Thought*. Oxford: Oxford University Press.

Glare, P. G. W. 1968. *The Oxford Latin Dictionary*. Oxford: Oxford University Press.

Gomme, A. W., and F. H. Sandbach, eds. 1973. *Menander: A Commentary*. Oxford: Oxford University Press.

Gould, John. 1973. *"Hiketeia." Journal of Hellenic Studies* 93: 74–103.

Graver, Margaret. 2007. *Stoicism and Emotion*. Chicago: University of Chicago Press.

Gregor, Mary, trans. 1997. *The Cambridge Edition of the Works of Immanuel Kant in Translation*. Cambridge: Cambridge University Press.

Griswold, Charles, and David Konstan, eds. 2011. *Ancient Forgiveness*. Cambridge: Cambridge University Press.

Griswold, Charles L. 2007a. "Plato and Forgiveness." *Ancient Philosophy* 27: 269–87.

— 2007b. *Forgiveness: A Philosophical Exploration*. Cambridge: Cambridge University Press.

Grossel, Cécile. 2008. "La Notion de συγγνώμη dans le *De Fraterno Amore* de Plutarque." *Revue des Études Grecques* 121: 373–92.

Gustafson Affinito, Mona. 2002. "Forgiveness in Counseling: Caution, Definition, and Application." In *Before Forgiving: Cautionary Views of Forgiveness in Psychotherapy*, ed. Sharon Lamb and Jeffrie G. Murphy. Oxford: Oxford University Press, 88–111.

Gutzwiller, Kathryn. 2011. "All in the Family: Forgiveness and Reconciliation in New Comedy." In Griswold and Konstan 2011.

Hallo, William W., and K. Lawson Younger Jr., eds. 1997. *The Context of Scripture*, vol. 1. Leiden, the Netherlands: Brill.

Hanna, Edward. 1907. "Absolution." In *The Catholic Encyclopedia*, vol. 1. New York: Robert Appleton Company. Available at http://www.newadvent.org/cathen/01061a.htm (accessed March 7, 2010).

Harré, Rom, and W. Gerrod Parrot, eds. 1996. *The Emotions: Social, Cultural, and Biological Dimensions*. London: Sage Publications.

Harvey, Steven. 1991. "A New Islamic Source of the Guide of the Perplexed." *Maimonidean Studies* 2: 31–59.

Hauptman, Judith. 2005. *Rereading the Mishnah: A New Approach to Ancient Jewish Texts*. Tübingen, Germany: Mohr Siebeck Verlag.

Heath, Malcolm. 2004. *Menander: A Rhetor in Context*. Oxford: Oxford University Press.

——— 1995. *Hermogenes on Issues: Strategies of Argument in Later Greek Rhetoricians*. Oxford: Clarendon Press.

Hegel, G. W. F. 1987. *Lectures on the Philosophy of Religion*, vol. 3, ed. Peter C. Hodgson. Berkeley: California University Press.

——— 1977. *Phenomenology of Spirit*. Trans. A. V. Miller. Oxford: Oxford University Press.

Henry, W. Benjamin, ed. 2009. *Philodemus: De morte*. Atlanta, GA: Society of Biblical Literature.

Hobbes, Thomas. 1996 (orig. 1651). *Leviathan*, ed. J. C. A. Gaskin. Oxford: Oxford University Press.

Hoffner, Harry A., Jr., ed. 2002. *Hittite Prayers*. Writings from the Ancient World Series, vol. 11. Atlanta, GA: Society of Biblical Literature.

Holstein, James A., and Jaber F. Gubrium. 2000. *The Self We Live By: Narrative Identity in a Postmodern World*. New York: Oxford University Press.

Hoz, María Paz de. 1999. *Die lydischen Kulte im Lichte der griechischen Inschriften*. Bonn, Germany: Asia Minor Studien 36.

Hübner, Hans, ed. 2004. *La Sapienza di Salomone: tre saggi di teologia biblica*. Studi Biblici Series, vol. 144. Brescia, Italy: Paideia.

Hunt, Hannah. 2004. *Joy-Bearing Grief: Tears of Contrition in the Writings of the Early Syrian and Byzantine Fathers*. Leiden, the Netherlands: E. J. Brill.

Janover, Michael. 2005. "The Limits of Forgiveness and the Ends of Politics." *Journal of Intercultural Studies* 26: 221–35.

Johnson, W. R. 1996. "The Rapes of Callisto." *Classical Journal* 92: 9–24.

Jones, L. Gregory. 1995. *Embodying Forgiveness: A Theological Analysis*. Grand Rapids, MI: William B. Eerdmans Publishing.

Jonge, M. de, and Johannes Tromp. 1997. *The Life of Adam and Eve and Related Literature*. Sheffield, UK: Academic Press.

Kaster, Robert. 2005. *Emotion, Restraint, and Community in Ancient Rome*. Oxford: Oxford University Press.

Klauck, H.-J. 1989. "Hellenistische Rhetorik im Diasporajudentum: Das Exordium des vierten Makkabäerbuchs (4 Makk. 1.112)." *New Testament Studies* 35: 451–65.

Kohler, Kaufmann. 1901–6. "Atonement." *The Jewish Encyclopedia*, vol. 1: 275–84. Available at http://www.jewishencyclopedia.com/view.jsp?artid =2092&letter=A&Search=atonement (accessed March 7, 2010).

Konstan, David. 2011. "Reading the Past with Suetonius." In *The Historian's Plupast: Introductory Remarks on its Forms and Functions*, ed. Jonas Grethlein and Christopher Krebs. Oxford: Oxford University Press, 2011.

2009a. "Reading Politics in Suetonius." In *Writing Politics in Imperial Rome*, ed. William J. Dominik, John Garthwaite, and Paul Roche. Leiden, the Netherlands: E. J. Brill, 447–62.

2009b. "Reunion and Regeneration: Narrative Patterns in Ancient Greek Novels and Christian Acts," in *Fiction on the Fringe: Novelistic Writing in Late Antiquity*, ed. Grammatiki Karla and Ingela Nilsson. *Mnemosyne* Supplements Series. Leiden, the Netherlands: Brill Academic Publishers, 105–20.

2006. *The Emotions of the Ancient Greeks: Studies in Aristotle and Classical Literature*. Toronto: University of Toronto Press.

2005. "Clemency as a Virtue." *Classical Philology* 100: 337–46.

2002. "Ressentiment ancien et ressentiment moderne." In *Le ressentiment*, ed. Pierre Ansart. Brussels: Bruylant, 259–76.

2001a. *Pity Transformed*. London: Duckworth.

2001b. "Ressentimento – História de uma emoção." In *Memoria e (res) sentimento: Indagações sobre uma questão sensível*, ed. Stella Bresciani and Márcia Naxara. Campinas, Brazil: Editora da Unicamp, 59–81.

1998a. "Philoctetes' Pity: Comment on Julius M. E. Moravcsik, 'Values and Friendship in the *Philoctetes*.'" *Proceedings of the Boston Area Colloquium in Ancient Philosophy* 13: 276–82.

1998b. "The Alexander Romance: The Cunning of the Open Text." *Lexis* 16: 123–38.

1994. *Sexual Symmetry: Love in the Ancient Novel and Related Genres*. Princeton, NJ: Princeton University Press.

Krašovec, Jože. 1999. *Reward, Punishment, and Forgiveness: The Thinking and Beliefs of Ancient Israel in the Light of Greek and Modern Views*. Leiden, the Netherlands: E. J. Brill.

Landman, Janet. 2002. *"Earning Forgiveness: The Story of a Perpetrator, Katherine Ann Power."* In *Before Forgiving: Cautionary Views of Forgiveness in Psychotherapy*, ed. Sharon Lamb and Jeffrie G. Murphy. Oxford: Oxford University Press, 232–64.

Lang, Berel. 1994. "Forgiveness." *American Philosophical Quarterly* 31: 105–15.

Langbein, John H. 2005. *Torture and the Law of Proof: Europe and England in the Ancien Régime*. Chicago: University of Chicago Press (orig. published 1976, without new preface).

Lange, Frits de. 2004. "Room for Forgiveness? A Theological Perspective." In *Incredible Forgiveness: Christian Ethics between Fanaticism and Reconciliation*, ed. Didier Pollefeyt. Leuven, Belgium: Peeters, 161–82.

Lauritzen, Paul. "Forgiveness: Moral Prerogative or Religious Duty?" *Journal of Religious Ethics* 15: 141–54.

Levinas, Emanuel. 1990. *Nine Talmudic Readings*. Trans. Annette Aronowicz. Bloomington: Indiana University Press.

Liddell, Henry George, and Robert Scott. 1940. *A Greek-English Lexicon*, 9th ed. Ed. Henry Stuart Jones and Roderick McKenzie. Oxford: The Clarendon Press (published with a supplement in 1968).

Luijten, Eric. 2003. *Sacramental Forgiveness as a Gift of God: Thomas Aquinas on the Sacrament of Penance*. Leuven, Belgium: Peeters.

MacLachlan, Alice. 2008. *The Nature and Limits of Forgiveness*. PhD diss., Boston University.

Macquarrie, John. 1998. "The Morality of Forgiveness." *The Franciscan* (The Society of Saint Francis). Available at http://www.sidings.org/franciscans/1999jan-macquarrie.html (accessed March 7, 2010).

McCabe, Mary Margaret. 2008. "Protean Socrates: Mythical Figures in the *Euthydemus*." In *Ancient Philosophy of the Self*, ed. Pauliina Remes and Juha Sihvola. New York: Springer Verlag, 109–23.

Mead, George Herbert. 1934. *Mind, Self, and Society from the Standpoint of a Social Behaviorist*. Ed. Charles W. Norris. Chicago: University of Chicago Press.

Meredith, Anthony. 2002. "Origen and Gregory of Nyssa on The Lord's Prayer." *Heythrop Journal* 43, no. 3: 344–56.

Merkelbach, Reinhold. 1973. "Fragment eines satirischen Romans: Aufforderung zur Beichte." *Zeitschrift für Papyrologie und Epigraphie* 11: 81–100.

Metzler, Karin. 1991. *Der griechische Begriff des Verzeihens: Untersuch am Wortstamm συγγνώμη von den ersten Belegen bis zum vierten Jahrhundert n. Chr.* Wissenschaftliche Untersuchungen zum Neuen Testament, Zweite Reihe Series, vol. 44. Tübingen, Germany: J. C. B. Mohr [Paul Siebeck].

Michel, Alain. 1987. "Le pardon dans l'antiquité de Platon à St. Augustine." In *Le pardon, ed. Michel Perrin*. Paris: Beauchesne, 49–60.

Milbank, John. 2001. "Forgiveness and Incarnation." In *Questioning God*, ed. John Caputo, Mark Dooley, and Michael J. Scanlon. Bloomington: University of Indiana Press, 92–128.

Miles, Jack. 1995. *God: A Biography*. New York: Alfred A. Knopf.

Milgrom, Jacob. 1974–5. "On the Origins of Philo's Doctrine of Conscience." *Studia Philonica* 3: 41–5.

Miller, William Ian. 2006. *Eye for an Eye*. Cambridge: Cambridge University Press.

——— 2003. *Faking It*. Cambridge: Cambridge University Press.

Milnor, Kristina. 2011. "Gender and Forgiveness in the Early Roman Empire." In Griswold and Konstan 2011.

Molnár, I. 1981. "Die Ausgestaltung des Begriffes des *vis maior* im römischen Recht." *Iura: Rivista Internazionale di Diritto Romano e Antico* 32: 73–105.

Montefiore, C. G., and H. Loewe, eds. 1938. *A Rabbinic Anthology*. London: Macmillan.

Montesquieu, Baron de. 1914 (orig. 1752). *The Spirit of the Laws*. Trans. Thomas Nugent, revised by J. V. Prichard. London: G. Bell and Sons.

Available at http://www.constitution.org/cm/sol.htm (accessed March 7, 2010).

Moore, George Foot. 1997. *Judaism in the First Centuries of the Christian Era: The Age of Tannaim.* 2 vols. (vol. 2 in this edition contains vols. 2 and 3 of original). Peabody, MA: Hendrickson Publishers (orig. Cambridge, MA: Harvard University Press, 1927 for vols. 1 and 2, 1930 for vol. 3).

Morgan, Michael L. 2011. "Mercy, Repentance, and Forgiveness in Ancient Judaism." In Griswold and Konstan 2011.

Morton, Adam. 2011. "What is Forgiveness?" In Griswold and Konstan 2011.

Most, Glenn. 2009. "Emotion, Memory, and Trauma." In Richard Eldridge, ed., *The Oxford Handbook of Philosophy and Literature.* Oxford: Oxford University Press, 442–63.

2008. "'Das Kind ist Vater des Mannes': Von Rushdie zu Homer und zurück." Trans. Sabine Franke. *Gymnasium* 115: 209–36.

Muffs, Yochanan. 1992. "Joy and Love as Metaphorical Expressions of Willingness and Spontaneity in Cuneiform, Ancient Hebrew, and Related Literatures." In *Love and Joy: Law, Language and Religion in Ancient Israel.* Cambridge, MA: Harvard University Press, 121–64.

Murphie, Jeffrie, and Jean Hampton. 1988. *Forgiveness and Mercy.* Cambridge: Cambridge University Press.

Naiden, F. S. 2006. *Ancient Supplication.* Oxford: Oxford University Press.

Nave, G. D. 2002. *The Role and Function of Repentance in Luke-Acts.* Atlanta, GA: Society of Biblical Literature.

Neusner, Jacob, trans. 1981. *The Tosefta: Fourth Division Neziqin or The Order of Damages,* vol. 4. New York: Ktav Publishing House.

Newberry, Paul A. 2001. "Joseph Butler on Forgiveness: A Presupposed Theory of Emotion." *Journal of the History of Ideas* 62: 233–44.

Newman, Louis. 1987. "The Quality of Mercy: On the Duty to Forgive in the Judaic Tradition." *Journal of Religious Ethics* 15: 155–72.

Nickelsburg, G. W. E. 1984. "The Books of Adam and Eve." In *Jewish Writings of the Second Temple Period,* ed. M. E. Stone. Assen, the Netherlands: Van Gorcum; Philadelphia: Fortress Press, 113–18.

North, Joanna. 1998. "The 'Ideal' of Forgiveness: A Philosopher's Exploration." In *Exploring Forgiveness,* ed. Robert D. Enright and Joanna North. Madison: University of Wisconsin Press, 15–34.

1987. "Wrongdoing and Forgiveness." *Philosophy* 62: 499–508.

Pagani, Karen. 2007. *Forgiveness and the Age of Reason: Fénelon, Voltaire, Rousseau and Staël.* 2 vols. PhD diss., University of Chicago.

Patillon, Michel, trans. 1997. *Hermogène: L'art rhétorique.* Paris: Belles Lettres (L'Age de l'Homme).

Peli, Pinchas H., ed. 1980. *On Repentance: The Thought and Oral Discourses of Joseph Dov Soloveitchik.* Jerusalem: Oroth Publishing House.

Perrin, Michel, ed. 1987. *Le pardon.* Paris: Beauchesne.

Pettigrove, Glen. 2007. "Hume on Forgiveness and the Unforgivable." *Utilitas* 19: 447–65.

Petzl, G. 1994. "Die Beichtinschriften Westkleinasiens." *Epigraphica Anatolica* 22.

Pirovano, Luigi. 2006. *Le Interpretationes vergilianae di Tiberio Claudio Donato: Problemi di retorica.* Rome: Herder.

Plumer, William S. 1864. *Vital Godliness: A Treatise on Experimental and Practical Piety.* New York: American Tract Society.

Quiroga, Alberto. Forthcoming. *"Quid Est Gloria, Si Tacetur?* Silence in Ambrose's *De Officiis." Latomus.*

Radice, Roberto, trans. 1998. *Stoici antichi: Tutti i frammenti secondo la raccolta di Hans Von Arnim.* Milan, Italy: Rusconi Editore.

Raith, Oskar. 1971. "Unschuldsbeteuerung und Sündenbekenntnis im Gebet des Enkolp an Priap (Petr. 133.3)." *Studia Classica* 13: 109–25.

Ramelli, Ilaria. 2010. "Unconditional Forgiveness in Christianity? Some Reflections on Ancient Christian Sources and Practices." In *Aspects of Forgiveness,* ed. Christel Fricke. Cambridge: Cambridge University Press.

——— 2008. Review of Griswold 2007b. *Rivista di Filosofia Neoscolastica* 100: 658–62.

——— 2007. "La colpa antecedente come ermeneutica del male in sede storico-religiosa e nei testi biblici." In I. Cardellini, ed., *Atti del XIV Convegno di Studî vetero-testamentarî dell'Associazione Biblica Italiana: Origine e fenomenologia del male: le vie della catarsi vetero-testamentaria (Roma-Ciampino, Istituto Il Carmelo, 5–7 settembre 2005).* Special issue of *Ricerche Storico-Bibliche* 19: 11–64.

——— 1998. "Il tema del perdono in Seneca e in Musonio Rufo." In *Responsabilità, perdono e vendetta nel mondo antico,* ed. Martha Sordi. Milan, Italy: Vita e Pensiero, 191–207.

Reese, James M. 1970. *Hellenistic Influence on the Book of Wisdom and its Consequences.* Rome: Biblical Institute.

Renehan, Robert. 1972. "The Greek Philosophical Background of Fourth Maccabees." *Rheinisches Museum* 115: 223–38.

Rodrigues, Marina Elena. 2006. *The Ethics of Interpersonal Forgiveness.* PhD diss., University of Minnesota.

Romilly, Jacqueline de. 1995. "Indulgence et pardon dans la tragédie grecque." In *Tragédies grecques au fil des ans,* ed. Jacquiline de Romilly. Paris: Les Belles Lettres, 62–77.

Rostad, Aslak. 2006. *Human Transgression – Divine Retribution: A Study of Religious Transgressions and Punishments in Greek Cultic Regulations and Lydian-Phrygian Reconciliation Inscriptions.* PhD diss., University of Bergen.

——— 2002. "Confession or Reconciliation? The Narrative Structure of the Lydian and Phrygian 'Confession Inscriptions.'" *Symbolae Osloenses* 77: 145–64.

Rubenstein, Mary-Jane. 2008. "Of Ghosts and Angels: Derrida, Kushner, and the Impossibility of Forgiveness." *Journal for Cultural and Religious Theory* 9: 79–95.

Rubinstein, Lene. 1993. *Adoption in IV. Century Athens*. Copenhagen: Museum Tusculanum Press.

Russell, Donald A. 2001. *Quintilian: The Orator's Education*, vol. 5. Cambridge, MA: Harvard University Press (Loeb Library).

Russell, H. M., and Rabbi J. Weinberg, trans. 1983. *The Book of Knowledge: From the Mishneh Torah of Maimonides*. New York: Ktav Publishing House.

Salzman, Michele. 2010. "Leo in Rome: The Evolution of Episcopal Authority in the Fifth Century." In *Istituzioni, Carismi ed Esercizio del Potere (IV-VI secolo d.C.)*, ed. G. Bonamente and R. Lizzi Testa. Bari, Italy: Edipuglia, 1–14.

Saunders, Trevor. 1991. *Plato's Penal Code: Tradition, Controversy, and Reform in Greek Penology*. Oxford: Clarendon Press.

Scarpat, G., ed. and trans. 1989–9. *Libro della Sapienza*. 3 vols. Brescia, Italy: Paideia.

Schaff, Philip, ed. 1988. *From Nicene and Post-Nicene Fathers*. First Series, vol. 6. Buffalo, NY: Christian Literature Publishing; and Edinburgh: T&T Clark (revised and edited for New Advent by Kevin Knight; available at http://www.newadvent.org/fathers/160364.htm [accessed March 7, 2001]).

Schaff, Philip, and Henry Wace, eds. 1895. *Nicene and Post Nicene Fathers*. Second Series, vol. 12. Buffalo, NY: Christian Literature Publishing (revised and edited for New Advent by Kevin Knight; available at http://www.newadvent.org/fathers/3603.htm [accessed March 7, 2001]).

Scheid-Tissinier, Evelyne. 2007. "Le rôle de la colère dans les tribunaux athéniens." In *Athènes et le politique: Dans le sillage de Claude Mossé*, ed. Pauline Schmitt Pantel and François de Polignac. Paris: Albin Michel, 179–98.

Scheper-Hughes, Nancy. 1999. "Un-doing: Social Suffering and the Politics of Remorse." In *Remorse and Reparation*, ed. Murray Cox. London: Jessica Kingsley Publishers, 145–70.

Schimmel, Solomon. 2002. *Wounds Not Healed by Time: The Power of Repentance and Forgiveness*. Oxford: Oxford University Press.

Schnabel, Eckhard J. 2003. "Divine Tyranny and Public Humiliation: A Suggestion for the Interpretation of the Lydian and Phrygian Confession Inscriptions." *Novum Testamentum* 45: 160–88.

Schneewind, Jeremy. 1998. *The Invention of Autonomy: A History of Modern Moral Philosophy*. Cambridge: Cambridge University Press.

Schneider, Carl. 2000. "What It Means to Be Sorry: The Power of Apology in Mediation." *Mediation Quarterly* 17: 265–80.

Seim, T. K. 2001. "Abraham, Ancestor or Archetype?: A Comparison of Abraham-language in 4Maccabees and Luke-Acts." In *Antiquity and Humanity: Essays on Ancient Religion and Philosophy Presented to Hans Dieter Betz on his 70th Birthday*, ed. A. Yarbro Collins and Margaret M. Mitchell. Tübingen, Germany: Mohr Siebeck, 27–42.

Silva, David De. 1998. *4Maccabees: Introduction and Commentary on the Greek Text in Codex Sinaiticus*. Leiden, the Netherlands: Septuagint Commentary Series.

Silver, Allan. 2003. "Friendship and Sincerity." *Sozialersinn* 1: 123–30.

Sissa, Giulia. 2006. "A Theatrical Poetics: Recognition and the Structural Emotions of Tragedy." *Arion* 14: 35–92.

Smith, Adam. 2002. *The Theory of Moral Sentiments*. Ed. Knud Haakonssen. Cambridge: Cambridge University Press.

Sorabji, Richard. 2006. *Self: Ancient and Modern Insights about Individuality, Life, and Death*. Chicago: University of Chicago Press.

Spade, Paul Vincent, trans. 1995. *Peter Abelard: Ethical Writings: His* Ethics *or* "Know Yourself" *and His* Dialogue between a Philosopher, a Jew and a Christian. With an introduction by Marilyn McCord Adams. Indianapolis: Hackett Publishing.

Stanton, Mike. November 3, 2007. "Martineau Pleads Guilty: Ex-Rep. admits selling office to CVS, Blue Cross." *Providence Journal*, A: 1, 5.

Stemm, Sönke von. 1999. *Der betende Sünder vor Gott: Studien zu Vergebungs- vorstellungen in urchristlichen und frühjüdischen Texten*. Leiden, the Netherlands: E. J. Brill.

Stern, Martin Stanley. 1979. "Al-Ghazzālī, Maimonides, and Ibn Paquda on Repentance: A Comparative Model." *Journal of the American Academy of Religion* 47: 589–607.

Sung, Chong-Hyon. 1993. *Vergebung der Sünden: Jesu Praxis der Sündenvergebung nach den Synoptikern und ihre Voraussetzung im Alten Testament und frühen Judentum*. Tübingen. Germany: J. C. B. Mohr.

Sussman, David. 2005. "Kantian Forgiveness." *Kant-Studien* 96: 85–107.

SVF. See Arnim 1964.

Swinburne, Richard. 1989. *Responsibility and Atonement*. Oxford: Clarendon Press.

Taylor, Gabrielle. 1996. "Guilt and Remorse." In *The Emotions: Social, Cultural, and Biological Dimensions*, ed. Rom Harré and W. Gerrod Parrot. London: Sage Publications, 57–73.

Thomas, Alan. 1999. "Remorse and Reparation: A Philosophical Analysis." In *Remorse and Reparation*, ed. Murray Cox. London: Jessica Kingsley Publishers, 127–33.

Thumiger, Chiara. 2007. *Hidden Paths: Self and Characterization in Greek Tragedy: Euripides' Bacchae*. Bulletin of the Institute of Classical Studies 99. London: Institute of Classical Studies.

Traill, Ariana. 2008. *Women and the Comic Plot in Menander*. Cambridge: Cambridge University Press.

Trilling, Lionel. 1971. *Sincerity and Authenticity*. Cambridge, MA: Harvard University Press.

Trollope, Anthony. 1989. *Can You Forgive Her?* London: The Folio Society.

Tromp, Johannes. 2005. *The Life of Adam and Eve in Greek: A Critical Edition*. Leiden, the Netherlands: E. J. Brill

Ure, Michael. 2007. "The Politics of Mercy, Forgiveness and Love: A Nietzschean Appraisal." *South African Journal of Philosophy* 26: 56–69.

Van Ness, Daniel W., and Karen Heetderks Strong. 2006. *Restoring Justice: An Introduction to Restorative Justice*. 3rd ed. Cincinnati, OH: Anderson Publishing.

Várhelyi, Zsuzsanna. 2011. "'To Forgive is Divine:' Gods as Models and Guides of Forgiveness in Early Imperial Rome." In Griswold and Konstan 2011.

Veyne, Paul, ed. 1987–91. *A History of Private Life.* Trans. Arthur Goldhammer. 5 vols. Cambridge, MA: Harvard University Press.

Wagatsuma, Hiroshi, and Arthur Rosett. 1986. "The Implications of Apology: Law and Culture in Japan and the United States." *Law and Society Review* 20: 461–83.

Walker, Lenore. 2000. *The Battered Woman Syndrome.* 2nd ed. New York: Springer Publishing.

Walker, Margaret Urban. 2006. *Moral Repair: Reconstructing Moral Relations after Wrongdoing.* Cambridge: Cambridge University Press.

Wallis, R. T. 1974–5. "The Idea of Conscience in Philo of Alexandria." *Studia Philonica* 3: 27–40.

Ward, Benedicta, S. L. G. 1987. *Harlots of the Desert: A Study of Repentance in Early Monastic Sources.* Kalamazoo, MI: Cistercian Publications.

Winston, David. 1995. "Philo's Doctrine of Repentance." In *The School of Moses: Studies in Philo and Hellenistic Religion, In Memory of Horst R. Moehring,* ed. John P. Keaney. Atlanta, GA: Publisher, 29–40.

1990. "Judaism and Hellenism: Hidden Tensions in Philo's Thought." *Studia Philonica Annual* 2: 1–19.

Wood, Allen, and George Di Giovanni, trans. 1998. *Immanuel Kant: Religion within the Boundaries of Mere Reason and Other Writings.* Cambridge: Cambridge University Press.

Yonge, Charles D., trans. 1888. *The Orations of Marcus Tullius Cicero,* vol. 4. London: George Bell and Sons.

Index